Performing
Women

Performing Women

FEMALE CHARACTERS, MALE PLAYWRIGHTS, AND THE MODERN STAGE

Gay Gibson Cima

Cornell University Press

Ithaca and London

First published 1993 by Cornell University Press.

International Standard Book Number 0-8014-2874-2
Library of Congress Catalog Card Number 93-17910

Printed in the United States of America

Librarians: Library of Congress cataloging information appears on the last page of the book.

⊗ The paper in this book meets the minimum requirements of the American National Standard for Information Sciences—Permanence of Paper for Printed Library Materials, ANSI Z39.48-1984.

To Ron, Gib, Anna,
and Geraldine Smith Gibson

Contents

Illustrations

Acknowledgments

To those friends and colleagues who offered critiques of individual chapters, I extend my warmest thanks: Marvin Carlson, whose generous assistance stretches over years and beyond the scope of this particular project; Raymond Reno and John Glavin, whose insights have challenged me for more than a decade; Lucy Maddox, Susan Lanser, Bert O. States, Timothy Murray, Michael Ragussis, and Bruce Smith, whose helpful responses prompted early revisions. Leona Fisher, who founded at Georgetown University a feminist community in which I could test my ideas, has earned my respect and appreciation.

I am also grateful to my colleagues who have chaired the English department during my tenure at Georgetown: Paul Betz, Jim Slevin, and Lucy Maddox; to the two deans who have presided over Georgetown College: Royden B. Davis, S.J., and his successor, Robert B. Lawton, S.J.; and to the dean of the Graduate School, Richard B. Schwartz. My thanks to Lynne Hirschfeld for her patience and her knowledge of computers, and to Joan Reuss for her assistance in word processing.

Without my feminist friends in the Women and Theatre Program of the Association for Theatre in Higher Education I could not have written this book. I also acknowledge my colleagues under the larger ATHE umbrella and within the American Society for Theatre Research, as well as the anonymous donor of the ASTR Younger Scholars' Prize and the others who responded to early discussions of the issues examined here.

Mabel Smith, trustee of Backsettown, generously granted me permission to publish materials from the Elizabeth Robins archives, which were provided through the assistance of Frank Walker, curator of the Fales Library at New York University. The Johns Hopkins University Press allowed me to reprint those portions of Chapters 1, 4, and 5 that originally appeared in *Theatre Journal:* "Discovering Signs: The Emergence of the Critical Actor in Ibsen," 35 (March 1983), 5–22; "Acting on the Cutting Edge: Pinter and the Syntax of Cinema," 36 (March 1984), 43–56; and "Shifting Perspectives: Combining Rauschenberg and Shepard," 38 (March 1986), 67–81. I extend special thanks to Carla Waal, who supplied me with slides of the Greta Gerell painting of Harriet Bosse as well as the photograph of Bosse in the role of the Daughter of Indra. Anita Brundahl, director of the archives and library of Dramaten, the Royal Dramatic Theatre in Stockholm, offered not only prompt assistance but also permission to reprint the painting. John Fuegi earned my appreciation for making his insights into the Brecht Collective available in advance of the publication of his book *Brecht & Co.* and for providing materials on the Beckett Directing Beckett project. Ute Eichel of the Berliner Ensemble was kind enough to send me a photo of the 1957 *Der Gute Mensch von Sezuan* poster. Particular thanks are due to the professional photographers who permitted me to reprint their work: Jan Deen, for his photograph of Rachel Rosenthal in *L.O.W. in Gaia;* Martha Swope for her photo of Billie Whitelaw in *Footfalls;* and Zoë Dominic, for the photograph of *Old Times.* The photo of Robert Rauschenberg's *Monogram* is reprinted courtesy of the Statens Konstmuseer; George de Vincent's photograph of Christina Moore in *Buried Child* courtesy of the Arena Stage; and the Zenchiku illustration courtesy of the Hosei University Institute of Nohgaku Studies, with special thanks to Aya Mihara.

Bernhard Kendler of Cornell University Press and his colleagues have provided invaluable assistance at every step.

Finally, I thank my family: my daughter, Anna, for her subversive stories; my son, Gib, for his sensitivity onstage and off; and my husband, Ron, for his love and laughter. I am deeply grateful to my mother, Geraldine Smith Gibson, who fostered my love of performing; to my father, Richard M. Gibson, who supported that love no matter what; to my brother, Richard, who encouraged me more than he knows; and to Judy, Rich, and Brock.

G. G. C.

Introduction

Acting styles reflect, enforce, and critique cultural models of behavior. New styles, often created collaboratively by actors and playwrights, can suddenly make visible the outdatedness of certain notions of performance, not only in the theatre but also in daily life. For that reason, feminists eager to transform social roles can benefit from examining the relationship between new playwriting and acting styles.

Recent works about the relationship between male playwrights and female characters in modern drama fall into one of two categories: books such as Gail Finney's *Women in Modern Drama*, which treat characters as real people and use psychoanalysis to explain the way in which male playwrights construct female characters as victims; and books such as Elizabeth Sakellaridou's *Pinter's Female Portraits*, which contend that male playwrights of genius can transcend gender boundaries and write "universal" women characters into their scripts.[1] Both of these views distort the intricate relationship be-

1. See Elizabeth Sakellaridou, *Pinter's Female Portraits: A Study of Female Characters in the Plays of Harold Pinter* (London: Macmillan, 1988). Sakellaridou places Harold Pinter in Shulamith Firestone's third category of male writer, the category of androgyny: "The playwright has, therefore, had to break his bond with this arid masculine world and to adopt an androgynous standpoint in order to achieve greater insight into the female psyche and give a fair and balanced picture of both aspects of the human condition" (p. 14). Sakellaridou explains Firestone's categories on p. 15. See also Linda Ben-Zvi, ed., *Women in Beckett: Performance and Critical Perspectives*

tween male playwrights and female characters, partly because they ignore or minimize female actors and the actual performance conditions and conventions, such as styles of performance, that help establish the meaning of any given character. Incorporating a consideration of these elements, this book analyzes structural models in representative scripts by canonical male playwrights and investigates the new performance styles that actors—female actors in particular—have created in conjunction with them. These innovative performance styles redefined the relationship between actor and character, actor and director, and actor and audience. By investigating and demystifing the authority of the playwright in hypothetical as well as actual performances featuring female actors, I hope to illuminate the history—and the potential political efficacy for feminists—of changing acting styles, and to clarify the complicated and sometimes contradictory relationships that may develop, especially between female actors and scripts by male playwrights.

Over the years different agents within the theatre have validated shifts in performance styles, introducing fresh ways to view the cultural codes that influence behavior. Certain eighteenth-century actors, such as Charles Macklin and David Garrick in England, were regarded as the initiators of new, more realistic paradigms of acting. But since the late nineteenth century the playwright and the director (or director/designer) have increasingly been seen as the agents of generating change in performance styles. Within the canon playwrights such as Ibsen, Brecht, and Beckett on the one hand and directors such as the duke of Saxe-Meiningen, Stanislavsky, Meyerhold, Craig, Appia, Reinhardt, and Artaud on the other have been said to have reconfigured the idea of performance.

Recent histories of the theatre have particularly emphasized the importance of the modern director in this process, declaring the twentieth century to be the age of the director; critics such as Roland Barthes and Jacques Derrida have even proclaimed the death of the author. Yet playwrights over the past century have nonetheless established and maintained a significant role in instituting the interpretive universe of a production, particularly in premiere productions

---

(Urbana: University of Illinois Press, 1990). In Chapter 6 I discuss aspects of Ben-Zvi's book. See also Gail Finney, *Women in Modern Drama: Freud, Feminism, and European Theater at the Turn of the Century* (Ithaca: Cornell University Press, 1989).

of their work. In fact, the late nineteenth century saw the emergence of a relatively new phenomenon, acting styles named for playwrights instead of actors or directors, as critics began to speak, for example, of "Ibsen actors," even in productions not directed by Ibsen. The male critical establishment, particularly in England, grew anxious about the new power assumed by female actors, who not only created a new acting style to portray the principal characters in Ibsen's scripts but also independently produced many of his plays. Perhaps to allay this fear, reviewers began to attribute the women's emerging acting style to the playwright's creativity rather than the performers', thus reversing a long tradition. This critical approach helped ensure Ibsen's place in the canon.

As early as 1891 George Bernard Shaw articulated the perceived uniqueness of Ibsen's claim on actors: "It is no more possible to get an Ibsen character out of [the old acting technique] than to contrive a Greek costume out of an English wardrobe."[2] Henry James emphasized Ibsen's "presence" onstage at the 1891 London premiere of *Hedda Gabler:* "The opportunity that [Ibsen] gives [actors] is almost always to do the deep and delicate thing. . . . He asks them to paint with a fine brush; for the subject that he gives them is ever our plastic humanity. This will surely preserve him (leaving out the question of serious competition) after our little flurry is over. It is what made the recent representation of *Hedda Gabler* so singularly interesting and refreshing."[3] When Elizabeth Robins, the actor playing Hedda, produced an Ibsen series two years later, James feared that she would be indelibly tagged an Ibsen actor (a figure he had helped create), conceding, however, that "it is doubtless as well to be that as any of the other 'only's' that seem open to others of the profession. It seems always, at best, a case of an 'only.'"[4]

William Archer strengthened the idea of Ibsen actors as a class apart when he deplored Herbert Beerbohm Tree's production of *An*

2. George Bernard Shaw, appendix to *The Quintessance of Ibsenism,* in *Shaw on Theatre,* ed. E. J. West (New York: Hill and Wang, 1953), p. 5. *The Quintessance of Ibsenism* was originally published in 1891.

3. Henry James, "On the Occasion of *Hedda Gabler,*" *New Review* 4 (June 1891): 529, reprinted in Michael Egan, *Ibsen: The Critical Heritage* (London: Routledge and Kegan Paul, 1972), pp. 242–43.

4. Henry James, Letter to Mrs. Bell, April 18, 1893, quoted in Elizabeth Robins, *Theatre and Friendship* (London: Jonathan Cape, 1932), p. 117.

Enemy of the People, which opened on June 14, 1893. He declared how grateful he was that the other Ibsen dramas had been "studied and staged by artists with special intellectual and technical qualifications for their work."[5] James urged Robins to accept the role of a melodramatic heroine in Henry Petitt's play *A Woman's Revenge,* which opened on July 1, 1893, to avoid being too closely associated with Ibsen, but when she did so, Clement Scott attacked her for being inconsistent: "If she is opposed to the popular form of drama, why does she play in it?"[6] In 1896, when Mrs. Patrick Campbell agreed to play the Rat Wife in Robins's production of *Little Eyolf,* the reviewer in the *Weekly Sun* maintained that she had done so only to repay Robins for relinquishing to her the title role in Pinero's *Second Mrs. Tanqueray,* for Mrs. Pat was "far too clever to identify herself largely with the Ibsen movement, as Miss Robins and Miss [Janet] Achurch have done to their cost."[7]

Robins tried to dispel the idea that she was solely an Ibsen actor, as is clear from an 1896 interview: "Miss Robins expressly disclaims the *aut Ibsen aut nullus* theory, which the exponents of the Norwegian dramatist are supposed to hold."[8] But by that time even the far-flung *Aberdeen Free Press* in northeastern Scotland was celebrating her as "the greatest Ibsen actress of the day."[9] Archer even felt unable to assess Robins's talent because he deemed it so intertwined with Ibsen's skill. When she played José Echegaray's Marianna in 1897, he wrote: "It has been my good fortune to work with Miss Elizabeth Robins in the preparation of five or six of Ibsen's plays, in which her performances have given me the keenest pleasure. But Ibsen stands by himself. To an actress of sympathetic intelligence he offers such unique opportunities that it is hard to bring her work into perspective, and see it in its true relation to the general work of the stage. Thus I have never been able to 'place' Miss Robins among

5. William Archer, *Theatrical World of 1893* (London: Walter Scott, 1894), p. 163.

6. Clement Scott, *London Illustrated News,* July 15, 1893, p. 67; see also July 8, 1893, p. 31.

7. *Weekly Sun,* November 8, 1896. This review, and all subsequent unpaginated newspaper reviews, may be found in Elizabeth Robins's *News Cuttings* scrapbook, Fales Library, New York University.

8. *Stage,* November 26, 1896.

9. *Aberdeen Free Press,* November 24, 1896.

her fellow-artists."[10] Criticizing Robins in one of the very last roles she ever played, a minor part in Stephen Phillips's 1902 *Paolo and Francesca,* Max Beerbohm speculated on the reasons why she over-acted: "I dare say that Miss Robins has toned down her performance since the first night, her own judgment being no longer obscured by fear that the stupid critics would call her 'Ibsenish.'"[11]

As a result of the process whereby acting styles were associated with playwrights, the term "action," which originally meant an ac-tor's gestures, came to mean the playwright's overriding line, the soul of the written text. And instead of championing Garrick's acting style over the Kembles', theatre critics began to speak of Ibsen actors, and later of Brechtian actors, the Pinteresque style, Beckett's style. These labels erased the achievements of the actors who had first created the performance styles, often in plays that featured women as central characters. Ironically, in order to make itself intelligible, my book must participate at least in part in that erasure while it seeks to reinstate the contributions of female actors within the modern and contemporary theatre.

This book identifies interconnections among the constituent parts of a theatrical production, investigating the role of male as well as female actors. It will be of interest, I hope, not only to feminists but also to anyone concerned with modern or contemporary theatre, with performance issues and dramaturgy in general, and with liter-ary theories of narrativity. I emphasize the issues facing female ac-tors working with scripts by male playwrights in the hope of articu-lating anew the complexities in that relationship. By examining specific structural models within canonized scripts and investigating the process through which actors, particularly female actors, devel-op a style of performing the script, thereby building a relationship with the character, the director, and the audience, I want to raise new questions about the relationship between the script and the performance text.

By refusing the diminutive "actress" and insisting instead on the nongendered term "actor" with the attendant adjectives "female"

10. William Archer, *Theatrical World of 1897* (London: Walter Scott, 1898), p. 63.

11. Max Beerbohm, *More Theatres, 1898–1903* (New York: Taplinger, 1969), p. 448.

and "male," I am taking the first step toward acknowledging and honoring the substantial contribution that female performers have made to the modern history of acting. In addition, I am simultaneously carving out a space in which I can foresee other female actors' going beyond what was possible at the historical moment when these various works were first performed. I therefore investigate both real and hypothetical performances as a means of understanding the relationship between the actor, particularly the female actor, and the male playwright.[12]

Acting is, of course, not simply a theatrical phenomenon but a cultural one as well, reflecting and reifying the worldview of a given society. As Erika Fischer-Lichte notes, acting participates in the mechanism of socialization: "The actors' bodies, as presented on the stage, are likewise culturally conditioned in accordance with the actual state of the civilizing process. Moreover, the particular mode of their presentation onstage may contribute to this ongoing process by representing and propagating new models of self-presence and self-presentation for audience imitation. The actor promotes and ridicules modes of behavior both uncommon and common for the time."[13] Actors are always governed by a complex technology of the body, disseminated through social and cultural institutions which determine how they may play their characters. Each male playwright

12. My emphasis here is on styles of acting rather than directing. I focus on the possibilities for feminist directing in "Strategies for Subverting the Canon," in *Upstaging Big Daddy: Directing Theater As If Gender and Race Matter*, ed. Ellen Donkin and Sue Clement (Ann Arbor: University of Michigan Press, 1993), pp. 91–105. A word on terminology is appropriate here: to highlight the way in which female actors can foreground their consciousness of performance even in their work on scripts by male playwrights, I have often employed the terms "acting style" and "performance style" interchangeably. I am aware that current usage commonly distinguishes between "acting" and "performing," associating scripted roles with the former and a non-scripted exploration of the self with the latter. This book acknowledges, however, that female performers are always already scripted in part by the patriarchy (therefore it is fundamentally impossible to work without some kind of implicit script, even if it is only a set of audience expectations), and also that even actors working with scripts can make their audience conscious of performance. The distinction between the two terms, then, is useful, but more as a matter of emphasis at a given moment than as a polarity determined by the presence or absence of an actual written text.

13. Erika Fischer-Lichte, "Theatre and the Civilizing Process: An Approach to the History of Acting," in *Interpreting the Theatrical Past: Essays in the Historiography of Performance*, ed. Thomas Postlewait and Bruce A. McConachie (Iowa City: University of Iowa Press, 1989), pp. 22–23.

examined in this book (indeed, any playwright) necessarily participates in that governance. According to Joseph Roach, acting styles even "regulate the intelligibility of performances by authorizing certain substitutions as appropriate and proscribing others as meaningless or false."[14]

With each new performance style female actors make visible, however, they focus attention on shifting and contested models of behavior. They thereby undermine, to a greater or lesser extent, the civilizing process. Successful feminist actors—such as the nineteenth-century actor Elizabeth Robins, or the Brecht Collective actor envisioned in Chapter 3—highlight competing codes, reminding audiences that their bodies cannot be subsumed into any given style. These resourceful actors oppose the technique associated with the eighteenth-century actor. Roach establishes convincing proof that "virtuosity, the physical mastery of a particular style, means subjection. In its name, the appropriate expressions and trills, the correct sequences and spatial designs, must be deeply inscribed upon the body. The virtuoso's muscles and nerves must remember at speeds often exceeding consciousness which procedures the style authorizes and which it proscribes."[15] This actor's body is subjected to the performative code, and the audience is in turn overcome by the virtuosity displayed. As initiators of novel and unpracticed performance styles (styles that necessarily carry with them vestiges of the old), the majority of female actors discussed herein reject virtuosity.

Despite the undeniable power of male playwrights and the theatrical and cultural systems they at once reflect and enforce, female actors since the late nineteenth century have actually assumed a collaborative and potentially disruptive role in creating new ways of performing the idea of woman. The picture that emerges in this book is not a story of female actors or characters victimized by male playwrights employing realistic narratives, nor is it a tale of women's instant liberation by the more experimental structures of French feminism or the bold, nonrealistic style of playwriting and acting which Brecht helped originate. These allegories, underlying much

14. Joseph R. Roach, "Power's Body: The Inscription of Morality as Style," in Postlewait and McConachie, *Interpreting the Theatrical Past*, p. 100.
15. Ibid., p. 109.

feminist writing about the theatre, obscure from view a more contradictory and unpredictable portrait.

My historical research on actual performance situations and my
work as an actor and director have prompted me to question one of
the basic premises of feminist theatre theory, indeed of feminist
literary theory: the idea that the structure of a script or text necessarily determines its political efficacy for feminists, and that the
traditional narrative structure of realism necessarily oppresses all
female actors and spectators. As Sue-Ellen Case argues, realistic
structures (such as Ibsen's are understood to be) are seen within
established feminist theatre theory as creating a "'prisonhouse of
art' for women, both in their representation on stage and in the
female actor's preparation and production of such roles. . . . The
form of the narrative itself is complicit with the psychocultural re-
pression of women."[16] Case writes: "From a feminist perspective,
the Method techniques for building these [realistic] characters lead
the female actor into inaccurate analyses of female sexuality. . . .
Objectives and through-lines might not be suitable acting techniques
for representing women's experiences."[17] Female spectators are also
subject to this entrapment, Jill Dolan contends: "If, as de Lauretis
argues, male desire drives all narrative and objectifies women, the
female spectator is placed in an untenable relationship to representation."[18]

The preferred response for feminists is either (1) to favor nonnarrative scripts (those that employ plots like the Brecht Collective's,
with episodes that break the narrative and expose the representational framework of the play, or those that borrow certain techniques
from French feminism) or (2) to champion Brechtian acting and
directing strategies that deconstruct onstage the workings of narrative. As Dolan writes: "Brecht's theories of alienation and historicization serve as a precedent for materialist feminist theatre practice
and criticism"; Brecht's "alienation effect, his theory of the social

16. Sue-Ellen Case, *Feminism and Theatre* (New York: Methuen, 1988), p. 124.
17. Ibid., p. 123.
18. Jill Dolan, *The Feminist Spectator as Critic* (Ann Arbor: University of Michigan
Press, 1988), p. 13. See Teresa de Lauretis, "Desire in Narrative," in *Alice Doesn't:
Feminism, Semiotics, Cinema* (Bloomington: Indiana University Press, 1984), pp. 103–
54.

gestus, and his description of an acting technique that asks a performer to quote, rather than psychologically become, a character,
are formulated to provoke a political critique that will lead to a
profitable change in class-based social relations."[19] Elin Diamond
and Janelle Reinelt have also established the importance of Brecht's
nonrealistic performance style for feminists. Diamond maintains
that "feminist theory and Brechtian theory need to be read intertextually, for among the effects of such a reading are a recovery of the
radical potential of the Brechtian critique and a discovery, for feminist theory, of the specificity of theatre."[20] Reinelt also acknowledges
Brecht's political efficacy: "Political theatre requires the ability to
isolate and manifest certain ideas and relationships that make ideology visible, in contrast with the styles of realism and naturalism,
wherein ideology is hidden or covert. Brecht's theorization of the
social gest, epic structure, and alienation effect provides the means
to reveal material relations as the basis of social reality, to foreground and examine ideologically-determined beliefs and unconscious habitual perceptions, and to make visible those signs inscribed
on the body which distinguish social behavior in relation to class,
gender, and history."[21]

Like Brecht, according to Dolan and Diamond, French feminists
such as Hélène Cixous provide useful nonnarrative alternatives to
realism. Of the experimental structure of *Portrait of Dora* Dolan
writes: "The play's narrative is fragmentary. . . . The articulation of
Dora's lesbian desire in Cixous's text resists inscription in Freud's

19. Dolan, *Feminist Spectator,* pp. 106, 14.
20. Elin Diamond, "Brechtian Theory/Feminist Theory: Toward a Gestic Feminist
Criticism," *The Drama Review* 32, 1 (Spring 1988): 82.
21. Janelle Reinelt, "Beyond Brecht: Britain's New Feminist Drama," in *Performing
Feminisms: Feminist Critical Theory and Theatre,* ed. Sue-Ellen Case (Baltimore: Johns
Hopkins University Press, 1990), p. 150. Reinelt acknowledges, however, that British
feminist actors such as Gillian Hanna of the Monstrous Regiment have in fact combined Brecht with the Method: "Out of the need to evolve a suitable dramatic form
for socialist-feminist drama, a new theatrical style may be evolving which synthesizes
older techniques" (p. 159). To illustrate, she quotes Hanna on acting: "My inclination
and experience is all to do with a kind of Brechtian acting, which doesn't deny
Stanislavsky but puts the emphasis elsewhere. . . . It doesn't work for me or for an
audience, if I'm doing it just on the level of remembering some sort of pain that I've
experienced. . . . Nor does it work on the level of 'I'm showing the audience something here.' The nights it seems to work best are when there is, and on a level that I've
not experienced before, a meshing of those two" (p. 159).

male, heterosexual narrative."[22] Diamond reads Samuel Beckett's work intertextually with French feminism, investigating formal similarities in the two bodies of work and considering their feminist possibilities.[23] These theories of feminist theatre are immensely useful, and their significance for female actors, directors, spectators, and critics should not be underestimated.

My examination of performances of Ibsen, Beckett, and the work of the Brecht Collective suggests, however, that just as feminist film theorists and scholars of popular culture are beginning to rethink the relationship between narrative structure and the production of meaning, theatre scholars may profitably do the same by reexamining how these narrative structures operate in historical performance situations. According to Rita Felski: "It is impossible to speak of 'masculine' and 'feminine' in any meaningful sense in the formal analysis of texts: the political value of literary texts from the standpoint of feminism can be determined only by an investigation of their social functions and effects in relation to the interests of women in a particular historical context, and not by attempting to deduce an abstract literary theory of 'masculine' and 'feminine,' 'subversive' and 'reactionary' forms in isolation from the social conditions of their production and reception."[24] As Patricia Schroeder notes, narrative forms "can be used for a variety of purposes."[25]

22. Dolan, *Feminist Spectator*, p. 102. See also Case, *Feminism and Theatre*, pp. 124–27.

23. Elin Diamond, "Speaking Parisian: Beckett and French Feminism," in Ben-Zvi, *Women in Beckett*, pp. 208–16.

24. Rita Felski, *Beyond Feminist Aesthetics: Feminist Literature and Social Change* (Cambridge: Harvard University Press, 1989), p. 2. In her critique of Jacques Lacan, Felski writes: "Critical analysis of existing discursive systems and conventions of representation has played an important part in recent feminist theory. To move, however, from the recognition of an androcentric bias in language use as exemplified in existing hierarchies of meaning to the assertion that social and symbolic discourse is inherently phallocentric is a highly reductive jump. Such an argument simplifies the complex nature of the interaction of feminism as a counter-ideology with a dominant patriarchal culture, a relationship necessarily defined by both dependence and critique; in attempting to avoid a voluntarism which assumes that language is a transparent instrument free of ideology, it falls into the opposite trap of a linguistic determinism, which interprets all discursive language as a reinforcement of patriarchal structures" (p. 42).

25. Patricia Schroeder, "American Drama, Feminist Discourse, and Dramatic Form: In Defense of Pluralism," paper delivered at the 1989 Association for Theatre in Higher Education Conference, New York City, p. 18.

Elizabeth Robins created a style of acting in Ibsen's realistic, narrative plays that allowed her to reveal and critique the roles expected of women. By contrast, the Beckett interpreter Billie Whitelaw and Brecht's female collaborators suffered physical pain and subjugation, despite the nonnarrative structure of their scripts.

A revised theory about the relationship between the structure of the script and the performance text may draw on the work in film theory by E. Deidre Pribram and Christine Gledhill. In *Female Spectators*, Pribram criticizes the ahistoricism of psychoanalytical-semiotic models of spectatorship and the attendant idea of a "monolithic" patriarchy: "The presumption that [the models] apply equally across all time and instances . . . leaves them open to justifiable charges of inaccuracy and inflexibility. When psychoanalysis is applied to film, the potential for theorizing alternative readings or interpretations within any given text is inhibited by a denial of viewing *contexts:* no place is allowed for shifts in textual meaning related to shifts in viewing situation."[26] As a result, this idea of spectatorship assumes that the text positions all women the same way—regardless of race, class, sexual orientation, or even historical period. Although this model explains the extraordinary success of the project of excluding women from power, its assumption of a monolithic ideology undercuts women's proven ability to envision and stage alternatives. Furthermore, as Pribram notes, defining all popular cultural activity as patriarchal presents an ironic danger: "If women do not seek to be included at the centre of cultural production, we only reinforce our exclusion from it, in opposition to many of feminism's political aims."[27]

Christine Gledhill, among others, proposes that instead of a monolithic model of cultural production we adopt a model that acknowledges negotiation: "Meaning is neither imposed, nor passively imbibed, but arises out of a struggle or negotiation between competing frames of reference, motivation and experience. This can be analyzed at three different levels: institutions, texts, and

26. E. Deidre Pribram, ed., *Female Spectators: Looking at Film and Television* (London: Verso, 1988), p. 2. Although feminist theatre theory has insisted that realistic structures and acting styles always imprison women, it has simultaneously argued for the importance of context.

27. Ibid., p. 4.

audiences—although distinctions between levels are ones of emphasis, rather than of rigid separation."[28]

In the theatre various factors compete to control meaning: the structure and system of representation promoted by the script; the actor's dynamic creation of an acting style which establishes a certain relationship between actor, character, and audience; the director's mode of mediating between playwright, actor, and audience; and the audience's active response to the resulting performance text; not to mention the designers, theatre architects, city planners, publicists, and critics' creative contributions.

Furthermore, in the theatre, production and reception of the performance text occur simultaneously; the (absent) male playwright does, paradoxically, appear, but his presence is mediated through a precise and ever-changing interrelationship among and between actor, character, director, and audience. It is particularly useful, then, for feminists to examine not only the structure of the male playwright's script and the female actor's style of acting but also the way these two factors intersect at specific historical moments, as well as in hypothetical contexts, as they compete to perform woman. The political efficacy of playwrights' structures and performers' acting styles cannot be judged independently of their connection to a particular script produced at a particular moment in history. To critique conventional behavior, an acting style must be visible to actors and audiences as a departure from the norm. Any style that enables actors and spectators to become once again conscious of performance may be illuminating for women, whether that style is Brechtian, naturalistic, or based in any of a number of other approaches. For late nineteenth-century audiences accustomed to the

28. Christine Gledhill, "Pleasurable Negotiations," in Pribram, *Female Spectators,* p. 68. Gledhill's theory draws "on a number of tenets of neo-Marxism, semiotics, and psychoanalysis, while at the same time challenging the textual determinism and formalism of these approaches. . . . In place of 'dominant ideology'—with its suggestion either of conspiratorial imposition or of unconscious interpellation—the concept of 'hegemony,' as developed by Antonio Gramsci, underpins the model of negotiation. According to Gramsci, since ideological power in bourgeois society is as much a matter of persuasion as of force, it is never secured once and for all, but has continually to be re-established in a constant to and fro between contesting groups. 'Hegemony' describes the ever shifting, ever negotiating play of ideological, social and political forces through which power is maintained and contested" (p. 68).

conventional codes of melodrama, realism made those codes seem strange, for in realism the female actor exceeded the womanly characters or styles of performance behavior the audience had grown to expect. And in that excess, that visibility, lay power.

Until recently many theatre historians viewed the developments of the nineteenth century as an evolution toward the opposing styles of realism and nonrealism or idealism.[29] As Thomas Postlewait observes: "Today, of course, we look with suspicion on an evolutionary theory of drama and theater history" because of its basis in outmoded positivistic thought; but the bipolar view of acting styles lingers, preventing us from understanding the significant differences among the plethora of performance styles that now exists.[30] The modern history of acting styles may be viewed as a site of the emergence of new models of behavior, similar to the scientific models discussed by Thomas S. Kuhn, which reconfigure our understanding of our position in the world by allowing us to accommodate new information, so that we may become once again aware of performance.[31] One possible avenue, then, for understanding the historical changes in the theatre is the replacement of acting styles that have become "normalized" (that is, so conventional as to be invisible) with styles that emphasize by their very newness the consciousness of performance. These uncommon styles enable the audience to see the seams, the gap between the actor and the character (where the potential for transformation lies), as well as the actor's mastery of (that is, submission to) the role.[32] For that reason, new styles can be particularly useful to feminists interested in altering standard roles.

29. See, for example, chap. 16 of a standard theatre-history textbook, Oscar Brockett's *History of the Theatre*, 3d ed. (Boston: Allyn and Bacon, 1977), pp. 467–507, a discussion of French, German, British, and Russian realism and nonrealism, or idealism.

30. Thomas Postlewait, "Historiography and the Theatrical Event: A Primer with Twelve Cruxes," *Theatre Journal* 43, 2 (May 1991): 175.

31. "When, that is, the [scientific] profession can no longer evade anomalies that subvert the existing tradition of scientific practice—then begin the extraordinary investigations that lead the profession at last to a new set of commitments, a new basis for the practice of science." Thomas S. Kuhn, *The Structure of Scientific Revolutions*, 2d ed. (Chicago: University of Chicago Press, 1970), p. 6.

32. There are two major and diametrically opposed styles of performance emerging on the margins of theatre in the United States: performance art or rituals that try to blur the distinction between daily "performances" and theatre, and

Each performance style that exposes conventions reminds the audience that the actor is *there:* performing according to a code but also existing beyond that code. By shifting conventions in this way, the emerging style keeps audiences focused on the performative nature of behavior. Audiences enjoy this process as long as enough vestiges of the old style remain to make it intelligible, for then the audience can see the difference between the conventional code and the actor's unique contribution, and can thereby witness both the stricture and the freedom of transformation. A new performance style makes visible the actor's movements and choices because the audience carries in mind the memory of an earlier style. Thus, it is in moments of stylistic change that we are best able to examine constructions of the body, including gender constructions. A female actor inaugurating what is perceived to be a novel performance style shows that, although a woman can succeed within existing models, she is not trapped in them. In the production situations I both study and envision, actors create or attempt to create new performance styles; the results resist neat or simple definition.

I do not mean to understate male playwrights' power over the styles adopted by actors, female or male. Academic theatre discourse, through acting textbooks, still frequently promotes the notion that it is the playwright and not the actor who generates changes in style, thus reinforcing the playwright's legal claim to controlling that style. The contradictory contention of directing textbooks that it is the director who establishes style creates an active debate about which agent does ultimately govern style. Playwrights still possess a great

---

dance/theatre work such as that of Martha Clarke, Ping Chong, and Robert Wilson, which separates the two so drastically that the performers at times resemble architectural shapes more than human figures. These phenomena may be viewed, I think, as different solutions to the same problem: how can the playwright, and in turn the actor and director, remind the audience that they are watching a *performance?* That consciousness of performance, according to Herbert Blau, constitutes theatre. Without an awareness of some mystery, some potentially transformative act, some *separateness,* there is no performance. The curious fact in current theatre is that the convention of psychologically realistic acting so pervades the mainstream that for a performance to create a sense of the theatrical, it must move either closer to daily life (as in some performance art) or closer to mechanization (as in much dance/theatre). Both moves satisfy the needs of the playwright, director, and actors for visibility. See Herbert Blau, *The Eye of Prey: Subversions of the Postmodern* (Bloomington: Indiana University Press, 1987), pp. 169–88.

deal of authority; their power has been upheld in many legal battles, most notably in productions of Samuel Beckett's scripts. There is, however, a difference between *production style,* which encompasses the entire artistic approach to any given staging (and which is traditionally viewed as the responsibility of the director in conjunction with or in opposition to the playwright or the script), and *performance style,* which commonly pertains to the actor's movement or pattern of gestures, and which is much more likely to be regarded, sometimes anxiously, as the actor's own province, despite the efforts of the playwright and the director (and the critic) to control it.

The idea of the playwright's "acting" in the script receives wide acceptance in contemporary textbooks, and is supported indirectly through the establishment of a canon and through separate academic societies devoted to individual playwrights (the Ibsen Society, the Strindberg Society, the International Brecht Society, the Harold Pinter Society, the Beckett Society—and even the Shepard "cult"). In this tradition actors are encouraged to focus on the playscript rather than on themselves or the director as the privileged source of style. Hardie Albright's *Acting: The Creative Process* is organized along lines that reveal how the academy trains actors to understand the genesis of performance styles. In part three, "Styles in Acting," Albright discusses Restoration and eighteenth-century styles under headings named for the actors who created them: David Garrick, Sally Kemble (Sarah Siddons), Edmund Kean. In discussing the nineteenth century, by contrast, he lists Oscar Wilde, Henrik Ibsen, Anton Chekhov.[33] Jerry Blunt concurs with the playwright-centered view: "A style is born because an artist—he is more likely to be a writer, painter, or musician than an actor—finds current forms of expression insufficient or wrong for his purposes."[34] Like Blunt, Albright acknowledges the eclecticism of the 1960s theatre scene in the United States: "The time has come when an actor must know many different styles of acting."[35] But, as another of their contemporaries remarks: "Style is inherent in the play script and therefore is not a mode which may be arbitrarily imposed. . . . It seems obvious

33. Hardie Albright, *Acting: The Creative Process* (Belmont, Calif.: Dickenson, 1968).
34. Jerry Blunt, *The Composite Art of Acting* (London: Macmillan, 1966), p. 342.
35. Albright, *Acting,* p. 123.

that for a particular script one style will be more appropriate than another."[36]

According to Robert Benedetti, style refers to "the unique intrinsic properties and manner of construction of an individual play"; he advises actors that "your objective is to make the style of your performance a direct expression and extension of the style of the play. . . . You cannot act a style; true style results from doing the specific job at hand in the manner demanded by the form of the play."[37] In a more recent acting textbook Jerry L. Crawford reflects the current interest in intercultural training by including a section on acting in "Oriental" theatre yet reinscribes the still lingering tradition that style, even an eclectic intermingling of styles, is authorized by the playwright rather than the actor or even the director: "The task of any actor relative to the delineation of style is to understand and find ways to execute or perform the author's/character's choices accurately and with a truthful sense of inevitablity."[38] In his study *Script Analysis*, David Grote defines style as "the manner in which all elements of a work are integrated into a whole. Hence, a style is indicated in the written script and must then be translated into the visual/aural style of the production."[39] Even Douglas A. Russell's *Period Style for the Theatre*, based on an examination of the styles of successive eras rather than playwrights or directors, holds that "each work generates its own style."[40] The playwright, rather than the actor, is viewed as the primary creative artist authorizing new types of performance; the actor's job is to locate and inhabit, to animate and interpret, that style. My own book complicates this configuration of the relationship between the actor and the script and rethinks the effect of specific styles of playwriting and acting.

36. Everett M. Schreck, *Principles and Styles of Acting* (Reading, Mass.: Addison-Wesley, 1970), p. 193.

37. Robert Benedetti, *The Actor at Work*, 3d ed. (Englewood Cliffs, N.J.: Prentice-Hall, 1981), pp. 243–44.

38. Jerry L. Crawford, *Acting in Person and in Style*, 3d ed. (Dubuque, Iowa: William C. Brown, 1983), p. 139. The question to answer, Crawford suggests, is: "How can the actor arrive at an authentic appraisal of the playwright's personal stamp or style?" (p. 140).

39. David Grote, *Script Analysis: Reading and Understanding the Playscript for Production* (Belmont, Calif.: Wadsworth, 1985), p. 239.

40. Douglass A. Russell, *Period Style for the Theatre*, 2d ed. (Boston: Allyn and Bacon, 1987), p. xv.

Because performance styles are constantly being normalized through repetition, the usefulness of any given style may be measured not simply by its nature but rather by its originality as perceived by a specific audience. To transform ourselves, we must be conscious of the nature of performance itself: we must be aware that performance is a repeated series of *acts,* and that "gender is in no way a stable identity or locus of agency from which various acts proceed [*sic*]: rather, it is an identity tenuously constituted in time—an identity instituted through a *stylized repetition of acts.*"[41] With each new definition of style comes a redefinition of the relationship between actor and character, director, and audience. And because of that new definition, the actor may once again become visible, foregrounding the nature of performance. Some of the playwrights I consider prompted more collaboration from actors, directors, and audiences than others; some found female actors who achieved unique performance styles during their lifetimes and others did not; but all of them share the effort to evoke a particular world onstage through specific new structural models.

Within the performance approach employed in this book, each chapter draws from a different body of theory in response to the precise nature of the playwright's and actors' work. Chapter 1, "Ibsen and the Critical Actor," analyzes the way in which female (and male) actors investigated Ibsen's use of retrospective action, collaborating with the playwright to convey past, present, and future dramatic action simultaneously. *Hedda Gabler* and *The Master Builder* serve as key scripts in explicating the critical acting style that female actor/directors originated in conjunction with Ibsen's retrospective structural mode. This chapter draws heavily on theatre history as well as on Lionel Abel's theory of metatheatre. At the turn of the century Elizabeth Robins, as a female interpreter of Ibsen's scripts, created a critical style that simultaneously placed on view the melodramatic and realistic bases of her character, complicating her position onstage and enabling audiences to become conscious of and critique the performance of woman.

Chapter 2, "Strindberg and the Transformational Actor," shows how August Strindberg employed a nonlinear, experimental struc-

41. Judith Butler, "Performative Acts and Gender Constitution: An Essay in Phenomenology and Feminist Theory," in Case, *Performing Feminisms,* p. 270.

ture, seeking a "dematerial" style of performance, with Harriet
Bosse's acting in *A Dream Play* providing the only successful realization of that attempt. A rereading of Strindberg's structural method,
rooted in Hindu tales of transformation, provides the alternative
"transformational" actor—newly envisioned in this chapter—an opportunity to expand somewhat the female actor's avenues of subversion by confusing the boundaries between reality and illusion in a
proliferating variety of performance styles. Strindberg's misreading
of Hindu myth, however, circumscribes that subversion, despite the
episodic breaks in the narrative. Hindu theories regarding the nature of reality and illusion inform this analysis.

Frank Kermode's concept of the parable as a site of mystery and
excess rather than closure provides the basis for my reassessment of
the Brecht Collective's structural and performance codes. Chapter
3, "The Brecht Collective and the Parabolic Actor," rereads *The Good
Person of Szechwan* to discover traces of Brecht's female collaborators,
particularly Ruth Berlau and Margarete Steffin, and to explain how
a revised reading of the Brecht Collective's methods of characterization permits the actor and the director to use the theatre as a labora-
tory in which to explore gender issues with an actively engaged and
argumentative audience. This chapter draws heavily on and recon-
siders feminist theatre theories regarding Brecht's work.

Chapter 4, "Pinter and the Cinematic Actor" employs the work of
Christian Metz and contemporary feminist film theorists to explain
acting in Pinter. A close analysis of the structure of *Old Times* reveals
cinematic codes that prompt the female actor to build a unique
"holographic" relationship with her character, her director, and her
audience. These codes are considered in light of responses to Laura
Mulvey's theory of the heterosexist male gaze in the cinema.

Chapter 5, "Shepard and the Improvisational Actor," draws from
the world of art theory, using Robert Rauschenberg's "combines" as
a metaphor to explain the way in which Sam Shepard jams two
dramatic actions together like found objects. This structural approach fosters an "improvisational actor," as well as a director and
an audience ready to make sense of the peculiar double actions
emerging from plays such as *Buried Child*. While demonstrating the
patriarchal basis of Shepard's narratives, this examination also sug-

gests ways in which female actors may employ Shepard's structures to their own advantage.

Chapter 6, "Beckett and the *Nō* Actor," explores the production situation encouraged by Beckett's late plays by comparing his structural system to that of Japanese *nō* drama. Spiraling toward *ma*, the blank time-space in which nothing (and everything) exists, Beckett's female actors resemble nothing so much as traditional *nō* performers, operating as if without a director in a highly controlled and encoded stage space for a coterie audience that knows the code. This final chapter utilizes *nō* theory, Buddhist theory, and feminist theories regarding Beckett to resituate his actors—particularly his female actors. Billie Whitelaw's portrayal of May in *Footfalls* figures prominently, revealing some of the rewards but more particularly the dangers of acting in Beckett.

Each of these canonized male playwrights creates key female characters: Ibsen's Hedda and Hilda, Strindberg's Daughter of Indra, the Brecht Collective's Shen Te/Shui Ta, Pinter's Kate and Anna, Shepard's Shelley, and Beckett's May. What I am concerned with is the position of female actors staging these characters. Whereas many feminist theatre scholars have dismissed all women's work in the canon as a process of simple victimization and others have tried to redeem the male playwrights as geniuses who write "universal" women's roles, I see a complex intertwining of hegemonic scripting and feminist countermovements. The implications for future theories of feminist theatre are significant. One cannot simply dismiss realism and psychologically based acting as patriarchal, or count on theories developed by the Brecht Collective or French feminists to create liberating performance spaces for women. The history of performance suggests that, given the number and complexity of the variables involved, the challenge is greater than that.

Chapter One

Ibsen and the Critical Actor

In historical analyses of acting styles, the phrase "realistic acting" is as ubiquitous as it is puzzling. The Kembles' style was supposedly more realistic than Garrick's, Booth's than the Kembles'. Frequently, the term is used to describe a type of movement and vocalization onstage, or the degree of reliance on traditional theatrical poses, both slippery footholds. Despite its popular usage, the phrase fails to define the precise relationship among the various elements that create the performance text, focusing instead on what the audience sees of the actor's craft. Too often it discourages an analysis of the actor's preparation for a performance and his or her relationship with the various other agents who compete to create meaning in a performance situation: the playwright, the other actors, the director, and the audience, not to mention the designers and technicians, the theatre architects, the urban planners, the publicists, the culture at large.

If one is to have a fuller understanding of the nature of acting (and of playwriting), it is necessary to study the forces that create the results we term either a "realistic" or a "nonrealistic" performance style. These terms serve as catchphrases signifying almost any new style of performance, any new development in the way an actor approaches a script or moves and speaks onstage. Instead of relying on them, we can analyze acting as an art, a process of creation, within the context of its materials, examining particularly closely the relationship between the actor and the script.

The playwright structures the script in such a way as to invite a specific mode of exploration, one the director and actors may or may not choose to realize in any given production. Frequently in the modern and contemporary theatre the most successful playwrights have been those whose work has prompted actors to imagine a startlingly new performance style, and to attempt to realize it. Ibsen's scripts did just that: they created opportunities for actors, who generated an innovative style that distinguished their work. Strindberg's attempt at a new acting style was thwarted by his lack of access to sophisticated technology, among other things, but the structural model with which he and some of his contemporaries experimented eventually succeeded in launching a variety of performance styles. This accomplishment depended in large part on the playwright's manipulation of structure to suggest for actors a different process of preparation and performance, thereby transforming the work of directors and audiences as well.

In the second half of the nineteenth century Henrik Ibsen adapted the structural method of retrospective action to his own ends, altering the traditional relationship between actors and their scripts. By opening his plays at the end rather than the beginning of a long, secret-ridden story line, Ibsen requires actors to reveal facts about the past in the present. As his retrospective dramas supplanted melodramas on stages in Britain and the United States, actors gradually had to alter the process of creating character. Partly because of this retrospective quality, Ibsen's scripts jolted actors into revising their attitude toward character and performance. As Ibsen's fame spread within the theatre and later within the academy, actors employed their revolutionary "Ibsen" acting style as they approached many other playwrights' scripts as well, including melodramatic scripts, which began to incorporate some of the elements of Ibsen's dramaturgy. The prime movers in this revolution were female actors and actor-managers, tired of the predictable women's roles offered by even the most sophisticated nineteenth-century melodramas. They were eager for a chance to transform themselves, to make the audience conscious of a new way of performing, particularly a new way of performing womanhood.

In the introduction to William Archer's *Masks or Faces?* Lee Strasberg, the doyen of modern American Method acting, argues against the idea that a new type of script requires a new acting methodology: "Some present-day theories of acting suggest that the actor's creative processes differ for different styles of plays, that while one approach may be right for the realistic play, another is necessary for the classic or poetic play. Does this imply that a painter or a musician working in the modern idiom feels less keenly or is less involved in his work than one working in the more conventional realistic style?"[1] Here Strasberg switches his focus from acting style to emotional involvement. Actors' creative processes do in fact differ as they approach different types of scripts, but not necessarily in terms of their emotional lives. The intellectual approach to the role—the process of studying the text and planning its execution— often changes for the actor, depending on the performance cues suggested by the script as well as the material conditions of the rehearsal process and actual production. The question to consider here is not whether a "realistic" actor *feels* the role more than a "classical" or a "nonrealistic" actor but what the nature of the process undertaken by the actor is. Furthermore, how did this process change for the actor as nineteenth-century melodramas were super-seded by realistic dramas?

New acting strategies may, of course, be generated by actors working collectively, or by visionary directors such as Vsevelod Meyer-hold (1874–1942) or Robert Wilson, or by the "importation" of a style of production adapted from another playwright or school of directing or design. In this study of the relationship between actors and playwrights in the canon, it is the playwright's structural conventions that provide the most logical starting point for an examination of acting styles, for in each case the writer has been widely understood to encode a specific performance style in the script, an acting style so unique that it has been given his name.

This process of naming the style for the playwright instead of the actor emerged, ironically, at a historical moment when female rather than male actors might have been recognized as the leaders of various revolutions in acting styles. As the character of "woman" became more visible and more complex within the male script in the late nineteenth century, the real women who played these complex char-

1. Lee Strasberg, Introduction, in William Archer, *Masks or Faces?* (New York: Hill and Wang, 1957), p. xiii.

acters were often denied the satisfaction of having a style named for them. But they forged a new performance approach nonetheless, frequently from the margins rather than in the spotlighted tradition of the actor-manager. And they did so even when the playwright was not present at rehearsals. To illustrate that fact, this chapter focuses on Ibsen's scripts as they were introduced into England by actors such as Elizabeth Robins, whose 1891 *Hedda Gabler* was produced in London, far from Ibsen's directorial control.

Robins, Marion Lea, and others like them may be seen as artists reshaping an age-old craft—not unlike painters or sculptors or musicians in the late nineteenth and early twentieth centuries. Clive Bell claims in his 1914 essay "The Aesthetic Hypothesis" that "significant form" is the most important element of any artwork, and that the essential quality for approaching a work of art is sensitivity to form. Actors and directors at the end of the nineteenth century responded to the new structural experimentation of playwrights, becoming artists in form. Actors discovered that form is created in performance, and consequently felt empowered by their new collaboration with playwrights.[2]

In his review of François-Joseph Talma's "Reflections on Acting," H. C. Fleeming Jenkin wrote: "Those who know what this study [of acting] means are driven almost to distraction when they hear an actor—perhaps a great actor—complimented on being able to remember the words of his part. But, on the other hand, it must be almost as galling when a great actor is told that he really understands his author's meaning."[3] Jenkin's attitude toward the script typifies the dominant nineteenth-century (pre-Ibsen) viewpoint. The written text was customarily viewed as a detailed skeleton, easily understood and visualized, requiring only the flesh and emotion of the actor to be brought to life. Since actors frequently received their texts through "sides"—that is, scripts containing only one character's lines and cues—their opportunities to ponder the meaning of an

2. Of course, many directors and actors (Meyerhold and the dadaists, for example) launched their own experimentation independent of playwrights; but the present study is concerned only with actors (and their directors) working with what seemed to them unique new playscripts—scripts that enabled them to develop a new performance style.

3. H. C. Fleeming Jenkin, "Review," in *Papers on Acting*, ed. Brander Matthews (New York: Hill and Wang, 1958), p. 61.

entire play were limited to the first company read-through and any other chances they themselves created.

Even nineteenth-century textbooks on acting seldom focused on textual problems. George Henry Lewes's 1875 *On Actors and the Art of Acting* introduces the idea of character psychology, but it does not contain a separate chapter on textual analysis, nor does it focus any more closely on "understanding the author's meaning" than its predecessor, Henry Siddons's *Practical Illustrations of Rhetorical Gesture and Action.*[4] Gustave Garcia's book *The Actor's Art* (1882), as well as Byron W. King's *Practice of Speech and Successful Selections* (1888) and Alfred Ayers's *Acting and Actors* (1894), follow the trend toward a concern with technical mastery of voice, movement, and gesture to illustrate or express the passions that were often listed in the table of contents.[5] This is not to say that Talma, Coquelin, the Kembles, Keans, Bancrofts, and others disregarded the script, but rather to suggest that they did not consider determining the play's or character's action or painstakingly analyzing structure to be the crux of the art of acting. The nineteenth-century domestic melodramas and French well-made plays which constituted typical British and U.S. theatrical fare required relatively little analysis, compared to Ibsen's plays with their hidden keys to the plot. Shakespearean dramas were, by custom, tailored to the skills of the leading male actor rather than vice versa. Even the psychologically dense melodramas of the late nineteenth century seemed more accessible than the structural recesses of Ibsen and his successors.

Later acting theorists, such as Stanislavsky and his fellow proponents of realistic performance, developed a methodology that placed the script rather than the actor in a central position, thereby potentially empowering modern playwrights in a new way. Chekhov's plays

4. G. H. Lewes, *On Actors and the Art of Acting* (Leipzig: Bernhard Tauchnitz, 1875); Henry Siddons, *Practical Illustrations of Rhetorical Gesture and Action* (London: Sherwood, Neely, and Jones, 1822). See Joseph R. Roach, Jr., "G. H. Lewes and Performance Theory: Towards a 'Science of Acting,'" *Theatre Journal* 32 (1980): 312–28, for an analysis of Lewes's theory. See also Roach, *The Player's Passion: Studies in the Science of Acting* (Newark: University of Delaware Press, 1985).

5. Gustave Garcia, *The Actor's Art* (London: T. Pettitt, 1882); Byron W. King, *Practice of Speech and Successful Selections* (Pittsburgh: W. T. Nicholson, 1888); and Alfred Ayers, *Acting and Actors, Elocution and Elocutionists* (New York: Appleton, 1894).

as well as Ibsen's require considerable study. By the early twentieth century, theorists such as F. F. Mackay in his *Art of Acting* (1913) were including in their textbooks special sections or entire chapters on script analysis, and troupes such as that led by Jacques Copeau at the Théâtre du Vieux Colombier devoted a portion of each day to the analysis of "literary texts."[6]

The previous attitude (before Ibsen and Stanislavsky) of indifference toward the script is reflected in the attendant perception of the actor's collaboration with the dramatist. Since the script was viewed not as something fixed and immutable but as a kind of template for performance, the actor, undaunted by the playwright's words, felt free to alter them. As John Hill wrote in 1750: "[The actor] is not to content himself with following his author strictly and faithfully; but in many places he must assist and support him; he must even in some instances become a sort of author himself."[7] Hill suggested several ways in which actors might collaborate with their playwrights: they might "artfully throw in a monosyllable," add stage business, express sentiments "not delivered in the play," or omit lines or scenes.[8] In making these alterations, he says, actors must be guided by their "understanding"; but Hill's use of this term refers to the actor's sensitivity to the type of delivery that is required, not to his or her comprehension of the play's plot or its overall movement. This "understanding" is the same faculty that Frédérick Lemaître used when, in 1823, he decided to play Robert Macaire in *Auberge des Adrets* as a comic instead of a serious character; it has little to do with the kind of analysis practiced in contemporary college classes on script analysis for the actor.[9] Another example of this early nineteenth-century style of collaboration occurred when the French tenor Adolphe Nourrit decided to accept the role of the Jew Eleazar in the 1835 production of Eugène Scribe and Jacques-François Fromental Halévy's *La Juive*. Nourrit requested that Halévy, the com-

6. F. F. Mackay, *The Art of Acting* (New York: F. F. Mackay, 1913). Jacques Copeau, "The Manifesto of the Vieux Columbier," trans. Joseph M. Bernstein, in *Actors on Acting*, ed. Toby Cole and Helen Krich Chinoy (New York: Crown, 1970), p. 218.

7. John Hill, *The Actor: A Treatise on the Art of Playing* (London: R. Griffiths, 1750; rpt. New York: Benjamin Blom, 1971), p. 5.

8. Ibid., pp. 248–49.

9. See Constant Coquelin, "Art and the Actor," in Matthews, *Papers on Acting*, pp. 22–23.

poser, substitute an aria for the fourth-act finale. Halévy scored music for Nourrit's lyrics, turning Nourrit, in Constant Coquelin's later estimation, into both "commentator and creator."[10]

In contrast, many late nineteenth-century scripts engendered a new attitude toward the necessary collaboration between playwright and actor. In Ibsen's plays (and in those of some of his contemporaries) performers often had to search for clues to unravel the plot. They had to study the entire script then link together the events of the narrative to make sense of the plot and the characters' past connections. The female actors who first staged many of Ibsen's scripts perceived the playwright's complex cues to interdependent character and action. Unlike romantic dramas and melodramas, which frequently set forth every significant event in the lives of the characters in chronological order, Ibsen's retrospective method typically began the action just before the moment of crisis, revealing crucial past events only through hints. The actor, therefore, had to detect these prior events, which could be revealed only through a word or gesture (signs of the absent scene), and then had to convey the necessary relationship between that past text and the present action. Paradoxically, this new process increased the power and responsibility of female actors while it granted the male playwright greater recognition. Of course, when at the turn of the century Janet Achurch, Elizabeth Robins, and other early Ibsen interpreters approached their roles, they were not venturing onto totally unfamiliar terrain. They had performed fairly realistic characters and stage business in the plays of Tom Robertson, and they had dealt with retrospective action in translations of Scribe's well-made plays. The rest of their stage work, however, consisted primarily of appearances in British melodramas, which may have contained some realistic characters but generally not retrospective action, and in Shakespearean revivals, which despite their psychological density were written in poetic language and used a plot structure that illustrated the entire story.

With Ibsen, the female actor for the first time faced the task of portraying a realistic character in a play that depended heavily on retrospective action. This aspect of performing Ibsen has been largely ignored by American and British studies of acting style,

10. Ibid., pp. 19–20.

which often trace the reason for the emergence of a more natural or realistic style to Ibsen's complex portraits of bourgeois life, his stage business, the box sets he helped promote, or the power of heredity and environment in his work. Nonetheless, the relationship between Rebecca and Dr. West in *Rosmersholm*, the nature of Nora's secret life in *A Doll's House*, the tenor of Hedda's past comradeship with Løvborg: these must be discovered by the actor, defined in terms of the past as revealed by the text. The actors who played these characters enjoyed the close study they viewed as a necessary prelude to staging Ibsen's scripts. In 1905 Minnie Maddern Fiske wrote:

> Sympathy and understanding between author and player is required to secure the best results with the dramas of Ibsen. Lack of success, from the popular standpoint, is due to the fact that the producer has not studied the play long and faithfully. . . . The producer of the Ibsen play must understand that the drama presented is but one phase of the whole story—the finale, the dénoument. The principal characters were living their lives many years before the visible presentation. . . . To intelligently portray those characters and conditions requires an understanding of all that has gone before. The producer must delve into the childhood of these characters and follow their lives down to the stage drama— that is the demand Ibsen makes upon his stage director. It is necessary that he shall know and be able to convey to the audience what he knows and the meaning of the drama as it is finally presented. The actors cannot always be asked to know the psychology of the parts or of the drama as a whole—the stage manager must be in a position to explain the parts and to convey the ideas that Ibsen wishes to express.[11]

Although she believed the final responsibility rested with the stage manager, Fiske herself developed a new method of study for approaching her Ibsen roles. Like other female Ibsen actors, she enacted imaginatively much of Hedda's past life: "In the study of Ibsen, I had to devise what was, for me, a new method. To learn what Hedda was, I had to imagine all that she had *ever* been."[12] Ibsen

11. Minnie Maddern Fiske, "Ibsen versus 'Humpty Dumpty,'" *Harper's Weekly*, February 4, 1905, p. 160.
12. Quoted in Alexander Woolcott, *Mrs. Fiske: Her Views on Actors, Acting, and the Problems of Production* (New York: Century, 1917), p. 62.

provided "keys" to "unlock [Hedda's] past," so Fiske could live through in her imagination "the scenes of [Hedda's] girlhood with her father," the first meeting between Hedda and Løvborg, "and all other meetings that packed his mind and hers with imperishable memories all the rest of their days."[13] Fiske also realized that when portraying Rebecca in *Rosmersholm*, the actor must consider carefully the character's past relationship with Dr. West: "It is the illumination of that past which she comes upon unexpectedly in a truth let fall by the unconscious Kroll—a truth so significant that it shatters her ambitions, sends her great house of cards toppling about her ears, touches the spring of her confession, and brings tragedy to its swift, inevitable conclusion. . . . I do not see how [an actor] could make this scene *intelligible* unless she had perceived and felt its hidden meaning: nor how, having perceived and felt it, she could help playing it well."[14]

Another of Ibsen's early interpreters, Elizabeth Robins, contended that actors not only had to unlock the past in Ibsen's scripts but also had to discover the playwright's "master-keys" to the characters' present concerns. She believed that Ibsen, unlike the melodramatists, offered the female actor a choice of keys. For instance, she was able "to see Hedda Gabler as pitiable in her hungry loneliness—to see her as tragic" because of the insight Ibsen granted her in the crucial scene at the end of act one, when Hedda tells Tesman that she still has one thing to kill time with—her pistols. This one line was for Robins a central symbol of Hedda's character: "It is perhaps curious Ibsen should have known that a good many women have found it possible to get through life by help of the knowledge that they have the power to end it rather than accept certain slaveries. Naturally enough, no critic, as far as I know, has ever noticed this governing factor in Hedda's outlook, her consciousness of one sort of power, anyway—the power of escape."[15] For Robins, suicide was not merely

13. Ibid., pp. 62–63.
14. Ibid., pp. 69–70.
15. Elizabeth Robins, *Ibsen and the Actress* (London: Leonard and Virginia Woolf, 1928), p. 30. In London during the 1890s Robins staged the first English productions of *Hedda Gabler*, *The Master Builder*, *Brand*, *Little Eyolf*, and *John Gabriel Borkman;* she revived *Rosmersholm* and also acted in *The Pillars of Society* and *A Doll's House*. For information on Robins's theatrical career, see Jane Marcus, "Elizabeth Robins: A Biography" (Ph.D. diss., Northwestern University, 1973); Joanne Gates, "'Sometimes

a melodramatic gesture. In 1887 her husband of two years, an actor named George Parks, had committed suicide by tying himself to a suit of medieval armor and drowning himself in the Charles River in Boston. In fact, Parks had pressured Robins into marrying him in the first place by threatening suicide. So Robins understood self-destruction as a potent weapon, a vehicle for manipulation as well as a means of violent protest and an escape from fixed gender roles, whether female or male. She thus viewed the process of enacting Hedda's suicide as a means of commenting on the role Hedda is asked to play in life.

Robins argued that an Ibsen script was open to more than one approach, precisely because of the type of collaborative effort it demanded:

> More than anybody who ever wrote for the stage, Ibsen could, and usually did, collaborate with his actors. I do not mean that he ever consulted one of them; the collaboration was a subtler thing than that. Ibsen was by training so intensely "un homme du théâtre" that, to an extent that I know in no other dramatist, he saw where he could leave some of his greatest effects to be made by the actor, and so left them. It was as if he knew that only so could he get his effects—that is, by standing aside and watching his spell work not only through the actor, but *by* the actor as fellow-creator. . . . By the power of his truth and the magic of his poetry he does something to the imagination that not only gives actors an impetus, but an impetus in a right direction. And I do not say *the* right direction.[16]

There was at least one major difference between Robins's and Fiske's idea of the key to Hedda. Whereas Robins believed that Hedda was, from the first, strong enough to take her life, Fiske unveiled General Gabler's "shining pistols" in her imaginative recreation of Hedda's

---

Suppressed and Sometimes Embroidered': The Life and Writing of Elizabeth Robins, 1862–1952" (Ph.D. diss., University of Massachusetts, 1987); Thomas Postlewait, *Prophet of the New Drama: William Archer and the Ibsen Campaign* (Westport, Conn.: Greenwood Press, 1986); Gay Gibson Cima, "Elizabeth Robins: The Genesis of an Independent Manageress," *Theatre Survey* 21 (November 1980): 145–63; and Cima, "Elizabeth Robins: Ibsen Actress-Manageress" (Ph.D. diss., Cornell University, 1978).
  16. Robins, *Ibsen and the Actress*, pp. 52–54.

past and determined that Hedda's cowardice was such that she would only "toy" with them.[17]

These actors, then, developed a new and more complex attitude toward the script and toward collaboration with the playwright. Responding to the demands of Ibsen's use of retrospective action, they studied their scripts with care, finding keys to elusive dramatic actions suggested by the playwright himself, but to be discovered and created onstage by the women themselves. Paradoxically, Ibsen, the master builder of a new structure, provided them with what they experienced as a novel freedom in performance: the ability to demonstrate, and to critique, the performative nature of the role of woman.

Earlier nineteenth-century actors had taken a very different approach, not only in their attitude toward the script but also in their view of character and action or motivation. They were accustomed to performing in melodrama. Whether in the rough-and-ready Sims and Buchanan melodramas or the drawing-room melodramas of the Kendal tradition, the actor's pattern of approaching a role was fairly standardized: accustomed to a particular "line of business" within an acting company (as ingenue leading lady or "first heavy," for example), the actor was assigned the usual character type, and at the first rehearsal was given a "side." The actor then proceeded to select from the prescribed code of performance regulating the theatre of the time the gestures and vocal patterns that would reveal the stock motivation for that specific character type. As Shaw argued in his appendix to *The Quintessence of Ibsenism:* "The old technique breaks down in the new theatre; for though in theory it is a technique of general application, making an artist so plastic that he can mould himself to any shape designed by the dramatist, in practice it is but a stock of tones and attitudes out of which, by appropriate selection and combination, a certain limited number of conventional stage figures can be made.[18]

17. When, in interviewing the actor, Alexander Woolcott described the guns as "those pistols that somehow symbolize so perfectly the dangers this little coward would merely play with," Fiske shook hands with him in enthusiastic agreement. Woolcott, *Mrs. Fiske,* p. 63.

18. George Bernard Shaw, appendix to *The Quintessence of Ibsenism,* in *Shaw on Theatre,* ed. E. J. West (New York: Hill and Wang, 1958), p. 5.

Partly because of their more circumscribed actions, early melodramas generated an acting style different from that prompted by Ibsen's scripts: the melodramatic protagonist, usually in conflict with external forces rather than divided against the self, struggles to win a battle, while the antagonist tries to block that action. The play usually moves toward an idealized, simplified truth: to show that right triumphs, or that suffering is rewarded. As Robert Corrigan notes: "One always knows where one is in melodrama. Moral principles are clearly established, and so, too, are the rules of proper conduct (factors which in large measure explain the stereotyped characters and rigid moral distinctions which are so characteristic of the form)."[19] It is no accident that character types, lines of business, the star system, and stock companies were all features of the nineteenth-century theatre. Customarily the actor's job was, in play after play, to follow a certain, very narrowly defined action: the hero's role was to save the day, the villain's to prevent him from doing so, the victim's to suffer bravely. In approaching a new part, the actor knew the line of action she was expected to play the moment she was offered it, even before reading the play, and she naturally enough focused not on determining the action, which was self-evident, but rather on individualizing the character type through use of her voice and body. Although psychological melodramas such as the Henry Irving vehicle *The Bells* would complicate this process, the general thrust, especially for female actors, remained the same: they suffered bravely.

Constant Coquelin in his "Art and the Actor" maintained that it is not enough for a playwright to create the "soul" of a character; "a body must be provided for it as well."[20] He perceived the actor's art to be one of embodiment, a filling-out or amplification of the character as delineated by the script. Dion Boucicault, among other writers of melodrama, discusses acting in similar terms: "Acting is to perform, to be the part: to be it in your arms, your legs; to be what you are acting, to be it all over, that is acting."[21] Boucicault then divides the practice of acting into voice, gesture and carriage, and

19. Robert Corrigan, ed., *Laurel British Drama: The Nineteenth Century* (New York: Dell, 1967), pp. 13–14.
20. Coquelin, "Art and the Actor," p. 21.
21. Dion Boucicault, "The Art of Acting," in Matthews, *Papers on Acting*, p. 147.

character study. Boucicault illustrates his notion of character analysis
with this anecdote about a production of *London Assurance:* "I was
producing a comedy in which Mr. Farren . . . played a leading part.
He did not ask what he was going to wear, but he came to me and
said, 'Who did you draw this party from; had you any type?' I said
'Yes, I had,' and mentioned the names of two old fogies who, at the
time, were well known in London society. One he knew, the other he
did not. He went and studied Sir Harcourt Courtly, and he studied
by the speediest method."[22] In another example Boucicault recounts
the time an actor came to him to inquire about Dazzle, another
character in *London Assurance.* "Do you know really a good type?" the
actor queried. Boucicault responded by telling a story about the
friend on whom he had modeled Dazzle, who, on hearing that a
friend had received £10,000 from the estate of a distant relative,
"looked at the ceiling and said, 'If I had only £10,000! Bless me! I
should be having £20,000 a year for six months.'" Boucicault then
confides to his reader: "From that he understood immediately what
the character was. That is the way to study character, to get at the
bottom of human nature."[23]

The actor's first task, Boucicault contends, is to define and copy
character type (always staying within the line of business) and then to
follow the technical rules outlined for voice and gesture. Boucicault
understood that characterization must be multidimensional. He believed three aspects are present in all characters: "First there is the
man by himself—as he is to himself—as he is to his God. That is one
man, the inner man, as he is when alone; the unclothed man. Then
there is the native man, the domestic man, as he is to his family. Still
there is a certain amount of disguise. He is not as he is to other men.
Then there is the man as he stands before the world at large, as he is
outside in society."[24] But these aspects were to emerge only one at a
time: for Boucicault, the master of melodrama, character was whole.

Since character action tended to be formulaic, it is not surprising
that to the eighteenth- and nineteenth-century actor, action meant
not motivation but gesture, or what a present-day actor might call
stage business. In *The Actor's Art* (1882), for example, Gustave Garcia

22. Ibid., p. 156.
23. Ibid., pp. 156–57.
24. Ibid., p. 158.

advises that "a calm thought will prompt a quiet action"; one chapter of his book is titled "Action of the Arms and Hands."[25] It was not until Ibsen, Stanislavsky, and their successors that the term *action*, so closely associated with gesture over the years, gradually evolved to mean motivation, and then the overall movement of a scene or entire play. To the eighteenth- and early to mid-nineteenth-century actor, action meant a gesture executed when a passion was felt.

In part because of the nature of the task these actors were asked to perform, sensibility, or the tendency to be susceptible to the various passions they would have to express through gesture, was often seen as their most valuable asset. François-Joseph Talma (1763–1826) identified the "two essential faculties" of acting as sensibility and intelligence. He defined sensibility as the emotional whirlwind that would offer the actor the key to his creation:

> To my mind, sensibility is not only that faculty which an actor possesses of being moved himself, and of affecting his being so far as to imprint on his features, and especially on his voice, that expression and those accents of sorrow which awake all the sympathies of the art . . . which associates the actor with the inspirations of the poet, transports him back to the past, and enables him to look on at the lives of historical figures or the impassioned figures created by genius—which reveals to him, as though by magic, their physiognomy, their heroic stature, their habits, all the shades of their character, all the movements of their soul, and even their singularities. I also call sensibility that faculty of exaltation which agitates an actor, takes possession of his senses, shakes even his very soul, and enables him to enter into the most tragic situations and the most terrible of the passions as if they were his own.[26]

This actor, whose career was launched in the eighteenth century but stretched into the nineteenth, was guided by his emotional sympathy with the character, and the almost mystical insight he gained through it.

Intelligence for Talma meant "prudent" acting; it was instrumental only as the performer monitored, selected, remembered, and

25. Garcia, *The Actor's Art,* p. 51.

26. François-Joseph Talma, "Reflections on Acting," in Matthews, *Papers on Acting,* pp. 48–49.

reproduced the effects—gestural or vocal—inspired by emotion: "The intelligence that accompanies sensibility judges the impressions which the latter has made us feel; it selects, arranges them, and subjects them to calculation. . . . Intelligence then passes all these means in review, connecting them and fixing them in his memory, to re-employ them at pleasure in succeeding representations."[27]

Intelligence as the ability to analyze the text, to probe its depths in a systematic way, was often seen at that time as antithetical to the art of the actor. Fanny Kemble (1809–1892), in her essay "On the Stage," says that "the reflective and analytical quality has little to do with the complex process of acting."[28] Even general intelligence in the sense of an awareness of social and cultural trends was seen as somehow threatening to the true actor. George Arliss, in his 1926 introduction to "On the Stage," restates Kemble's observation that "greater intellectual cultivation and a purer and more elevated taste are unfavorable to the existence of the true theatrical spirit."[29] The late nineteenth-century actors involved in productions of Ibsen's plays disagreed, however; they felt justified in using all their critical faculties to analyze the scripts they staged.

Because in staging Ibsen the first task was to discover the line of action for both play and character, rather than merely to choose from a stock of passions and accompanying gestures, the actor required a new technique of study. Central to this approach was the concept of action as the overall movement of the play, the confluence of all the characters' motivations. F. F. Mackay was one of the first to explain this approach in the language that we now associate with Stanislavsky and Chekhov: "Dramatic art in its greatest perfection requires a group of artists, working together, and the correct result depends entirely on their harmonious action. In order to develop the intentions of the author, the group of artists seeking to represent the author's dramatic personae must rehearse the memorized words for the purpose of discovering the individual action of the several characters of the play, and so to conjoin those actions as to preserve the unity of purpose that a dramatic author must have, if he would present a successful play."[30]

27. Ibid., pp. 49–51.
28. Fanny Kemble, "On the Stage," in Matthews, *Papers on Acting*, p. 208.
29. George Arliss, introduction, to ibid., p. 202.
30. Mackay, *The Art of Acting*, p. 261.

Another acting text published before Stanislavsky's work was translated into English is Enid Rose's *Dramatic Art*, which also elucidates the Ibsen actor's approach to character: "Dramatic characters are once removed from the natural, being the result of contemplation and an imaginative choice on the part of the dramatist who has created an imaginary 'line' of consciousness for each of the persons in his drama."[31] This "'line' of consciousness" is parallel to a character's central motivation—the puzzle that Ibsen's performers first attempted to solve. Rose also echoes their concern with discovering the action or form of the play as a whole: "Unity of performance can only be attained when each player realized his part as a contribution to the whole; all his shades of variation in time, force, and pitch are conditioned by the whole 'line' of the drama."[32] Furthermore, as Mackay makes clear, this new actor concentrated on trying to perform actions in keeping with the intentions of the author.

Thus actors, particularly female actors, created the beginnings of what we now call psychologically real acting—and they did so through Ibsen. Of course, the full-blown articulation of this technique was realized by Stanislavsky, who directed his students not to read a text and decide on a passion but to read a script and determine its action:

> When you are choosing some bit of action leave feeling and spiritual content alone. Never seek to be jealous, or to make love or to suffer, for its own sake. All such feelings are the result of something that has gone before. Of the thing that goes before you should think as hard as you can. *As for the result, it will produce itself.* The false acting of passions, or of types, or the mere use of conventional gestures—these are all frequently faults in our profession. But you must keep away from these unrealities. You must not copy passions or copy types. You must live in the passions and in the types. Your acting of them must grow out of your living in them.[33]

In other words, although an actor may feel the conventional passions or portray a character reminiscent of conventional types,

31. Enid Rose, *Dramatic Art* (London: W. B. Clive, 1926), p. 9.

32. Ibid., p. 12.

33. Constantin Stanislavsky, *An Actor Prepares* (New York: Theatre Arts, 1936), p. 38.

the primary duty is to discover the *motivation* for the passion (what the character wants) and the *reason* for the type (what has made the character want it), and the result "will produce itself." Detailed illustrations of gestures or types are no longer necessary; the actor must, however, determine what Stanislavsky describes as the superobjective of the plot and the "spine" of the character, a process that establishes the (male) playwright securely in the position of author, the (female) actor as a visible but unnamed co-creator.

Ibsen's dramas were perceived as more complex than formulaic melodramas, in part because of the playwright's use of irony, which in turn broadened the range of possible choices of action for the play. In 1893 an anonymous reviewer for the *Spectator* complained of *The Master Builder* that "the dramatist's habit of hiding plot within plot, and issue within issue, makes it almost impossible to give a fair idea of the main lines upon which the play is laid."[34] That was not generally the case with melodramas, or even with some of Ibsen's predecessors who flirted with realism. In *Camille*, for instance, the overall action might be described as the sacrifice of self to save another—applicable equally to Camille and her lover. And though there might be variations on this superobjective, the movement of the play holds fairly rigidly to that single line of action. Yet in Ibsen's plays the choices of action are wider. In the final moment of *Ghosts*, for example, the actor playing Mrs. Alving must decide which motivation is stronger—to save her son's life or to ease his pain by honoring her promise to end it. Twentieth-century critics, like those actors who first staged Ibsen, espouse opposing views of the action of *Hedda Gabler*. For example, Orley I. Holtan contends that "the principal action . . . is the temptation and destruction of Eilert Løvborg," while David Richard Jones sees it as Hedda's search for greater freedom.[35] Holtan's choice requires the actor to portray a relatively hard, wily Hedda, in comparison with Jones's frustrated but presumably idealistic Hedda. Actors playing Nora Helmer face similar choices: one might interpret the action as self-discovery; an-

34. "Ibsen's Last Play," *Spectator,* March 4, 1893, pp. 285–86, reprinted in Michael Egan, *Ibsen: The Critical Heritage* (London: Routledge and Kegan Paul, 1972), p. 296.
35. Orley I. Holtan, *Mythic Patterns in Ibsen's Last Plays* (Minneapolis: University of Minnesota Press, 1970), p. 81. David Richard Jones, "The Virtues of Hedda Gabler," *Educational Theatre Journal* 29 (1977): 447–62.

other might focus instead on playing the game (thus undercutting Nora's exit while emphasizing the self-dramatizing, ironic quality of the ending).

Contemporary feminist readings of realistic scripts such as Ibsen's emphasize their closed quality, the patriarchal imperative embedded in the retrospective narrative and its negative effect on the representation of woman. Sue-Ellen Case, for example, warns that "the closure of [the] realist narrative chokes women to death and strangles the play of symbols."[36] Jill Dolan writes: "Unmediated realism has . . . been theorized as a site in which ideology intervenes in a very material way to inflect the meanings of the text. The mystification of the author, and his or her singular authority over the construction of meaning in the text; the position of the spectator as the competent interpreter of the realist text; and the mimetic function of realism as a mirror that truthfully records an objective social portrait, have all been analyzed as elements of the pernicious operation of a form with dire consequences for women."[37] These readings of realism illuminate crucial elements of Ibsenian dramaturgy. Certainly Ibsen was assumed to have drawn his portraits from life, portraits made all the more dangerous by their "hidden secrets." As his scripts and others like them have been placed in the academic canon, the figure of Ibsen as author has continued to haunt the interpretation of the scripts as surely as contemporary theatregoers are teased into perceiving themselves as the subjects of his plays. Furthermore, Ibsen's name as playwright-author hovered over the female actors who created the style of the period, thereby mystifying the creative process underlying the production of the scripts.

Nonetheless, to the actual women who staged Ibsen premieres and to their audiences the scripts offered a real chance for change, for power, however deeply circumscribed from the point of view of the present. Today's audiences, accustomed to the lens of realism, may not experience a consciousness of performance while watching real-

36. Sue-Ellen Case, "Towards a Butch/Femme Aesthetic," in *Making a Spectacle: Feminist Essays on Contemporary Women's Theatre,* ed. Lynda Hart (Ann Arbor: University of Michigan Press, 1989), p. 297.

37. Jill Dolan, "'Lesbian' Subjectivity in Realism: Dragging at the Margins of Structure and Ideology," in *Performing Feminisms: Feminist Critical Theory and Theatre,* ed. Sue-Ellen Case (Baltimore: Johns Hopkins University Press, 1990), p. 42.

istic productions because the conventions of viewing are invisible
to them; but the customary lens for the London audiences of the
1890s was melodrama, and consequently they were—like the actors
themselves—aware of the Ibsen premieres as performances of a new
order. Both "woman" and women, the characters and the actors,
were changing performance, performing change. And the female
actors who staged Ibsen's scripts made visible the lever of this
change. Doubtless the production of *Hedda Gabler,* for example, re-
inscribed patriarchal assumptions about the dangers of female sexual desire, about compulsory heterosexuality and maternity, about
female competitiveness and deceit, not to mention amorality. But
Elizabeth Robins and her partner Marion Lea showed that women
could make visible the roles granted to "woman," and could make
perceptible the negative effect of those roles.

They also proved that women could raise the necessary funds to
produce the scripts of their choice and star in productions of them
without relying on a male actor-manager or dramatist for the opportunity to perform. As Robins later remarked: "The chances which
are given are never such good chances as those chosen, insisted on at
the inner prompting. The chances given are such extraneous
chances as suits some man to put in a beautiful woman's way."[38]
Albeit without credit, Robins also contributed to the translations of
several of the scripts, thereby adding another layer of choice to her
work. It is important, too, to acknowledge the extremely modest and
fleeting but nonetheless independent economic power these Ibsen
productions could grant: owing to the financial success of the *Hedda*
run, Robins envisioned creating a theatre in which "ability would be
the one open sesame,"[39] perhaps even a theatre in which "a disciplined democracy" would "give the trained actor some share in the
decisions on moot points (such as all of us have heard discussed
between the Theatre Proprietor or the Producer and the Stage
Manager)"—posts generally held by men.[40] Robins wielded artistic
power over these premieres far beyond that exercised by a well-

38. Elizabeth Robins, *Ancilla's Share* (London: Hutchinson, 1924), p. 70.
39. Elizabeth Robins, diary, August 16, 1891, Fales Library, New York University.
40. Elizabeth Robins, "Killed by Stage Management," Fales Library, New York University.

established female actor in a settled company, such as Ellen Terry, whose career Nina Auerbach has described so tellingly.[41] Realistic dramas at that particular moment in history thus promoted a certain kind of power for the women who staged them. In fact, Robins went on to become involved in the suffrage movement, even writing an Ibsenian "thesis play" titled *Votes for Women*.

In part because of the broader choice of action for the whole play, Ibsen's characters were not easily discernible types, at least not to the late nineteenth-century actor. Whereas her more conventional counterparts understood immediately upon being assigned a role both the play's action and the character's functional motivation, the Ibsen actor (often not even a member of an established company) had to struggle to locate the character after first determining which line of action was appropriate for the drama. The figures were polysemous, full of multiple meanings. Male as well as female actors tackled their task with vigor. Many, such as the British actor Herbert Waring (1857–1932), began to read the newly published *A Doll's House* as if it were a melodrama, only to be surprised and challenged:

> I had confidently anticipated that the prosaic husband would wake up for a moment to his sense of responsibilities as a hero, and take the onus of his wife's misdemeanor upon his shoulders; that all would be forgotten and forgiven, and that the drama would hurry to its obvious and commonplace conclusion. But when I came to the catastrophe, and the extraordinary subsequent conversation between husband and wife, I became dimly conscious that I was reading a work that was either utterly imbecile or something very great indeed. . . . Nora and Rank and Helmer were living and breathing entities, not conventionally embellished with the ordinary stock attributes of stage figures, but concerned and developed with a masterly knowledge of the intricacies of human nature.[42]

Critics as diverse as Clement Scott and Henry James pondered the fact that Ibsen avoided character types in his plays. In the *Daily*

41. Nina Auerbach, *Ellen Terry: Player in Her Time* (New York: W. W. Norton, 1987).
42. Herbert Waring, "Ibsen in London," *Theatre*, October 1, 1894, pp. 164–69, quoted in Egan, *Ibsen*, p. 327.

Telegraph Scott wondered: "In what category of human beings are we to place Halvard Solness? . . . He is a new order of man."[43] James expressed even more puzzlement over the "quality" of Ibsen's characters, extolling the dramatist's "habit of dealing essentially with the individual caught in the fact," but countering: "Sometimes, no doubt, [Ibsen] leans too far on that side, loses sight too much of the type-quality and gives his spectators free play to say that even caught in the fact his individuals are mad. We are not at all sure, for instance, of the type-quality in Hedda."[44] To contemporary audiences Hedda seemed an indeterminate figure in the carpet, an ever-changing transference of perspectives.

James, however, acknowledged Robins's contribution toward ensuring that the characters were not forced into a type. Of her Hedda he wrote: "One isn't so sure she is wicked, and by no means sure (especially when she is represented by an actress who makes the point ambiguous) that she is disagreeable. She is various and sinuous and graceful, complicated and natural; she suffers, she struggles, she is human, and by that fact exposed to a dozen interpretations, to the importunity of suspense."[45] Robins, then, successfully met a novel challenge: to control her audience's shifting sympathies and make them uneasy with any attempt to pigeonhole her character. In Hedda there seemed to be something more, or other, than the customary character type—some excess. Robins, in fact, embodies Northrop Frye's figure of irony: "shifting ambiguities and the complexities of individualized existence . . . the phase of most sincere explicit realism," a definition that applies to critics' descriptions of her acting as realistic.[46]

Although the critics were often frustrated by Ibsen's refusal to depend on character types, the performers—particularly the women—reveled in the ambiguities. Alla Nazimova (1879–1945), the Russian-born actor who introduced many American audiences to Ibsen's women, typified this attitude toward Ibsen's characters:

43. Clement Scott, *Daily Telegraph*, February 21, 1893, p. 3, reprinted in Egan, *Ibsen*, p. 270.

44. Henry James, "On the Occasion of *Hedda Gabler*," *New Review* 4 (June 1891): 519–30, reprinted in Egan, *Ibsen*, p. 243.

45. James, "On the Occasion of *Hedda Gabler*," p. 241.

46. Northrop Frye, *Anatomy of Criticism* (Princeton: Princeton University Press, 1957), pp. 223, 237.

"They are in a way difficult to understand, it is true, not because they are artfully mysterious, but because they are real and therefore like all real people not to be classified by a simple formula. They are full of the pettinesses, the peculiarities, the inconsistencies, the contradictions that we find in everybody we know intimately. That is what makes them so fascinating; that is why we want to learn more of them."[47] Because of the apparent lack of a character typology, Ibsen actors had to possess the kind of incisive, analytical intelligence that Fanny Kemble so distrusted. The Ibsenian "type," a figure of shifting ambiguity, required an "actor type" with the skill and agility to transform the figure: "various and sinuous and graceful, complicated and natural."

Herbert Waring, who created Solness in *The Master Builder* for London audiences in 1893, vouched for the amount of study necessary for an actor to assess the play's action and the character's "spine": "I confess that I read the play through at least three times before I could assure myself that I comprehended the author's intention, and at least three times more before I felt I had grasped the character of Bygmester Solness."[48] Female actors recommended even more extended application. Nazimova, who studied Hedda for four years, counseled that "to portray [Ibsen's] characters one must think, think, think."[49] Mrs. Fiske went so far as to suggest that "to properly produce 'Hedda Gabler' requires at least two years' study. It would not be extravagant to say that a play like Ibsen's 'Rosmersholm' should occupy three years' study and preparation."[50] Actors faced a difficult challenge in their attempts to penetrate the seemingly unambiguous, plain, prosaic dialogue to uncover the characters' psychological motives. Waring's efforts enabled him to perceive how Hilda channels Solness's character in act two: "The apparently nugatory dialogue develops with perfect artistic graduation the painful workings of the unhappy architect's self-tortured mind; and it is in the new impetus given to this stagnating mental development by the brilliant and dominating influence of Hilda

47. Alla Nazimova, "Ibsen's Women," *Independent,* October 17, 1907, p. 909.
48. Waring, "Ibsen in London," p. 329.
49. Quoted in Ada Patterson, "An Interview with a Multiple Woman," *Theatre Magazine* 56 (1907): 220.
50. Fiske, "Ibsen versus 'Humpty Dumpty,'" p. 160.

Wangel that the whole meaning of 'The Master Builder' lies"[51] Waring's reliance on close study, his critical and intellectual preparation
for his performance, echoes the strategy of the female actors with
whom he worked.

In addition to possessing the specific analytical skills necessary for
understanding the subtext, Ibsen actors had to keep an open mind
toward their characters' morality. Any actor unable to perceive a
justification for Nora's leaving Torvald or for Hedda's suicide would
be unable to play either character. Shaw noted of Janet Achurch,
Florence Farr, Marion Lea, and Elizabeth Robins: "All four were
products of the modern movement for the higher education of
women, literate, in touch with advanced thought, and coming by
natural predilection on the stage from outside the theatrical class, in
contradistinction to the senior generation of inveterately sentimental actresses, schooled in the old fashion if at all, born into their
profession, quite out of the political and social movement around
them—in short, intellectually naive to the last degree."[52] The questions Ibsen raises with regard to character are frequently moral
issues of guilt and responsibility. The actor had to be able to understand (if not necessarily to accept) what was sometimes an unconventional, and perhaps even an unacceptable, evaluation of a character's
guilt and responsibility. By contrast, the actor in a melodrama was
usually faced with a situation in which "the protagonist is a victim
who is acted upon: his moral quality is not essential to the event, and
his suffering does not imply an inevitable related guilt—in fact,
there need not be any meaningful relation between the suffering of
the protagonist and the cause and nature of the disastrous event."[53]
In Ibsen the female actor was suddenly able to demand that audiences consider the moral issues embedded in characterizations of
women.

With the earlier nineteenth-century methodology of acting, the
relationship between the actor and the character during a performance was fairly simple: most theorists and performers agreed that
during a performance the actor had a dual consciousness, with one
part of the mind focused on character and one part on self, that is,

51. Waring, "Ibsen in London," p. 329.
52. Shaw, *Shaw on Theatre*, pp. 4–5.
53. Corrigan, *British Drama*, p. 9.

on emotions or technique. William Archer asked several London actors in the era before Ibsen's dramas stormed onto British stages: "Can you give any example of two or more strata of consciousness, or lines of thought, which must coexist in your mind while acting? In other words, can you describe and illustrate how one part of your mind is given up to your character, while another part is criticising minutely your own gestures and intonations, and a third, perhaps, is watching the audience, or is busied with some pleasant or unpleasant recollection or anticipation in your private life?"[54] The many actors who responded to Archer's detailed inquiry all talked in terms of only one possibility: that one part of the mind rests with the character and the other part or parts monitor the self in relation to character, audience, or daily life. Janet Achurch (1864–1916), for example, who had not as yet performed any Ibsen, claimed that the only "double line of thought" she was aware of while she was onstage was "a mental criticism of her own performance," which she tried to stamp out as soon as possible. Many admitted to levels of thought focused not on character but on minute details of technique or the like.

They did not, however, mention what a modern actor—an actor since Ibsen—would readily admit to: a double layer of consciousness concerning *character.* In Ibsen's dramas performers for the first time faced characters who were pursuing a bifurcated action. The actor could no longer speak of the dual consciousness of self and character but rather had to discuss the treble strata of self, character, and *the role* the character plays, a metatheatrical phenomenon that produced a radical change in the actor's art. Before Ibsen, as William Archer wrote, "the Player is both a participator in the action and a spectator. He looks before and after; he cannot divest his mind of a knowledge of the past and future; the irony of things, which is, by hypothesis, concealed from the personage he represents, is patent to him."[55] But in Ibsen's dramas the characters, even minor ones such as Engstrand, are conscious of "the irony of things." Hedda is often fully aware of the ridiculousness of her situation, and can even joke caustically about it. She is capable of self-dramatization, of creating a role for herself different from the role she has been assigned. Con-

54. Archer, *Masks or Faces?*, p. 184.
55. Ibid., p. 116.

sequently, the actor who portrays her must play a double line of action while also being aware of her own self: this treble consciousness is one of the skills frequently demanded in psychologically real acting since Ibsen.

The double line of action that the Ibsen character demands takes several forms. While at times it is the product of the self-dramatizing quality of a character, at other times it is generated by the use of retrospective action or simultaneous staging. Perhaps the most important change Ibsen and his actors brought about, however, was the creation of self-dramatizing characters operating in what Lionel Abel has called "metatheatre," or "theatre pieces about life seen as already theatricalized. . . . The persons appearing on the stage in these plays are there . . . because they themselves knew they were dramatic before the playwright took note of them. . . . They are aware of their own theatricality."[56]

In Ibsen's scripts this self-consciousness is often caused by the playwright's planting his characters in two plays in one, by mixing genres within a single drama. For example, even in Ibsen's most realistic plays his characters sometimes behave as if they were characters in a melodrama (thus fooling some early interpreters into thinking they were simply that). Melodramatic characters "conceive of themselves constantly in histrionic terms," as Hedda, Nora, Stockman, Borkman, and other Ibsen heroes do.[57] Janet Achurch's approach to Rita in *Little Eyolf* incorporated this distinction. A reviewer wrote: "Miss Achurch chose another reading, and one easily to be justified: she made [Rita] . . . a being of strong and no doubt genuine passions, but an external 'poseur,' for ever acting to him or herself and to other people."[58] To offer another, more specific example, in *A Doll's House* the actor playing Nora must portray not only the Nora of the realistic play—a woman strong enough to forge her signature, to work secretly to repay a debt, and to walk out on her husband—but also the Nora of the melodrama unfolding in the character's mind, the birdlike, game-playing Nora who has hero-

---

56. Lionel Abel, *Metatheatre: A New View of Dramatic Form* (New York: Hill and Wang, 1963), p. 60.

57. Corrigan, *British Drama*, p. 10.

58. J. T. Grein, *Sunday Times*, November 29, 1896, p. 4, quoted in Egan, *Ibsen*, p. 353.

ically "saved" Torvald, and who envisions herself "tied to the tracks" as Torvald, in turn, rescues her heroically. The actor must reveal where Nora *thinks* she is headed as well as where she actually *is* headed. What Nora, Hedda, and other Ibsen characters envision as they dramatize themselves differs considerably from the outcomes of the realistic plays in which they are confined.

The director Ingmar Bergman explored this facet of *Hedda Gabler* when, in June 1968, the Stockholm Royal Dramatic Theatre played the Aldwych World Theatre Season in London. Through the setting he helped the actor Gertrud Fridh reveal Hedda's inner life. According to the critic Irving Wardle, "The stage is a red vault bisected by a screen, and while the cozy domestic chatter occupies one acting area, Hedda occupies the other, eavesdropping and practicing solitary rituals. Coming into the company, she draws her iron features into the animation befitting General Gabler's dazzling daughter; when she retires again becomes the woman who bores herself to death and whose pleasure with her father's pistols suggests the sickly fantasies of an incurable fetishist."[59] Fridh succeeded in this production in disclosing both lines of fictive action: Hedda's motivation in the melodrama in which she has cast herself, the foreground of the stage and of her thoughts, as well as her action in the realistic social world that forms the background of the stage and of her life. By creating a dual stage, however, Bergman's production separated the public and the private Hedda, thereby encouraging the actor to play these fictive actions separately. Instead of emphasizing the female character's (and actor's) negotiation of an imbricated action—the potentially subversive consciousness of performance staged by Robins—Bergman's production characterized the play as "a drama of destiny and entrapment."[60]

His direction contrasted markedly with Robins's attempt to reveal the simultaneity of the melodramatic and the "real." The Ibsen actor's task, as she saw it, was to reveal the two lines of action simultaneously, both Hedda's motivation within her private melodrama and her action in the realistic play of which she is a part. To negoti-

59. Irving Wardle, "Bergman Stages Ibsen in London," *New York Times*, June 5, 1968, p. 39.

60. Frederick J. Marker and Lise-Lone Marker, *Ibsen's Lively Art: A Performance Study of the Major Plays* (Cambridge: Cambridge University Press, 1989), p. 179.

ate that divide was to suggest a consciousness of performance, which in turn offered subversive potential. Contemporary female actors, emphasizing the melodrama rather than the realism, might not only recreate the turn-of-the-century Ibsen style but also reveal interesting gaps in the fabric of those performances.

Because of his structural method of retrospective action, Ibsen requires another kind of double motivation as the actor reveals the character's past actions through present ones. To clarify this conflation of past and present action, the actor portraying Hedda, for example, has to show the audience a glimpse of the electricity that drew her to Løvborg in the past as she "playacts" the album scene with him in the present. Mrs. Fiske described this need for a double consciousness of past and present: "To Hedda the very sight of Løvborg standing there on the threshold of her drawing-room brings a flood of old memories crowding close. It must not show on the surface. That is not Ibsen's way . . . but if the actress has lived through Hedda's past, and so realized her present, that moment is electrical. Her blood quickens, her voice deepens, her eyes shine."[61]

Early Ibsen actors also sometimes mixed past and present time frames in a subtler way. Elizabeth Robins, for example, enlarged the act-four scene in which Brack informs Hedda that Løvborg did not die as she fancied he did. According to William Archer: "Instead of starting, where Brack says he must dispel her pleasant illusion, Miss R[obins] used to speak three speeches: 'Illusion?' 'What do you mean?' and 'Not voluntarily?' quite absently, looking straight in front of her, and evidently not taking in what Brack was saying. She used to draw deep breaths of relief (*befrielse*), quite intent on her vision of Eilert lying *i skönhet* [in (a state of) beauty], and only waken up at her fourth speech: 'Have you concealed something?'"[62] In her prompt-book for Hedda, Robins wrote "grave and absent" beside the line "Illusion?" and next to the line "Not voluntarily?" she penned this direction: "sad, farlooking eyes and a smile that says softly how much better I know Eilert than you."[63] Robins's action was intended not only "to avoid Brack's presence" (present action) but also "to envision Løvborg's death" (action related to past as well as present).

61. Woolcott, *Mrs. Fiske*, pp. 64–67.
62. Charles Archer, *William Archer* (London: Allen and Unwin, 1931), p. 187.
63. Robins's promptbook is in the Fales Library, New York University.

Archer's description and Robins's promptbook both indicate how she revealed Hedda's melodramatic, self-dramatizing, past-oriented action as well as her present struggle to keep Brack at bay. And the audience, trying to negotiate meaning out of the resulting gap, could see Robins quoting a melodramatic gesture within a realistic play.

The actor confronts yet another type of metatheatre when Ibsen stages his scenes simultaneously. In *Hedda Gabler,* for instance, the actors must play multiple lines of action, "performing" in scenes they are not directly a part of as well as the three-tiered action in the scenes in which they are physically present. An often-cited example of double or simultaneous staging is the Hedda-Løvborg album scene, played within view of the concurrent scene between Tesman and Brack in the inner room. All four of the actors must play not only against their partner but also against the opposite twosome. Hedda's focus on Løvborg shifts to take into consideration the possibility that Brack is eavesdropping, is an audience to her performance—and she must also appear faithful to her husband. This technique of simultaneous staging occurs again, most obviously, toward the end of the play, in act four, when Hedda and Brack remain downstage as Thea and Tesman huddle upstage, piecing together Løvborg's manuscript. Thea and Tesman may be directed by a single action—to restore Løvborg's book—but Hedda follows a tiered or imbricated line of action: she must decipher Brack's insinuations, attend to overhearing Thea and Tesman, and simultaneously devise a way out of the roles offered her by the two scenes in which she is already playing.

The actor's process of treble consciousness—that is, of playing a double line of action while also being aware of herself as an actor— distinguishes the female Ibsen actor from many of her predecessors and contemporaries, who were all too often considered merely to be playing themselves prettily onstage. According to Lesley Ferris, this time-honored critical stance is a "patriarchal premise that conveniently and skillfully removes women from any possibility of cultural creativity."[64] By contrast, the female actors who first produced Ibsen's scripts in England were perceived, at least by the more liberal

64. Lesley Ferris, *Acting Women* (New York: New York University Press, 1989), p. xi.

critics, as intelligent artists who not only negotiated the divide between actor and character but also revealed that the character herself was divided.

This new performance style complicates the realistic character
read in the script by contemporary feminists. Gail Finney, for instance, holds that Hedda is hysterical because she has been reduced
to her femaleness,[65] but this critical stance does not reflect the record that emerges from actual audience responses to productions
during the late nineteenth century, largely because these viewers
perceived, as we cannot at this remove, a revolutionary performance
style at work: they saw the actor (1) as an actor; (2) as the character;
and (3) as the role the character plays. This third layer, the actor's
creation of Hedda's awareness of the absurdity of the role she plays,
is what constituted, for female actors and audience members, a new
subversive lever in the theatre.[66] When critics maintain that the staging of Hedda's suicide affirms nothing, they ignore one small but
important qualification: Hedda's suicide may be played in such a way
as to affirm her comic stance, her contention that life, as she is being
asked to act it as a woman, is ridiculous. The actor and the audience
can see this fact and are therefore able to apprehend the implications of (to reject as well as to be seduced by) the conventional
solution of the woman's suicide. Hedda simultaneously mocks and
enacts the role of woman as ideal victim. At least one battle is won:
audiences may recognize these roles as roles, and as ridiculous,
stultifying roles at that.

Critics called Robins's performance variously realistic ("she is the
very woman") and melodramatic (her Hedda was "a very melodra-

65. "Hedda Gabler, like Hauptmann's Rose Bernd, can be seen as the personifica-
tion of the hysterization of the female body, or the reduction of the woman to her
status as female, and it is this process that brings about her downfall." Gail Finney,
Women in Modern Drama: Freud, Feminism, and European Theatre at the Turn of the Century
(Ithaca: Cornell University Press, 1989), p. 151.

66. Turn-of-the-century audiences, it should also be noted, did not necessarily see
the script performed in its entirety, as Finney assumes: in the 1891 London premiere
of *Hedda Gabler*, for example, William Archer's "cowardice" led to the omission of the
essential act-one reference to Hedda's pregnancy. See George Bernard Shaw, *Collected
Letters*, ed. Dan Laurence (New York: Dodd, Mead, 1965), pp. 292 and 295, and
Archer's letters to Robins, April 23, 1891, and April 22 or 29, 1891, Fales Library,
New York University.

matic, highly effective creation").[67] (See figure 1.) In fact, Robins made the audience conscious of both the old style and the new, and in that gap—in that consciousness of performance—lies the essence of theatre but also a potential site of power for real women both onstage and in the auditorium. Robins's staging played out the death of a "demonic" woman, a "hysteric," to use Finney's terms. But it also attempted to enact and kill off the melodramatic image of the self-sacrificing woman, to show the ludicrousness as well as the seductiveness of her very sacrifice. Hedda Gabler the character kills herself—beautifully, melodramatically, seductively—just as Hedda the self-conscious actor kills the role foisted on that character. As Tracy Davis remarks: "Actors who built their reputations on Ibsen performances did so in controversial roles that combined realistic characteristics with sensational behaviour. Success in such parts was obtained by striking the right balance between truthful embodiment and theatricalized effect in accordance with the audience's taste for modernism and long experience of presentational acting."[68]

In her publicity for the premiere Robins wrote a mock interview in which a "Philistine" questions her about playing Hedda. This interview reveals Robins's attitude toward the subversive potential of Ibsen's structuring of this complex, metatheatrical character. When the interviewer/"Tormentor," who reduces Hedda to a flat melodramatic character type, asks if Hedda is not a rather repulsive person, she replies:

> Robins: Yes. She objects to anyone using her drawing-room as a hat-rack and she has AN UNPARDONABLE SENSE OF HUMOR.
>
> Interviewer: But she's perhaps—clever?—
>
> Robins: Ah, very, for she finds out her husband isn't as brilliant as his family hope.
>
> Interviewer: But Ibsen's heroine is immoral, of course?
>
> Robins: I'm afraid so. As an unmarried woman she threatens to shoot her would-be lover when he oversteps the bounds of cama-

67. See A. B. Walkley, *London Star*, April 21, 1891, for example, and Justin McCarthy, "Pages on Plays," *Gentleman's Magazine* (June 1891): 638, quoted in Marker and Marker, *Ibsen's Lively Art*, p. 164.

68. Tracy C. Davis, "Acting in Ibsen," *Theatre Notebook* 39, 3 (1985): 113.

Figure 1. Elizabeth Robins as Hedda in *Hedda Gabler* (1891), courtesy Trustees of Backsettown and Fales Library

raderie (although she has a secret passion for him) and later she takes her own life, in order, among other things, to avoid breaking her marriage vow to her delightful husband. Yes, she's not very moral.

Interviewer: And worst of all, being depraved, she's unsympathetic?

Robins: Very true, she never tells you she was badly brought up, and wasn't really to blame. . . . Depravity and vice? Yes, I've often wondered how any actress could DESCEND TO LADY MACBETH.[69]

Robins's subversive preproduction publicity tactics invited the audience, especially the female spectators, to exercise their own "unpardonable" sense of humor, to see the way in which Hedda's behavior is generated by the very system of patriarchal morality that condemns it. It is immoral, Robins suggests, to have to pretend that one's husband is brilliant if he is not; to have to protect a marriage vow in this way; to judge Hedda, rather than General Gabler, as depraved.

The complicated and varied motivations of the Ibsen characters could not be signified by the types of gestures available to the melodramatic actor. The codification of gestures, a skill practiced carefully in early nineteenth-century texts such as the Reverend Gilbert Austin's *Chironomia*, was usually based on the function of each gesture. Austin, typically, lists five types of gestures—commencing, discriminating, auxiliary, suspended, and emphatical—all of which are indicative or emphatic in purpose.[70] Albert M. Bacon in his manual divides gestures into descending and horizontal categories, and discusses how they function to illustrate or imitate states of passion.[71] Dion Boucicault follows Austin's and Bacon's tradition in his "Art of Acting," which again outlines "universal" rules of gesture, all supposedly indicative of emotional states.[72] In 1833 J. W. Shoemaker published his *Practical Elocution,* which listed the three standardized

69. *London Star,* March 23, 1891. This review and all subsequent unpaginated reviews may be found in Elizabeth Robins's *News Cuttings* scrapbook, Fales Library, New York University.

70. Gilbert Austin, *Chironomia* (London: T. Cadell and W. Davies, 1806), pp. 386–92.

71. Albert M. Bacon, *Manual of Gestures* (Chicago: John W. Dean, 1870).

72. Boucicault, "The Art of Acting," pp. 30–32.

types of gestures: those whose purpose was "location" (indication), "illustration," or "emphasis,"[73] Although Henry Siddons seemed to be creating original categories when he divided gestures into the "picturesque" and the "expressive," the three types of gestures he labels picturesque are either simply imitative (as with the "instructional" gesture) or a combination of imitative and emphatic (as with the "correction" and "justification" gestures). The "expressive" gestures Siddons outlines are also all illustrative: those made by design or "those that paint the object of a thought" (as in inclining toward a desired object); analogous gestures, or "those that paint the situations, effects, and modifications of the soul" (as in walking at a slow or fast pace); and physiological or involuntary gestures (as in tears, blanching, or blushing).[74]

Before Ibsen's dramas reached England, then, acting texts reflected a codified system of typical signs or gestures designed to "index" (indicate, illustrate, or emphasize) various emotional states, without considering the complication of the verbal sign system and its ability to contradict and to metatheatricalize the meaning of the gestures. With the advent of Ibsen's plays and their individualized characters, however, a revised category of gestures became necessary: the *autistic gesture,* or subtle visual sign of the character's soliloquy with herself or himself. This type of introspective gesture allowed the Ibsen actor to reveal the dialogue taking place within the character and the various lines of action it implied. Often the actor gestured through subtle facial expressions, especially eye and lip movements, or through the movement of the hands in relation to the body, such as, perhaps the frenzied motions of Hedda's hands when she is left alone after Miss Tesman's exit. Robins employed the autistic gesture liberally, as her annotated sidebook suggests. For instance, when Robins, as Hedda, heard Thea admit that she had left Sheriff Elvsted to follow Løvborg "straight to town," she delivered her response, "My dear good Thea, how did you find the courage?" while "still sitting on arm of chair and looking off into space."[75] The gesture of looking into space allowed Robins an introspective facial

73. J. W. Shoemaker, *Practical Elocution* (Philadelphia: National School of Elocution and Oratory, 1883), p. 141.
74. Siddons, *Practical Illustrations,* pp. 31–44.
75. Robins's promptbook, Fales Library, New York University.

sign, not unlike those positions of the head and eyes described by Michael Fried in his study of absorption and theatricality.[76] This type of gesture transfigured the gestures of the earlier actor, signaling a new age of acting.

With the autistic gesture Ibsen actors revealed the role the character thinks she is playing a well as the role she is actually playing. They opened a gap through which the audience could see the actor mediate the character's performance of conflicting roles. Oddly enough, the acting style of psychological realism fostered by Ibsen's actors enabled contemporary audiences to see the performance of gender as a series of repeated melodramatic acts, as a system of illustrative gestures quite separate from the character's more subversive, more critical autistic communication system. In this way the actors permitted their audiences to understand gender identity as "a performative accomplishment compelled by social sanction and taboo," and asked them to consider that "in its very character as performative resides the possibility of contesting its reified status."[77] Judith Butler defines gender as "an identity instituted through a *stylized repetition of acts*."[78] This is what Janet Achurch, as Nora, allowed her audience to see: the character as she plays the melodramatic and therefore ridiculous role of "woman," which is constituted through a stylized repetition of acts. And Herbert Waring, who played both Helmer and Solness, typified the male Ibsen actor in his effort to reveal the character's "self-tortured mind," the distance between the melodramatic stance of manhood expected of him (even by the female characters who sought release from their own melodramatic traps) and the more realistic role of the "prosaic husband."

Even the secondary characters in Ibsen's scripts challenged the

76. Michael Fried, *Absorption and Theatricality: Painting and Beholder in the Age of Diderot* (Berkeley: University of California Press, 1980).

77. Judith Butler, "Performative Acts and Gender Constitution: An Essay in Phenomenology and Feminist Theory," in Case, *Performing Feminisms*, p. 271. Butler continues: "In opposition to theatrical or phenomenological models which take the gendered self to be prior to its acts, I will understand constituting acts not only as constituting the identity of the actor, but as constituting that identity as a compelling illusion, an object of *belief*." (Butler is discussing ordinary life here, as opposed to theatre.)

78. Ibid., p. 270.

actors to construct a double line of action. A character such as Thea in *Hedda Gabler,* for example, cannot simply be reduced to the status of pawn in the mythical game of "literary paternity," as Gail Finney asserts. It is true, as Finney contends, that Thea serves the role of female muse to Løvborg's author and thereby promotes the patriarchal appropriation of the creative role in the public sphere (men write books, women have babies).[79] It is also true that the female Ibsen actors played roles authorized by a male writer and that, as we have seen, even their creation of a new style of performance carried his name. Nonetheless, in actual production what the audience witnesses is the actor creating a character: a female actor publicly reveals her creative ability to negotiate an imbricated action. She presents a character split between the melodramatic portrayal of the muse which Finney explores and the realistic picture of a woman who walks out on a loveless marriage. Many members of the audience were aware of the actor's careful delineation of this action. As one critic noted of an early matinee performance, the audience may have been self-selecting, but it came prepared "to think on the play and critically watch the acting."[80]

At least in part because of the different demands facing the actor in the fledgling realistic theatre of Ibsen and his contemporaries, as opposed to the melodramatic theatre, the director's responsibilities differed as well. In a complex process that had begun earlier in the century but coalesced in the production of realistic scripts such as Ibsen's, the stage manager of the melodramatic theatre—the one who selected the scripts for the season, who distributed roles according to lines of business, who made sure that the stage movement emphasized the importance of the company's star—evolved into the modern (as opposed to the postmodern) director: one who shapes the dramatic action in concert with the actors and offers the audience an explanation of that action in the program notes.

As we have seen, the women who first directed Ibsen in England and America broke with many theatrical traditions. They frequently formed their own companies to produce Ibsen's plays—companies without lines of business or an enthroned actor-manager as star. In traditional companies the actor-manager reigned. In the late nine

79. Finney, *Women in Modern Drama,* p. 154.
80. *The Theatre,* May 1, 1891.

teenth and early twentieth centuries he was a powerful social phenomenon, a cultural icon of special interest: "The pride and the
place of the actor-manager were comparable then to those of men
born to a great hereditary position; the companies of actors were
like small courts to the heads of the profession and the public their
willing slaves. . . . Men were not believed equal then, stars shone
without impropriety on their fellows, and acting was expected of the
actor, both on and off the stage."[81] This status contrasts markedly
with that of the Ibsen actor-managers, women drawn to the complexity of the scripts, and dedicated to mounting productions under
less than auspicious conditions. Elizabeth Robins and Marion Lea,
for example, sold Robins's jewelry in order to launch a subscription
drive to produce *Hedda Gabler;* they collected from various other
companies the actors they wanted in their cast, rented a theatre for
the short run of the show, and worked in a roughly ensemble fashion
in rehearsal. The directorial duties were dispersed among several
people: Henry James and William Archer attended rehearsals and
offered guidance, as did Robins and Lea. The actor playing Hedda
in the London premiere thus had control over the production finances, played a part in the directing, and even contributed to the
translation of the Norwegian text into English.

Whenever Robins differed with one of the well-known men associated with the early Ibsen productions—such as when she decided
that as Hilda in *The Master Builder* she should wear hobnail boots
instead of looking "pretty," as Henry James advised her to do—
she simply ignored him and followed her own inclinations. In a
midnight postrehearsal note to Robins, James wrote: "Don't be
fantastic—be *pretty,* be agreeable, in the right key. I can't help being
sorry you have only one gown; if so it ought to have a very positive
felicity. . . . Be better, be darker, be longer! And wear something else
in Act II. The speech about the 'same dress' doesn't matter—it's
arbitrary."[82] Robins ignored James and wore boots and a plain cotton
dress with bloused sleeves and a skirt tied up with a bit of twine to
allow for free movement and to suggest both practicality and negli-
gence. (See figure 2.) She could do so only because she had helped

81. Frances Donaldson, *The Actor-Managers* (Chicago: Henry Regnery, 1970), p. 11.
82. Quoted in Elizabeth Robins, *Theatre and Friendship* (London: Jonathan Cape, 1932), p. 99.

Figure 2. Elizabeth Robins as Hilda in *The Master Builder* (1893), courtesy Trustees of Backsettown and Fales Library

manage the finances and could use her power to serve her own goal: making visible her nontraditional concept of Hilda as a woman. As a result she enjoyed a sense of agency in performing that few women onstage at that time possessed. As a female actor and as a manager-director, then, Robins relished her independence, despite the difficulties of raising money for each production; of finding a theatre and hastily assembled, inadequate sets; of gathering a new cast and crew each time.

As a director and actor, she felt the challenge of working with a dramatic action that was not immediately apparent to her, as the assumed line of action had been for those who staged melodrama. Consequently, even though the structure of retrospective action and the genre of realism promoted the dominant ideology almost as fiercely as melodrama had, the female Ibsen actor-managers detected a possible means of subversion and took full advantage of it. Partly because of their sense of the wider possibilities offered by the world of Ibsen production, these new actor-managers envisioned the theatrical company differently than did their male counterparts such as Sir Henry Irving, Sir Herbert Beerbohm Tree, Sir Johnston Forbes-Robertson, or even the more democratic Sir George Alexander. Since their livelihoods depended on their star status, the knighted actor-managers protected their turf very carefully. "Because the position of the actor-manager was so exalted, it was heavily guarded. As a result, young actors with unusual gifts had often little choice between chancing their own arm in management—with all the attendant risks but with all the additions to personality that success in the role would bring—or restricting their performances to a few lines spoken in the shade of some existing luminary. The play was not the thing."[83]

In contrast, Robins pictured a company that would shun the hierarchy of the actor-manager–led troupes and instead would share power equally, even in terms of the directorial function. In a typescript titled "Killed by Stage Management," Robins writes: "Despotism may do to death as many fine possibilities on the stage as elsewhere in the human arena. Perhaps a disciplined democracy may be the best medium for a well-chosen cast and staff to work in. It seems

83. Donaldson, *The Actor-Managers*, pp. 11–12.

at least arguable that to give the trained actor some share in the
decisions on moot points (such as all of us have heard discussed
between the Theatre Proprietor or the Producer and the State Manager), and to give the actor some liberty to develop his part in his
own way, always provided he doesn't clash with the reasonable liberty
of others, might bring a sense of responsibility."[84] Nor did the new
breed of Ibsen actor-managers necessarily take the largest roles as
their own, in part, perhaps, because they saw the possibilities inherent in the minor characters as well. For example, Lea encouraged
Robins to play Hedda to her Thea, though it was Lea's idea to produce the play in the first place. Ibsen helped to sustain a new kind of
thinking about directing as well as a new mode of acting.

His work also made possible a different relationship between the
actor and the audience. During the heyday of the actor-manager in
London, "playgoers went to the theatre, not so much to see a new
play, as to see a new actor in an old play. Actors were expected to
make their mark in the roles of their predecessors."[85] The cult of the
star, then, and the attitude toward acting in the pre-Ibsen era in
England, encouraged the audience to derive pleasure from being
swept away by the hero-star's mastery. In direct contrast, the audience attending Ibsen premieres was curious about the plays themselves. The play was the thing. Furthermore, this early Ibsen audience was a diverse one, including "playgoers of all classes and
persuasions": "Ibsen attracted people who were interested in contemporary literature (whether or not they had literary aspirations
themselves), publicity-seeking socialites, genuine devotees of the
drama and acting, and ordinary playgoers whose curiosity was
raised by the plethora of press attention."[86] There was no knighted
actor-manager by whom the audience could be mastered but rather
a gathering of actors from various companies working in a balanced
if underrehearsed ensemble. Some audience members were puzzled
or outraged by the productions, but others were fascinated by the
novel sensation of freedom, by the chance to figure out for oneself

84. Elizabeth Robins, "Killed by Stage Management," Fales Library, New York University.

85. Donaldson, *The Actor-Managers*, p. 12.

86. Tracy C. Davis, "Ibsen's Victorian Audience," *Essays in Theatre* 4, 1 (November
1985): 35, 23.

what really happened to Solness, or what Mrs. Alving finally did about her son. Because of the double line of action, the audience was free to choose how the two actions related to each other, a choice that was never offered by the single line of action of the melodramatic theatre. Actors such as Robins "pointed up subtle character affinities and interconnections that had not occurred to literary critics."[87] Even as sophisticated a reader as Henry James admitted that *Hedda Gabler,* "on perusal, left one comparatively muddled and mystified, fascinated, but—in one's intellectual sympathy—snubbed. Acted, it leads that sympathy over the straightest of roads with all the exhilaration of a superior pace."[88] And as George Bernard Shaw remarked of Robins's portrayal of Hedda: "You were sympathically unsympathic, which was the exact solution of the central difficulty of playing Hedda."[89]

In response to Ibsen's new structural strategies, then, female actors experimented with creating the form of a drama rather than just "filling it out"; they approached character from the standpoint not of type but of action; they discovered a new and complex understanding of their self-dramatizing characters; and they created new modes of gesture to aid them in their portrayals. Although the creative freedom accompanying these changes was circumscribed, it was nonetheless apparent as these actors staged the relationship between the representation of "reality" and melodrama. For both the director and the audience there was a similar, potentially subversive sense of freedom and a concomitant awareness of risk. At issue was the question: What is the nature of reality?

87. Marker and Marker, *Ibsen's Lively Art,* p. 166.

88. Henry James, "On the Occasion of *Hedda Gabler,*" reprinted in James, *The Scenic Art,* ed. Allan Wade (New York, 1967), pp. 245–46.

89. George Bernard Shaw, *Collected Letters,* vol. 1, *1874–1897,* ed. Dan H. Laurence (London: Max Reinhardt, 1965), p. 292.

Chapter Two

Strindberg and the Transformational Actor

In his often-quoted author's note to *A Dream Play,* August Strindberg writes that in his late plays he "sought to reproduce the disconnected but apparently logical form of a dream. Anything can happen; everything is possible and probable. Time and space do not exist; on a slight groundwork of reality, imagination spins and weaves new patterns made up of memories, experiences, unfettered fancies, absurdities, and improvisations. The characters are split, double, and multiply; they evaporate, crystallise, scatter and converge."[1] This passage reveals Strindberg's awareness of the novelty of his structural model and outlines the radical differences between his peripatetic method and the linear, well-made plays of his contemporaries. It establishes the primacy of this experimental structure and clarifies its effect on Strindberg's concept of character. Within the dream structure the human spirit is no longer necessarily locked into time or space; characters may drift in and out of actors' bodies. This structure prompts the actor, director, and audience to investigate not the nature of material reality, as in Ibsen, but rather the nature of the ever-transforming, often, in Strindberg's term, "dematerial" reality within a waking dream.

Strindberg himself tried to originate a "dematerial" actor, that is,

1. Elizabeth Sprigge, trans., *Six Plays of Strindberg* (New York: Doubleday, 1955), p. 193. All subsequent references to *A Dream Play* are to this edition, unless otherwise noted.

one who would reflect his concept of the waking dream, but he failed to create a unified performance style. This failure occurred partly because, given the limited technology of the theatre at the time, most actors could not envision this unconventional acting style that Strindberg sought, nor were they prepared, either by their own training or by Strindberg's direction, to discover the alternative "transformational" performance style suggested by the script. One female actor, however, did manage to create the incorporeal style Strindberg hoped to foster. Harriet Bosse's performance of the Daughter of Indra as an ethereal goddess set a precedent that survives, especially in Sweden, to this day, locking female actors into a damaging stereotype.

An examination of the structure of *A Dream Play*, especially in light of the playwright's interest in Eastern religions, reveals an alternative path for the female actor in Strindberg: the actor is invited to employ a wide variety of performance styles, not just a "dematerial" style, thus transforming the story from its base in Eastern mysticism to fairy tales, then to naturalism, to dreams, and back again. If we refuse to cast the female actor in Strindberg as an ethereal woman without a body, we can envision another approach—a *transformational* approach—to acting, directing, and understanding Strindberg's scripts. This style varies the representation of woman and complicates the position of the female actor, taking advantage of the episodic nature of Strindberg's scenes to break the narrative flow and to reposition the story. But the playwright's skewed version of Hindu myth, a worldview that permeates his work, limits the possibilities open to women precisely because of its misreading of Hinduism.

In a passage originally intended for the preface to *A Dream Play*, Strindberg hinted at his understanding of life as a Hindu dream: "Whoever follows the author during the brief hours of his sleepwalker route will perhaps find a certain similarity between the apparent jumble of a dream and life's motley, unmanageable canvas, woven by the 'World Weaver'—she who sets up the 'warp' of human destinies and then constructs the 'woof' from our intersecting interests and our variable passions."[2] Strindberg compares the structural

---

2. Quoted in Harry G. Carlson, *Strindberg and the Poetry of Myth* (Berkeley: University of California Press, 1982), p. 140.

elements and experiential quality of the dream to those of life itself, represented as a deceptive tapestry woven by a woman.

Shortly after Strindberg began writing *A Dream Play* in 1901, his new bride and third wife, the Norwegian actress Harriet Bosse, became pregnant. Within two weeks of the confirmation of that fact, she announced that she was leaving him. Strindberg railed at "this ghost story which is our marriage."[3] It is not surprising that he alluded to his relationship with Bosse as ghostly, repetitive, for he seemed to follow the same tortured pattern with each successive wife. He continually sought to reconcile himself with mundane life through an idealized notion of woman, only to encounter failure, and to vilify the woman. During the tumultuous first year of his marriage to Bosse, as Strindberg worked on *A Dream Play,* he was incensed by the idea that Bosse had left him "without having reconciled [him] to humanity—and woman!"[4] Like the Poet, he anticipated a scene of redemption through Bosse: "And she leads him toward the sunshine. . . . And he thanks her who has reconciled him to mankind and woman."[5] When he recalled Bosse's early sexual taunts that he "was not a man," that she would take a lover, he exploded in bewilderment and anger: "It was in this manner you sought to give me back my faith in woman—and in humanity!"[6] Repeatedly he positioned Bosse as an untouchable Other, outside humanity, a goddess whose job was to save him, a role that she, like her predecessors, vehemently rejected in real life. In her stage life, however, in 1907, cast as the original Daughter of Indra, Bosse, now divorced from Strindberg, played the ethereal goddess who solves the riddle of life by blaming woman for the misery of creation, and only *then* walks out, leaving the Poet to suffer. In that process Bosse, as Indra, assumed the blame for her own disappearance, and launched a performance tradition that has trapped female actors ever since in an inaccurate and unsettling version of Hindu myth. (See figure 3.)

3. Quoted in Michael Meyer, *Strindberg: A Biography* (New York: Random House, 1985), p. 426.
4. See Strindberg's letter to Bosse, June 27, 1901, in *The Strindberg Reader*, ed. Arvid Paulson (New York: Phaedra, 1968), p. 418.
5. Ibid., p. 419.
6. Letter to Bosse, August 28, 1901, in Paulson, *Strindberg Reader*, pp. 420–21.

Figure 3. Harriet Bosse as the Daughter of Indra in *A Dream Play* (1907), courtesy Carla Waal

Critics have often noted Strindberg's awareness of the repetitious nature of life, but they have rarely shown how this sensitivity reinforced his interest in Hinduism, with its view of life as a series of karmic repetitions and rebirths. Strindberg's interest in this myth intensified at the turn of the century. In *A Dream Play* he lifted the final dialogue between the Daughter and the Poet, in which the Daughter explains the creation myth, "almost verbatim, from one of [his] favorite reference books, a survey of world literature by Arvid Ahnfelt"; and though he may have encountered the idea of the world as a waking dream in Arthur Schopenhauer's *World as Will,* he had read other volumes on Eastern thought as well, including G. de Lafont's *Buddhisme* and a book titled *Dans l'Inde.*[7] His diary entry for November 18, 1901, the day he finished *A Dream Play,* establishes the connection he perceived between his script and Eastern philosophies:

> Am reading about the teachings of Indian religions. The whole world is but an illusion (—humbug or relative meaninglessness). The Divine Primary Force (Mahann-Atna, Tad, Aum, Brahma [*sic*]) let itself be seduced by maya of the impulse of procreation. In this the Divine Primary Element sinned against itself. (Love is sin; that is why pangs of love are the greatest hell that exists.) Thus the world exists only through sin, if it exists at all, for it is only a dream picture (hence my Dream Play is a picture of life), a phantom the destruction of which is the mission of the ascetic. But this mission conflicts with the instinct of love, and the sum of it all is a ceaseless wavering between sensuality and the pangs of remorse. This seems to me the answer to the riddle of life. . . . All day I read Buddhism.[8]

Nor was this a fleeting interest: on October 4, 1905, Strindberg wrote Bosse: "I find my only comfort now in Buddha who says plainly that life is a phantasma, an illusion, the truth of which we shall see in another life. My hope and my future lie on the other side, that is why life is so difficult for me to live."[9]

Syncretistically jamming Hinduism and Buddhism together,

7. Carlson, *Strindberg,* pp. 141, 146–47.
8. Meyer, *Biography,* p. 432.
9. Ibid., p. 457.

Strindberg omits one important element in his diary account of the Hindu myth of creation: in Hindu thought absolute reality—pure spirit—exists only within Brahman, the divine primordial and neuter force which is "without attribute and consequently has no relation to human beings."[10] Brahman, in order to create the world, manifested itself as Brahmā, the active masculine principle. Strindberg, however, conflates Brahmā with Brahman, thereby raising the masculine principle to the position assigned to godhead. Manhood becomes godhead in Strindberg's misguided reading. According to the myth, Brahmā—the male principle—allows *māyā*, the female world of reality which is an illusion, to seduce him in order to increase and multiply himself. In the words of the Daughter of Indra in *A Dream Play:* "This mingling of the divine element with the earthly was the Fall from heaven. This world, its life and its inhabitants are therefore only a mirage, a reflection, a dream image."[11]

In Strindberg's revision of the myth, then, the earthly, illusory female seduces the divine male godhead, creating the hellish dream play of a life plagued by sin. Woman is the earth goddess who deludes the man-god, dragging the world into misery. "Do you understand now what woman is?" the Daughter of Indra asks the Poet, disclosing the answer to the riddle of life: "Woman, through whom sin and death entered into life."[12] The patriarchal basis of Strindberg's modification of the myth assumes particularly grotesque reverberations when one considers Bosse's role as Indra, Strindberg's customary association with the Poet, and the fact that Bosse's approach to performing the character persists.

A Dream Play may be read as a misogynistic parable of Strindberg's life: aligning himself with the conflated figure Brahmā/Brahman, Strindberg creates himself in the script as the dreamer (split into the Officer, Lawyer, and Poet) who is seduced by *māyā*, the image of woman as seductress and Earth Mother. He is thereby mired in *saṃsāra*, the Hindu term indicating both marriage and earthly life. To escape he must destroy the phantom of the world, returning to the spirit world of Brahman, which for Strindberg meant all-powerful, independent manhood.

10. Carlson, *Strindberg*, p. 181.
11. Sprigge, *Six Plays*, p. 257.
12. Ibid., p. 258.

Despite Strindberg's widely chronicled interest in Eastern models in his writings after *Inferno,* his later dramas have often been compared to Christian passion plays in terms of their structure. Walter H. Sokel remarks, for example, that in expressionist plays in general "a loosely connected 'life story,' a series of 'stations,' pictures, and situations takes the place of a well-knit plot."[13] This reading of the structure of *A Dream Play* posits the Daughter of Indra as a Christlike paragon, leaving a heavenly father so that she might take on and explore the burdens of humankind, finally shedding her earthly existence to rejoin her father. But if the Daughter of Indra is "a Christ figure with differences," as Walter Johnson writes, those differences are profound.[14] She is a woman—a woman of color from the East. Furthermore, she is a student as much as a savior: Indra sends her to find out if the complaints of men and women are justified. A Christian reading of Strindberg's structural strategies erases these crucial elements from the script.[15] Without them it is difficult to see that this "paragon" leaves without truly redeeming anyone. She tires of married life on earth, says good-bye, and departs.

Strindberg invented this female child for Indra, the legendary king of all the Hindu gods. In Hindu mythology he lives in a magic city in the sky. Typically the city is composed of clouds, precisely as in Strindberg's prologue, and it serves "to pry us loose from our conviction that cities we inhabit are real."[16] From the opening image noted in the script, we are encouraged to think of life in terms of Hinduism

13. Walter H. Sokel, ed., *Anthology of German Expressionist Drama* (Garden City, N.Y.: Doubleday, 1963), p. xxi.

14. August Strindberg, *A Dream Play and Four Chamber Plays,* trans. Walter Johnson (New York: W. W. Norton, 1975), p. 9.

15. Ingmar Bergman's 1970 staging of *A Dream Play* at the Dramaten in Stockholm followed this critical approach to its logical conclusion and cut many of the Eastern elements from the script: "Indra's Daughter and Agnes are split into two characters played by different actresses, and the Daughter, now deprived of all but her most 'divine' lines and no longer used to open the play, could almost as well have been (as Bergman apparently first intended) eliminated altogether. . . . The Poet, seated at his desk surrounded by the other characters who, dreamlike, await his call, opened and closed the play with speeches originally given by the dramatist to Indra's daughter." Frederick J. Marker and Lise-Lone Marker, *The Scandinavian Theatre: A Short History* (Oxford: Basil Blackwell, 1975), p. 272.

16. Wendy Doniger O'Flaherty, *Dreams, Illusion, and Other Realities* (Chicago: University of Chicago Press, 1984), p. 275.

as well as Christianity. The fact that Strindberg added the prologue after the first performance of the play to clarify his desired emphasis only strengthens the importance of this initial impression. The daughter's name, Agnes, calls to mind not only Agnus Dei but also Agni, the Hindu god of fire, the mediator between gods and humans. This is the role assumed by Agnes in the play: she is not, or at least not simply, a Western savior sent to redeem people but an Eastern messenger sent to discern whether the complaints of earthbound creatures are justified. For Strindberg the Poet she offers reconciliation and release, but she does not, like Christ, die a human death to take away sins. Instead, she decides rather abruptly that she has had enough of human misery; she recites Strindberg's misreading of Hinduism, then vows to report to her father that "human beings are to be pitied." Finally, like Strindberg's wives, she leaves without having reconciled earthlings to their lot. (In that action Bosse as the Daughter simultaneously enacted her liberation and her entrapment.) She goes, but it is her fault, or so we are to believe, that those left behind continue to suffer.

Against the glow of the burning castle into which she exits, the audience sees two images: the giant chrysanthemum which has bloomed in response to the warmth of the fire that consumed her earthly existence, and the wall of faces of those she leaves behind on earth, "questioning, mourning, despairing."[17] Her victory in escape is thereby juxtaposed against the continuing complaints of those whom—like the Poet, like Strindberg—she abandons in their despair. Strindberg represents the Daughter of Indra, the role he wrote for Bosse, as an exotic womanly Other whose father has sent her to learn, but who suddenly aborts her student status, just as Bosse abruptly rejected Strindberg as husband.

Luciano Codignola calls Strindberg's later, post-*Inferno* plays "dramas of repetition."[18] The series of short scenes in *A Dream Play* repeat the same action over and over again: in almost every scene a man and woman fail to negotiate their way toward happiness, complaining that "human beings are to be pitied." Codignola wrongly

17. Sprigge, *Six Plays*, p. 261.
18. Luciano Codignola, "Two Ideas of Dramatic Structure: Strindberg's Last Period and Pirandello's Third Period—A Confrontation," in *Strindberg and Modern Theatre* (Stockholm: Strindberg Society, 1975), p. 39.

concludes, however, that "this type of drama does away with all the dramatic conventions, except the supreme and fundamental one, according to which whatever happens on the stage is an imitation of life and not life itself."[19] In Hindu thought this separation of imitation (or illusion) and reality does not exist.[20]

In Strindberg the repetitive karmic law of transformations and repetition has replaced the linear law of cause and effect underlying Ibsen's use of retrospective action. Karma has been defined as "the law of universal causality, which connects man with the cosmos and condemns him to transmigrate indefinitely."[21] The new reality implied in Strindberg's structural mode is not that the unified self is varied and shifting in a complex figure/ground as in Ibsen, but that the very ground is itself a shifting illusion—*māyā*—and the figure a body that at any moment might transform itself into someone else,

19. Ibid., p. 40.

20. Many other scholars have discussed Strindberg's structural techniques, most notably Henry G. Carlson and Evert Sprinchorn. Grounding his analysis of the structure of *A Dream Play* in the playwright's interest in Eastern religions, Carlson suggests that the script employs the shared dream structure which frequently appears in Hindu stories and which he thinks Strindberg may have encountered in Rudyard Kipling's story "The Brushwood Boy" (*Strindberg*, p. 139). According to Carlson: "The structure I have suggested in the play of four dreamers experiencing three sets of reciprocal dreams—Agnes and the Officer, Agnes and the Lawyer, Agnes and the Poet—might also be viewed as two dreamers—the woman and the man—sharing one dream. Evert Sprinchorn suggests that Strindberg intended that all the men coalesce into one male and all women into one female" (pp. 144–45). Sprinchorn further develops this line of reasoning: "Finally, remembering *the bisexual nature of man* [emphasis added], the subjective nature of the play, and the egocentric nature of dreams, we must allow the two characters ultimately to fuse into one; and it is absurd to ask, as some caviling critics have, which of the thirty characters in the play is the dreamer." Evert Sprinchorn, *Strindberg as Dramatist* (New Haven: Yale University Press, 1982), p. 160. Sprinchorn thus invites a reading of the play as a dream dreamed by one dreamer, but this dreamer, like Carlson's paired dreamers, is both Western and white, not to mention male, and is interpreted by way of Freud and Schopenhauer. Strindberg, says Sprinchorn, "read a book on Indian religion and adapted some of its ideas to his own use in the final dialogue between the Daughter and the Poet. But Brahma has little to do with the rest of the play. It is much more helpful to invoke Schopenhauer and especially that awakener of modern time, Freud" (p. 157). This despite Sprinchorn's admission in the very next sentence that "Strindberg never read a word written by Freud." I take seriously Strindberg's fascination with Hinduism, using it as a lever to pry loose our Westernized readings of his structural strategies so that we may consider both the Eastern and the Western implications of his work.

21. Mircea Eliade, *Yoga, Immortality, and Freedom*, trans. Willard R. Trask (New York: Pantheon, 1958), p. 3.

or into a different time frame. Early in the play, for example, the scene changes from a theatre alleyway to a law office, a gate is transformed into an office railing, the Doorkeeper's lodge into a cubbyhole for the Lawyer's desk, the lime tree into a hat stand, the cloverleaf door into a cabinet. In a similar fashion the Officer keeps transforming—from youth to aged gentleman to middle-aged suitor. Feminists have come to regard this kind of transformational production style as potentially liberating because of its rejection of the narrativity of realism, the cause and effect of Ibsen. But Strindberg's skewed version of Hinduism, in which manhood is elevated to godhead, disarms in large part the potentially disrupting effect of nonrealistic structure and staging techniques.

In Hindu myths, as in *A Dream Play, The Ghost Sonata,* and Strindberg's other dream plays, this structural pattern reveals the transformational nature of the storyteller's worldview. A story may begin as a tale of illusion and be transformed midstream into a tale of magic or of dreams. This happens in Indian narratives because "one of the points of the story is to demonstrate how difficult it is to tell one sort of transformation from another."[22] In a similar fashion, *A Dream Play* shifts narrative styles in successive scenes, suggesting a variety of performance styles. Like the dream with its kaleidoscopic variousness, each scene presents a new mode of representation of a different kind of reality. The dancelike ritualism of the opening scene, with its mythic diction, exudes mysticism and seems to call for an ethereal figuration of Agnes:

Indra's Voice: Where art thou, Daughter?

Daughter: Here, Father, here!

Indra's Voice: Thou hast strayed, my child. Take heed, thou sinkest. How cam'st thou here?

Daughter: Borne on a cloud, I followed the lightning's blazing trail.[23]

Moments later this mythic tale transmutes into a fairy tale as the Daughter of Indra is reincarnated as the prescient Daughter of the

---

22. O'Flaherty, *Dreams,* p. 3.
23. Sprigge, *Six Plays,* p. 197.

Glazier. The Glazier and his daughter gaze at the growing castle in wonder:

> Glazier (*to himself*): I've never seen that castle before—and I've never heard of a castle growing . . . but . . . (*to the Daughter with conviction*) yes, it's grown six feet. . . .
>
> Daughter: Ought it not to blossom soon? We are already halfway through the summer.[24]

As they approach the castle, its walls dissolve, admitting into the fairy tale a curious admixture of the opening scene's mysticism and the subsequent scene's earthy realism. The Daughter tries to free the castle's prisoner, the Officer:

> Daughter: What do you see in me?
>
> Officer: The beautiful, which is the harmony of the universe. There are lines in your form which I have only found in the movement of the stars, in the melody of strings, in the vibrations of light. You are a child of heaven.
>
> Daughter: So are you.
>
> Officer: Then why do I have to groom horses, clean stables, and have the muck removed?
>
> Daughter: So that you may long to get away.[25]

A screen is pulled aside to reveal a scene within a scene, deeply entrenched in the gritty details of life associated with the naturalism of Zola. The Officer transforms into Alfred, son of a dying mother and discontented father, as the Daughter becomes identified for the first time as Agnes. The audience sees firsthand the joy and agony of *saṃsāra*—earthly life and marriage—and, like the characters themselves (indeed, like Strindberg), the audience wants out. The tale has descended, like the Daughter, to a level that prompts a desire for release, for *mokṣa*. At this moment the Daughter voices, for the first time, the play's refrain: "Det är synd om människorna," which, as Elizabeth Sprigge notes, may be translated as "human beings are to be pitied," but which also suggests the sense of: "It's a shame about

24. Ibid., p. 199.
25. Ibid., pp. 200–201.

human beings."[26] Agnes learns her lesson, then, ten minutes into
the play, and all that follows reviews the lesson through various
lenses and performance styles, each of which explores the nature of
reality as a waking dream. At the end of the play the earthbound
characters, including the Poet, remain below in despair, as only the
goddess Agnes ascends to the High Ether: pain, for the characters
Agnes leaves behind, as for Strindberg, is experienced not merely as
an illusion but as a complex and concrete reality.

Wendy Doniger O'Flaherty's view of karmic rebirths serves as a
vehicle for understanding Strindberg's repeated scenic actions if one
thinks of the play's action as its "soul" seeking rebirth in successive
scenes, unable to relinquish its own complaint, its illusion. She
writes: "The cause of rebirth—excessive attachment to the ways of
the world—is also the cause of the failure to see through the decep-
tion and illusion of the world. . . . The unwillingness to let go, the
inability to leave things unavenged and unfinished, is the drive to
rebirth."[27] Strindberg's inability to "leave things unavenged" leads
him to refigure, again and again, the fight between male and female.
Halfway through *A Dream Play* the Lawyer-husband reminds Agnes
that she must return to their home to experience the worst fate of
all: "Repetitions, reiterations. Going back. Doing one's lessons
again."[28] Indeed, each major character—as in most of Strindberg's
scripts, even the realistic ones such as *The Dance of Death I and II*—
remains locked in painful repetitions. The Daughter's status as goddess and her willingness to leave things unfinished saves her. The
Officer, in scene after scene, searches for Victoria, the idealized
woman, and must return to school as a man-child after having won
his laurel wreath; the Lawyer listens to confession after confession
then relives his few pleasures as distorted nightmares the next day;
the Poet and the earthbound Agnes, just before the opening of the
door, reprise their Fingal's Cave discussion of the relationship between dreaming, poetry, and reality. Reality is defined as dream, as
poetry:

Poet: I seem to have lived through all this before.

Daughter: I, too.

26. Ibid., p. 190.
27. O'Flaherty, *Dreams*, p. 220.
28. Sprigge, *Six Plays*, p. 237.

Poet: Perhaps I dreamt it.

Daughter: Or made a poem of it.

Poet: Or made a poem.

Daughter: You know then what poetry is.

Poet: I know what dreaming is.

Daughter: I feel that once before, somewhere else, we said these
words.

Poet: Then soon you will know what reality is.

Daughter: Or dreaming.

Poet: Or poetry.[29]

In the never-ending repetition of life, and in the repetition of scenes
in this script, reality is *māyā*, cosmic illusion. But in actual Hindu
practice *māyā* serves the important function of generating a need for
transcendence: "The more man suffers (that is, the greater is his
solidarity with the cosmos), the more the desire for emancipation
increases in him, the more intensely he thirsts for salvation."[30]

The characters in *A Dream Play* fail to distance themselves from
suffering in part because, like Strindberg himself, they do not finally
believe that the spirit is already free. They do not recognize Brahman, the neutral godhead who offers release into pure spirit. Instead, again like Strindberg, they want to blame the seductive world
of *māyā* represented as a female principle, to rail against it as the
source of their misery. This occurs because of Strindberg's mis-

29. Ibid., pp. 250–51.
30. Eliade, *Yoga*, p. 11. Eliade further describes the process: "The first stage of the
conquest . . . is equivalent to . . . denying suffering as something that concerns us, to
regarding it as an objective fact, outside of Spirit, that is to say, *without value* and
without meaning (since all 'values' and all 'meanings' are created by intelligence in so far
as it reflects *purusa* [Spirit]). Pain exists only to the extent to which experience is
referred to the human personality regarded as identical with *purusa*, with the Self.
But since this relation is illusory, it can easily be abolished. When *purusa* is known,
values are annulled; pain is no longer either pain or nonpain but a simple *fact*. . . .
From the moment that we understand that the Self is free, eternal, and inactive,
whatever happens to us—sufferings, feelings, volitions, thoughts, and so on—*no
longer belong to us*. All such things constitute a body of cosmic facts, which are conditioned by laws, and are certainly real, but whose reality has nothing in common with
our *purusa*. Suffering is a cosmic fact, and man undergoes that fact, or contributes to
its perpetuation, solely in so far as he allows himself to be seduced by an illusion"
(p. 28).

reading of the Hindu myth, because these characters live in a world in which Brahman is conflated with Brahmā.

One of the reasons for Strindberg's rejection of *puruṣa* (spirit) as an immediate release is that, despite his longing for the spirit world and his fascination with the concept of the world as illusion, Strindberg also perceived that the suffering in the material world is quite real, and is based on class differences and economic oppression. After examining the Officer's repeated efforts to woo Victoria, first as a dashing young man and then, suddenly, as an aged gentleman, Strindberg changes the scene to the Lawyer's office. There Agnes meets the Lawyer, who puts human suffering into the social context so keenly felt by the playwright, this self-proclaimed "son of a servant":

> Lawyer: And what people live on is a mystery to me. They marry with an income of two thousand crowns when they need four. They borrow, to be sure, they all borrow, and so scrape along somehow by the skin of their teeth until they die. Then the estate is always insolvent. Who has to pay up in the end? Tell me that.
>
> Daughter: He who feeds the birds.
>
> Lawyer: Well, if He who feeds the birds would come down to earth and see the plight of the unfortunate children of men, perhaps He would have some compassion.[31]

Perhaps the most clear-cut example of Strindberg's concern with class oppression emerges in the Coal Heavers' scene, which voices thematic concerns and employs a style now associated with Bertolt Brecht:

> 1st Coal Heaver: Nothing to eat! We, who do the most work, get the least food. And the rich, who do nothing, get it all. Might one not, without taking liberties with the truth, call this unjust? What has the Daughter of the Gods up there to say about it?
>
> Daughter: I have no answer. . . . Is it true those poor men aren't allowed to bathe in that sea? . . . Can't they go and bathe outside the town—in the country?

31. Sprigge, *Six Plays,* p. 213.

Lawyer: There is no country. It's all fenced in.

Daughter: I mean where it is open and free.

Lawyer: Nothing is free. Everything is owned. . . . Help them. . . .
It's not the people who are so bad, but . . .

Daughter: But?

Lawyer: The system.[32]

The tenor as well as the content of this scene reveal Strindberg's critique of the system of private ownership and his deeply rooted anger at a society that forces some to suffer more than others. Class divisions, however, punish the rich as well as the poor in *A Dream Play*. When the Daughter and the Officer arrive in Foulstrand, they discover that the grotesquely wealthy there suffer from their abuse of excess money. The Quarantine Master exhorts them: "Look at that man on the rack. He's eaten too much pâté-de-foie-gras with truffles, and drunk so much Burgundy that his feet are knotted . . . and that one lying on the guillotine has drunk so much brandy that his backbone's got to be mangled."[33]

The Georg Grosz quality of this scene and the Brechtian performance style of the Coal Heavers' scene contrast, of course, with the poetic mysticism of the Fingal's Cave scene and the chilling, Robert Wilson-like robotics of the scene in which the servant Kristin pastes shut the cracks in the Lawyer's home. Other performance styles present themselves, too: there is the absurdism of the scene in which the Officer-turned-schoolboy witnesses a schoolfellow prove, Peter-Pan fashion, that he is Time, because while the others speak, he (like time) flies; and the burlesque of the fight among the Four Faculties to establish their contradictory edicts on the meaning of life. In fact, Strindberg employs a multitude of styles within the repeated scenes of suffering. His adoption of the karmic dream structure enables him to examine carefully the varied states of being that are associated with dreaming sleep, and to hint at the stylistic challenges facing his actors.

This kaleidescope of performance styles engendered by Strindberg's repetitive structural method contrasts markedly with the sin-

32. Ibid., pp. 240–42.
33. Ibid., p. 224.

gular critical or realistic acting approach fostered by Ibsen's narrative structure. Instead of permitting actors to discover clues to his elusive dramatic action, Strindberg presents the same action over and over again in play after play. It is a pity about human beings, whose lives seem like nightmare versions of reality: that line of action might serve to describe his scripts from *The Father* to *To Damascus*. Even the supposedly realistic *Miss Julie* focuses on a moment that is hinged between reality and Midsummer's Eve nightmare. In *The Ghost Sonata* the Student learns in scene after scene, as more is disclosed, that the reality he believed in is in fact an illusion; and when he tries to speak his reality, it kills the Girl whom he has loved. He pronounces his benediction over her as the play ends: "You poor little child, child of this world of illusion, guilt, suffering and death, this world of endless change, disappointment, and pain. May the Lord of Heaven be merciful to you upon your journey."[34] Here again, embedded within a repetitive structure, is the Eastern worldview of reality as illusion, but without the Hindu acceptance of the way out of *saṃsāra*. Instead, in play after play, the characters, locked into the painful and illusory battle of the sexes, must die to achieve release into a Christian heaven. And unlike Ibsen's characters, who are usually represented as having at least the illusion of choosing their own ironic deaths, Strindberg's characters are frequently silenced by the sheer weight of repeating the waking dream itself. The Strindberg actor cannot find *the* key to a character's reality (as in melodrama), or even *a* key, (as in Ibsen): *all* is illusion-as-reality, and to create and maintain that illusion challenges the actor's every reserve.

The Hindu-oriented reading of Strindberg's repetitive structure prompts actors to see the characters in *A Dream Play* as reincarnations of one another, souls or spirits nominally and momentarily attached to individual forms but ceaselessly fluid and seeking release from their material existence. As early as his preface to *Miss Julie*, Strindberg articulated his idea of character, which may be reexamined in light of his later Hindu ideas of the self. The most striking facet of even this early credo is his dismissal of the term "character" in preference to "soul": "My souls (characters) are conglomerations

34. August Strindberg, *The Ghost Sonata*, in Sprigge, *Six Plays*, p. 304.

of past and present stages of civilization, bits from books and news-
papers, scraps of humanity, rags and tatters of fine clothing, patched
together as is the human soul. And I have added a little evolutionary
history by making the weaker steal and repeat the words of the
stronger, and by making the characters borrow ideas or 'suggestions'
from one another."[35] Strindberg contrasts his "souls" with the customary idea of character, with the static, simple roles of melodrama
linked to bourgeois values and old-fashioned styles of theatrical production.

In his ideal theatre, then—an alternative, experimental one—
Strindberg hoped to redefine character as soul. And, unlike Ibsen's
characters, who shift as we view them through a linear double action, Strindberg's souls evade us because they emerge as "bits,"
"scraps," "rags and tatters" which steal one another's very essence. In
Hindu terms they try to escape karma and be reborn into a higher
incarnation. They are, as Strindberg describes them, "inconsistent
characters, disjointed, broken, erratic characters."[36] He compares
his delineation of characters to the fragmentation of the cine-
matographer's art: "Notice how many shots must be taken in sequence by the cinema photographer to reproduce a single movement, and even so the image is blurred. . . . How many myriads
would not be needed to depict a movement of the soul?"[37]

In assessing this facet of Strindberg's characterization, critics tend
to link his work to the later German expressionists, viewing all of
Strindberg's characters as fragments of his own psyche. Ingmar
Bergman's production of *A Dream Play,* with the Poet figure onstage
from the opening scene, best illustrates this approach: Strindberg as
Poet dreams his subconscious into the public arena, staging, for
example, the "feminine within himself" as the Daughter of Indra.
Maurice Gravier explains the goal of expressionistic theatre:

> Instead of describing and imitating "characters," superficial labor
> without significance, [the playwright's] business is to express the
> profound movements of the soul. This is the very principle of the

35. Sprigge, *Six Plays*, pp. 64–65.
36. August Strindberg, *Open Letters to the Intimate Theatre*, trans. Walter Johnson
(Seattle: University of Washington Press, 1967), p. 29.
37. Ibid., pp. 81–82.

expressionistic theatre. Since, moreover, the author cannot know any other consciousness than his own, the new theatre will necessarily be autobiographical and confessional. The poet mistrusts logic and its artifices, and the drama he writes will seem inarticulate and even arbitrary to the layman. Since so-called conscious life conceals the more substantial truth and is only a form of sleepwalking, we can reach the realm of the subconscious only by the royal highway of the dream.[38]

The Westernized bias that this type of theatre must "necessarily be autobiographical and confessional" has led us to view Strindberg's characters as projections of his tormented psyche, as they may indeed be; but if we also consider Strindberg's handling of character in Hindu terms, we see quite a different picture. Characters then become transitory individuals in a dream chain, reborn in particular forms because they want something: "There is a hunger, unsated in their present lives, that propels them across the barrier of death into a new birth, where this still unfulfilled longing leads them to do what they do."[39]

These souls may be regarded not merely as patches of Strindberg's unconscious but rather as selves that are not aware of their karmic traces and therefore suffer misery and delusion. Karmic memory traces are "bits of experience that adhere to the transmigrating soul," and, according to the Sanskrit text *Yogavāsiṣṭha*, "people who are not aware of their karmic traces find it hard to give up their bad habits."[40] So these incarnations of female and male repeat, over and over again, and in various guises, the same misguided desires. Harry Carlson envisions the Officer, the Lawyer, and the Poet as ironic treatments of the Indic divine trinity, composed of Siva the destroyer, Viṣṇu the preserver, and Brahmā the creator: "The Officer is part of the military, the chief purpose of which is to be ready to make war. . . . The Lawyer's vocation is in the maintenance of social order. . . . And the Poet as artistic creator emulates the original creator."[41] Each of these gods might be viewed as an

---

38. Maurice Gravier, "The Character and the Soul," in *Strindberg: A Collection of Critical Essays,* ed. Otto Reinert (Englewood Cliffs, N.J.: Prentice Hall, 1971), p. 83.

39. O'Flaherty, *Dreams,* p. 220.

40. Ibid.

41. Carlson, *Strindberg,* p. 178.

improved reincarnation of his predecessor: "Where the Officer and the Lawyer are both blinded by māyā . . . the Poet's perspective is not limited to the past or the present; he is free to soar higher and see farther than his predecessors."[42] At the end of the play the Poet seems to have progressed further than any of the others toward understanding that "suffering is redemption, and death release [from *māyā*]." Kristin, perhaps the most elementary incarnation in the play, by contrast collapses into her task of pasting the windows shut; she focuses so entirely on shutting out the heavens that she becomes an automaton, in ironic contrast to the Daughter of Indra, who seeks to open the cloverleaf door, to burn the castle down in an act of subversion.

Whereas Ibsen's shifting characters seek desperately to find, to choose, to know the imbricated self, Strindberg's disjointed, converging souls ultimately desire the release from self that Agnes finds in the purging fire at the end of the play. As O'Flaherty notes: "In the West, the loss of the sense of self (ego)—for which the Sanskrit *ahaṃkara* is a pejorative parallel—is often regarded as a sign of madness, but in India the loss of the sense of Self (*ātman*) as distinct from God (*Brahman*) is the key to enlightenment."[43] To seek *mokṣa* means to avoid "the same failures, losses, embarrassing mistakes, and ruined opportunities that had plagued the countless lives of the past" and to opt instead "to enter bliss (*ānanda*)."[44] This solution, however, does little to set the stage for an empowering or liberating representation of woman in the here and now.

The short scene between the lovers He and She illuminates the concept of character as reincarnation in *A Dream Play*. The Poet and the Officer watch as He, an allegorical representation of man, glides by with an "ideal" female, She/Victoria. But their karma is no better than that of any of the other characters. Just like the Father and the Mother, the Officer and the elusive Victoria, the Lawyer and Agnes, and the newlyweds who arrive shortly thereafter to commit joint suicide, He and She realize that their chance for happiness in this material world is an illusion. As if in atonement for his desire for the female principle—*māyā* as incarnated in Victoria—moments later

42. Ibid., p. 179.
43. O'Flaherty, *Dreams*, p. 121.
44. Ibid., pp. 299–300.

the Officer is incarnated as a grown-up schoolboy, unable to remember his lessons, and the motif of reincarnation and repetition erupts once again on stage.

Strindberg's repetitive structure and reincarnated characters presented his actors with a challenge. Instead of signifying an absent scene or double line of action as an Ibsen actor might in an effort to represent reality, the Strindberg actor must evoke successive transformations of illusion as reality, employing Strindberg's "dematerial" style of production. Whereas the actor playing Hedda portrays her shifting motivations to signal both a psychological reality and a melodramatic role, the actor performing the Daughter of Indra has to assume a different attitude toward the reality of her character in each successive scene. As the herald of godhead in the opening scene, she floats toward earth, landing in a fairy tale that is suddenly transformed, first into a naturalistic drama, then into absurdism and burlesque. As the herald of *māyā* as well as of the Brechtian character as type, the Strindberg actor-magician explores both the illusion of acting in the real world and the fluctuating reality of that world. While in character the actor is sometimes distanced, in yogin fashion, from the ordinary world. Through this process of "disembodiment" the Strindberg actor in effect acknowledges the spirit's freedom from the body: at any moment we may become someone else, or find ourselves in a different kind of reality. This sudden and complete transformation distinguishes Strindberg's actor: a moment-to-moment willingness to jump into a different mode of reality. The actor presents characters that are types—but not the caricatures of melodrama or the tortured expressions of the playwright's soul, as in the later German expressionists. In Strindberg's late plays the actor presents the transformational type, hinged between *sat* (the real) and *asat* (the unreal). This transformation entails more than the alteration of outward appearances or the adoption of successive roles (such as in the early Sam Shepard scripts). It involves sudden and drastic fluctuations in the nature, function, and condition of the relationship between reality and illusion from one scene to the next.

Obviously the actor's task outlined here differs substantially from the Ibsen actor's careful pondering of intellectual choices and adoption of secret autistic gestures. As John Ward writes: "Many of

[Strindberg's] major roles defy virtuoso performance. The protagonists of *To Damascus, A Dream Play* and *The Great Highway,* for example, are not the neatly delineated, well-structured psychological entities that actors are likely to appreciate. *Prima facie,* they are amorphous, inconsistent, and dramatically implausible . . . characters that are constantly changing. Moreover, this dynamism does not easily appear as growth; often the protagonists are so mercurial, so evidently lacking in rationality, that their behavior seems to lose all consistency."[45] Actors need not search for keys to the past in playing Strindberg's characters but may instead focus on the considerable variety of performance styles prompted by the script.

Female actors do not have to follow Bosse's lead in attempting a "demateriel" style of performance, of course. Seeking to counteract the effect of Strindberg's misogynistic myth, they may wish to accent the breaks, the disruptive potential of these transformations from scene to scene, highlighting their obvious theatricality. In that way the female actor can make apparent the construction of womanhood in its various guises. In the transformation from the opening scene to the second scene of *A Dream Play,* for example, the actor playing the Daughter can switch abruptly from playing the wayward and willful goddess who has followed the lightning to escape her father's domain to portraying the impatient and all-knowing heir of the castle's potential: "Ought it not to blossom soon?" In these transformations the actor can reveal the possibility of change and set the stage for the character's eventual exit from the earthly repetition of misguided desires.

Advances in film technology and experiments in mixing projections, film, dance, and theatre onstage—work by artists such as Robert Wilson, Ping Chong, and Martha Clarke—now enable Strindberg's directors and actors to achieve what Strindberg, Castegren, and Falck could not: a production of *A Dream Play* that explores the demateriel as well as the material bases of the script. Strindberg's desire for nonrealistic staging emerged even before its fullest articulation in *A Dream Play* or its predecessor, *To Damascus.* He originally conceived of dematerialism not as an acting style but as a production

45. John Ward, *The Social and Religious Plays of Strindberg* (London: Athlone Press, 1980), p. 6.

style, an inexpensive way to provide necessary scenery by means of optical projection. A detailed investigation of these efforts to achieve a nonrealistic production style can clarify the playwright's attempt at a dematerial acting style.

As early as 1889 the playwright tried to interest the actor-director August Lindberg in a chronicle play which he described as "a half-fantastical romance about the French Revolution, with cheap illusions using a large *laterna magica*."[46] A decade later his interest was reignited by a trip to Paris, where he, along with other symbolists, viewed the dreamy shadow plays of Henri Rivière's famous Chat Noir cabaret in Montmartre. "'I don't want to use ordinary theatre decorations for my new plays,' he declared shortly later in *Svenska Dagbladet* (21 January 1899). 'All these old-fashioned painted theatrical rags must go! I only want a painted background representing a room, a forest, or whatever it may be, or perhaps a background could be produced by a shadow picture painted on glass and projected onto a white sheet.'"[47] This simplified theatre with its projected pictures also meant for Strindberg scenery and stage properties that transformed from one scene to the next, as in *A Dream Play*, as well as an unadorned "Shakespearean" platform stage.

The movement toward the dematerial theatre was, of course, pervasive in the era of Gordon Craig, William Poel, and Harley Granville-Barker.[48] Emil Grandison, who directed the premier to *To Damascus I* at the Royal Dramatic Theatre, Dramaten, in Stockholm in 1900, launched Strindberg's first campaign of that revolution. Although the effort to use projected scenery failed, Grandison arranged for Karl Grabow to design highly stylized painted backdrops on which were sketched, in emblematic form, the necessary furniture and scenic elements which were normally placed onstage in all their three-dimensionality. A second proscenium arch framed an inner stage, lit in a nonillusionistic fashion to emphasize the faraway, dreamlike movements of the actors. The *Aftonbladet's* critic reported

46. Göran Söderström, "Strindberg's Sceneographic Ideas," in *Strindberg on Stage*, ed. Donald K. Weaver (Stockholm: Swedish Centre of the I.T.A., the Strindberg Society, and the Swedish Institute, 1981), p. 34. For information on Strindberg and film, see Rune Waldekranz, "Strindberg and the Silent Cinema," in *Essays on Strindberg*, ed. Strindberg Society (Stockholm: Beckmans, 1966), pp. 87–107.

47. Marker and Marker, *The Scandinavian Theatre*, p. 189.

48. Ibid., p. 190.

that the actors' entrances and exits appeared magical: "It is easy to imagine oneself in a hallucinatory state caused by fever."[49]

After the opening Strindberg wrote his future wife, Harriet Bosse, who played the Lady in the premiere, applauding her work but cautioning her against the unified mystical approach which she later repeated in the premier of *A Dream Play*. He requested a lighter, more complex and varied performance with "small traces of roguishness and with more expansiveness. A little of Puck. . . . A laugh in the midst of suffering indicates hope, and the situation certainly does not prove to be hopeless!"[50] By this time, indeed by the time of the *Damascus* dress rehearsal (at which he advised Bosse how to kiss the Unknown), Strindberg had fallen in love with Bosse, for whom he later wrote the role of the Daughter of Indra.

But by the time *A Dream Play* reached the stage, on April 17, 1907, at the Swedish Theatre in Blasiehomen, Bosse had left Strindberg, and Grandison's earlier nonillusionistic staging efforts had been scrapped. Strindberg documented his unsuccessful search for a production style to frame his "demateral" actors. In *Open Letters* he discusses the difficulties he and his director, Victor Castegren of the Swedish Theatre, faced:

> We began to discuss means of transforming the dream into visual representations without materializing it too much. The sciopticon was first used. We had already tried that in the production of *To Damascus* at the Royal Theatre. Sven Scholander actually projected a backdrop sufficiently large and clear, but, since it had to be kept dark in front of the backdrop so that it would show up, the actors could be seen less clearly. Another disadvantage was that the electric light showed through the fabric, but this could be improved by placing the lights below the level of the stage floor. That was too low, and we wearied.[51]

Strindberg suggested several solutions to the problems presented by the sciopticon, including red lights to illuminate the actors in addition to overhead lighting, but Castegren (unlike Strindberg) feared

49. My description of the premiere of *To Damascus* relies on the account of Marker and Marker, ibid., pp. 189–90.

50. Ibid., p. 193.

51. Strindberg, *Open Letters*, p. 293.

"getting the same lighting effects 'as used in variety shows.'"[52] The theatre manager, Albert Ranft, rejected the Grandison strategy of employing arches and multiple backdrops, so Castegren finally hired Karl Grabow to paint the traditional scenery.

Strindberg criticized the resulting production elements and the actors' performances as "too material for the dream. . . . The construction on stage disturbed the actors' dedication of spirit and called for endless intermissions; besides, the whole performance became 'a materialization phenomenon' instead of the intended dematerialization."[53] Tor Hedbert, the critic for *Svenska Dagblad*, remarked that "the task is so incredibly difficult that one hardly even has a right to make comments." but he had to admit the failure of the premiere.[54]

Strindberg, however, maintained his interest in a dematerial production style, if not his hope for achieving this style through his actors. His later plan for the Intimate Theatre's production of *A Dream Play* included the scenic use of simple draperies with colored lights, allegorical properties, and bright costumes for "all ages" ("just so they are beautiful, because here in the dream there is no question of reality").[55] "But," he said, "instead of painted sets, which in *this case* cannot reproduce unfixed and moving mirages or illusions, we intend to seek only the effect of colors."[56] In another experiment Strindberg developed a set for *A Dream Play* in his own toy model theatre, with a frame painted to resemble a poppy field, behind which "he had placed a backdrop of flowers, in which was an opening for exchangeable masks."[57]

Strindberg sought to stage a moving mirage in many of his plays, focusing on production elements, which were, after all, more malleable than he had found his actors to be. According to Göran Söderström, "among Strindberg's effects are several lists from 1900 of plays, written and unwritten, suitable for a sciopticon theater. Among those he lists are *The Dance of Death, Advent,* the then-

---

52. Ibid., p. 294.
53. Ibid.
54. Marker and Marker, *The Scandinavian Theatre*, p. 195.
55. Strindberg, *Open Letters*, p. 295.
56. Ibid., p. 294.
57. Söderström, "Strindberg's Scenographic Ideas," p. 45.

unwritten *Easter,* and *To Damascus.* An outline of a family drama, later *The Pelican,* was also designated 'sciopticon.'"[58] This attempt to utilize film techniques in order to dematerialize the set stemmed from the same impulse that led Strindberg to suggest that J. M. W. Turner's hazy painting style would be appropriate for a production of *A Dream Play.* These attempts are all to graft a nonrealistic style onto the established realism of the day. But each of these early efforts failed in one way or another. The stage history of the script since that time traces the efforts of various directors, from Max Reinhardt in the 1920s and Olof Molander in the 1930s to Ingmar Bergman in 1970, to accomplish two goals: to help actors master the complex interweaving of performance styles required by the script, and to establish a suitable production style. After seven separate attempts Molander concluded: "The resources not the least on the acting level, which this Strindbergian masterpiece requires in order to, in my opinion, come even close to doing it justice are so colossal that no theatre has them at its disposal."[59]

Bosse's biographer Carla Waal concludes that *A Dream Play* "was an innovative masterpiece in symphonic form, making technical demands beyond the resources of the Swedish Theatre and the directorial imagination of Victor Castegren."[60] It was not only the director who faced difficulty in staging Strindberg's script, however; the actors, too, struggled unsuccessfully with the problem of performance style. While some used highly stylized speech, others spoke naturally.[61] Bosse stressed the dreamlike quality of her character by wearing a flowing plain white gown and moving in a way that suggested otherworldliness. According to one critic, Bosse's "soft, slightly swaying walk had the right ethereal quality."[62] After her retirement years later Bosse posed for Greta Gerell's portrait of her as the

58. Ibid., p. 44.
59. Marker and Marker, *The Scandinavian Theatre,* p. 237.
60. Carla Waal, *Harriet Bosse: Strindberg's Muse and Interpreter* (Carbondale: Southern Illinois University Press, 1990), p. 229. For a stage history of *A Dream Play,* see Egil Törnqvist, "Staging *A Dream Play,*" in *Strindberg's Dramaturgy,* ed. Göran Stockenström (Minneapolis: University of Minnesota Press, 1988), pp. 256–90. For an account of the Open Space Theatre Experiment's 1981 New York production, see Susan Einhorn, "Directing *A Dream Play:* A Journey Through the Waking Dream," in Stockenström, *Strindberg's Dramaturgy,* pp. 291–302.
61. Waal, *Harriet Bosse,* p. 230.
62. Quoted ibid.

Daughter of Indra, reciting her lines from *A Dream Play* as Gerell recreated her airy, incorporeal portrayal on the canvas. (See figure 4.) Bosse thereby initiated one of the two traditional approaches to the role—characterizations that persist to this day: "She is either played as an elevated, mystical figure who represents Eastern wisdom (as played by Harriet Bosse and Tora Teje) or as a rather ordinary, everyday person (as played by Gun Wallgren, Marika Lagerkranz, and Malin Ek)."[63] Recent portrayals have emphasized the naturalistic approach. Both performance strategies fail, however, to probe the vacillating transformations within the central female character. And both restrict the representation of women to univocal rather than ever-shifting characters, thereby limiting the actor's opportunities to make the audience conscious of performance.

Audiences familiar with a variety of technically sophisticated production styles can now acknowledge the diverse performance codes that Strindberg fostered in his writing, and can perceive the kind of acting that his dramaturgy invites. With female and male actors devoted to transforming their bodies and voices into multiple and merging illusions and bits of naturalism, the director of Strindberg's various scripts can adopt "a production-concept equal to the length and breadth of the original work" instead of suffering from the "Psychological Realistic Hang-Up" as the director Charles Marowitz calls it.[64]

Strindberg himself, as director of the Intimate Theatre, failed to articulate for his actors what his demterial production style meant for them. In his *Open Letters* he advises them, "Follow the text!" but then defines his collaboration with them in a way that is reminiscent of the pre-Ibsen director.[65] Instead of showing them the keys to interpreting the shifting scenes of his demterial style, he suggests, "Tamper with your speeches, if you can get them to go better, stretch them a bit, if you want to," only "see to it your speeches fit in with the others'" (p. 142). He even suggests that the actor, not the director,

63. Gunnar Ollen, "Performing Strindberg—Problems of Role Interpretation," in Weaver, *Strindberg on Stage*, p. 165.

64. Charles Marowitz, "Approaching Strindberg by Passing Him By," in Weaver, *Strindberg on Stage*, pp. 60–61.

65. Strindberg, *Open Letters*, pp. 104–5; subsequent references to this work are cited by page in the text.

Figure 4. Greta Gerell's portrait of Harriet Bosse as the Daughter of Indra in *A Dream Play*, courtesy Carla Waal, by permission of Dramaten

should determine the final contours of the character sketched by the playwright: "When something is expressed in several ways the artist should independently decide what is right for his purpose" (p. 143). This laissez-faire attitude stems more from a desire to escape the actors, however, than from a coherent directorial agenda. Describing the way in which the Intimate Theatre cast staged *The Ghost Sonata, The Bond,* and *Queen Christina* without a director (before he assumed the post for *The Father* and *Swanwhite*), Strindberg writes, "If I add that I could not bear hearing my own words out of the past drummed into my ears day after day and if I confess that my writing fascinated me, I have stated the principal reasons for my withdrawal as director" (p. 143).

In fact, at times Strindberg seems to regard acting as a mystical accomplishment rather than an art requiring study and technique. He promotes the concept of the naive actor, one who instinctively senses the demands of the script. This conception of the female actor is diametrically opposed to that of the Ibsen actor, who must be alert to the complexities of the script and the intellectual currents of the time, including women's issues. According to Strindberg, however: "The person who considers himself an artist, that is, looks at his art as art and does not brood about universal suffrage or emancipation, who does not speculate about world problems and zoology, will become a good actor. If the actor can live unreflectively, naïvely, a little carelessly, not read too much rather be with people but not to study them but really live with them now and then, and have fun, his art will benefit most" (p. 133). Whereas Ibsen actors such as Elizabeth Robins worked actively for women's rights, Strindberg's ideal female actor is not to "brood" about such things. This portrait of the actor as a naive interpreter coincides with Strindberg's image of the actor as being in a waking dream: "The actor acts so unconsciously, so much like a sleepwalker that he literally does not understand what the director says" during rehearsal (p. 137). Strindberg complains that actors often treat him like an unauthorized intruder offering performance suggestions either too early or too late in the rehearsal process (pp. 137–38). Like Bosse, they seem impervious to his commands. Given Strindberg's concept of the actor as a naive "dream-walker," best left alone unless guilty of a major violation, it is not surprising that his desire for a dematerial production style manifested itself primarily in his efforts to control the set rather than the actors.

To his credit, Strindberg nonetheless perceived the complexities of the audience's reception of performance styles. Acting styles, he says, are linked to the worldview and even the nationality of the audience. An acting style must be contemporary to move its audience: "If the time is skeptical, insensitive, and democratic as ours is, there is no point in using grand airs of sentimentality" (p. 138). When he watched Jean Mounet-Sully act in *Rome vaincue* at the Théâtre Français in the late 1870s, he found the acting style stilted instead of beautiful, "possibly because [he] was not a Frenchman," (p. 139). Strindberg therefore advocated a style of acting that would change continuously with the repertory and the audience's sensibility: "If there comes a period when people become more sensitive and another view of the world succeeds the biological we have passed through, there will be needed another repertory, which will have to be acted in another way" (p. 140). Although Strindberg recognized that successive eras would generate a need for new approaches, the transformational approach prompted by his structural experimentation still receives validation not only from current attitudes toward a director's artistic rights but also from his own concept of the relationship between the audience and the actors' styles of performance.

A Dream Play, like Mounet-Sully's *Rome vaincue*, missed its target audience at its premiere in 1907 in part because it was ahead of its time in its call for a dematerial mixture of performance styles. Keve Hjelm, a self-confessed "malcontent" at a 1981 symposium on staging Strindberg, contended that Strindberg has not yet truly been performed, for the "literary acting style" or psychological realism which has pervaded the Swedish theatre has prevented any genuine exploration of his scripts.[66] At that same gathering other participants disagreed, noting a current trend toward mixing or breaking performance styles: "Breaking style as a mode concerns not only gestures but entire productions. It is usually an attempt to create scenic richness and diversified style."[67] They perceived "a tendency toward style breaking even in Strindberg's texts. The tendencies

66. Quoted in Weaver, *Strindberg on Stage*, pp. 65–67.
67. Group Report, ibid., p. 164.

swing between Romanticism and Realism," citing the influence of the opera and the baroque stage on his dramaturgy.[68] To these influences on Strindberg's performance style, however, must be added two elements: first, his long-standing interest in the possibilities of photography and film in the theatre, an interest that enabled him to envision a dematerial theatre that would present the world as a world of dreams; and second, his readings in Eastern religions, which confused the boundary between dream and reality and thereby helped infuse his writing with an ever more complicated series of character transformations and performance styles.

Bruce Wilshire cites three "methods of fictive variation" in his analysis of Robert Wilson's dramas, techniques that should be useful to Strindberg actors and directors faced with similar dramaturgical devices. These techniques are repetition, "action slowed down," and "action aborted, unconsummated."[69] One of the most intriguing ruptures in *A Dream Play* offers an instance of repeated action: Kristin's insistent "I paste, I paste," a phrase that echoes as she attempts again and again to patch the unmendable cracks in the Lawyer and Agnes's marital home. Wilshire writes: "If action is not employed merely to get on to something else, but is repeated, it is framed; it stands out. . . . Hence the nature of *normal* action comes through being violated. . . . We cease to be absorbed in it as an exclusive possibility of existence."[70] The effect of Kristin's repeated activity is to render it useless and frustrating, a form of suffocation, an ineffectual and pointless attempt to create warmth within the marital home. The actor can, Wilson-style, break down the gesture into its constituent parts, emphasizing its robotic qualities. Like Kristin, the Officer repeats his primary activity of wooing Victoria, achieving a similar result. As the actor playing the Officer appears in his courtship scenes first as a young man, then as an aged gentlemen, and finally as a middle-aged man, this repetition of the activity of romantic pursuit not only subverts the traditional romance narrative but also frames and highlights the ineffectuality of the actor's repeated, almost mechanized movement—at a physical and emo-

68. Ibid., pp. 164–65.

69. Bruce Wilshire, *Role Playing and Identity: The Limits of Theatre as Metaphor* (Bloomington: Indiana University Press, 1982), pp. 118–20.

70. Ibid., p. 118.

tional cost, of course, to the actor. Wilshire's discussion of Wilson's strategy also applies to Strindberg: "When the action of meeting and encounter is unconsummated and our expectations are disappointed, we finally see, through contrast, what *consummation* always amounted to, and what some of its conditions are. . . . Suggested principles of relevance, without which the texture of human being-together would be impossible, include: meeting, distance, deference, encounter, and joint absorption in a common subject of concern."[71] This describes precisely the kind of joint absorption the Ibsen actor, director and audience shared.

In the Ibsen theatre the female actor articulates the superobjective of the script, experimenting with spines and beats to create a shifting but concrete psychological reality. This attempt to recuperate a psychological reality frequently leads to the choice of realistic sets and stage properties which reinforce the actors' and therefore the characters' grounding in a specific, predictable environment— which in turn, of course, symbolizes a greater "reality." In Strindberg's plays, however, the world onstage does not always signify reality but may also signal its lack, or a complex meshing of illusion and reality. Consequently the female actor, the director, and the designer face a difficult challenge.

Through his unique structural method Strindberg urges female actors, and their directors and audiences, to explore the liminal zone between illusion and reality instead of examining a particular representation as reality, as Ibsen does with his retrospective method. Strindberg's transformational actor faces a task as complex and as difficult as that confronting Ibsen's critical actor—a task that entails portraying the very nature of a waking dream. Whereas Harriet Bosse, in the premiere production of *A Dream Play*, was trapped in an isolated attempt at devising a demateral style of performance, one that recapitulated her own problematic relationship with Strindberg, contemporary female actors can adopt the transformational style suggested by his scripts, a style that offers new possibilities and potentials for subversion.

71. Ibid., p. 120.

Chapter Three

The Brecht Collective
and the Parabolic Actor

Whereas Strindberg's dream structures explore the karmic transformations of characters perched between reality and illusion, Bertolt Brecht roots his plays firmly in material reality. That much seems obvious. In fact, his work is so widely associated with materialist concerns, with the dialectical structure, contradictory characters, and acting style of the epic theatre, that one may well ask how anything new or worthwhile can be said about Brechtian structure or performance style, much less about the relationship between the actor and the character, director, or audience in the Brechtian theatre. Furthermore, we know that Brecht operated pragmatically as a director; he did not always concern himself with his own theoretical concepts or with techniques such as the much-discussed *Verfremdungseffekt* (alienation effect). So why yet another examination of Brecht's structural strategies and their impact on acting style?

Earlier studies of Brechtian performance have assumed that Brecht is the authority on his plays because he is their author, but more recent scholarship has begun to clarify the collaborative nature of the Brecht script, its production through a collective. A consideration of the several authorial voices in the scripts prompts me to rethink Brechtian acting, positing a style that includes not only what Brecht himself calls for but also what seems necessary to the other sources, especially the female sources, in the Brecht canon. It becomes important to picture not the Brechtian actor but the performer of the Brecht Collective, a performer who focuses less on the parable than on the parabolic way in which the parable turns against itself. Instead of playing out the "not this *but* that" of the familiar alienation effect, the Collective actor juggles both dialectical choices presented to the character, thus suggesting the character's desire to do "not this *and* not that." The Collective actor imagined herein gestures toward the past and the present to suggest future possibilities, encouraging the audience to write beyond the ending.

Although *The Good Person of Szechwan* has typically been read as a Marxist allegory about the difficulty of being good in an evil capitalistic world, this script also reproduces the ambivalent social relations involved in its long and complicated collaborative history: good and evil are inseparable in this script from considerations of gender. Two members of the Brecht Collective, Ruth Berlau and Margarete Steffin, collaborated with Brecht on this particularly taxing project, which was written over a period of a decade and a half, and which Brecht himself never staged. It is very likely that Elisabeth Hauptmann, another of Brecht's collaborator-lovers, also contributed to the early drafts. In its examination of the ways in which gender is constructed, the script reflects the tensions inherent in its own genesis and serves as a paradigm of the Brecht Collective performance style. As a parable it both enacts and critiques the way in which faltering patriarchal institutions such as Christianity attempt to entrap women into being "good." Simultaneously the play calls on women and men in the audience to disengage themselves from the bungling ineptitude of their institutional gods and the outdated ethical and gender codes they promote. This revised approach to the parable structure of the Collective's work, which reflects women's voices in the writing of the script, suggests a strategy for approaching other Brecht Collective scripts, and poses new challenges for Collective actors, directors, and audiences.

In a telling footnote to *The Essential Brecht,* John Fuegi reports that Brecht himself was the prototype for one of the three gods in *The Good Person of Szechwan.* As Fuegi explains, in 1926 Brecht, with his friends Arnolt Bronnen and Alfred Döblin, received a less than satisfactory welcome at a Dresden theatre festival, which prompted Brecht to write "a satirical ballad on a city's failure to recognize the arrival of three visiting gods."[1] Brecht may, then, be present in *The Good Person of Szechwan* as the First God, who sets up the project: to produce a good person in order to justify his existence, that is, to commodify the female, Shen Te, in order to justify his own life. As the First God explains his object: "We must find someone. For two thousand years we have been hearing the same complaint, that the world cannot go on as it is. No one can stay on earth and remain good. We must at last be able to show some people who are in a position to keep our commandments."[2] Like the gods, Brecht invents the narrative which seems to control the collective venture; he creates a situation in which love is treated as a commodity. Although the gods in Brecht's script eventually seem to lose control, in fact, they never had it in the first place. They seek in Shen Te a collaborator who will shore up a narrative in which even they themselves cannot thrive, in a world that commodifies the most intimate of relations.

Like the gods in the parable, Brecht in his personal life set up the means of production in the form of the rules by which his female collaborator-mistresses lived. These rules, despite their misogynistic basis, were designed to permit the inclusion—if not the acknowledgment—of the women's work. These women were central

1. John Fuegi, *The Essential Brecht* (Los Angeles: Hennessey and Ingalls, 1972), p. 259. Ronald Hayman gives a fuller version of this story: "In March Brecht was invited, together with Bronnen and Alfred Döblin, to give a poetry reading in Dresden, where Verdi's *La Forza del Destino* was to be premiered in Franz Werfel's translation. Humiliatingly, though, the three guests of honor were allocated inferior seats in the opera house, and were not invited to the gala reception for Werfel. Infuriated, they returned their tickets, and it was only after a publisher, Leo Franck, had stepped in as mediator that they agreed to go ahead with the reading. Brecht included a freshly written allegory about three gods who visit Alibi where no one pays homage to them because the people are all celebrating the great Alea. One citizen of Alibi, Sibillus, persuades the gods to go with him 'to the table of the fat Alea . . . to pick up the crumbs that fall from his rich table.' Though Werfel was quite plump, the audience would have missed the point if the impulsive Bronnen had not denounced Werfel and the management, describing the previous day's events. A scandal ensued, and years later, when he wrote *Der Gute Mensch von Sezuan*, Brecht went back to the idea of three visiting gods who are given a poor reception." Ronald Hayman, *Brecht: A Biography* (New York: Oxford University Press, 1983), pp. 115–16.

2. Bertolt Brecht, *The Good Person of Szechwan*, trans. John Willett, in *Bertolt Brecht: Collected Plays*, ed. John Willett and Ralph Manheim, vol. 6, pt. 1 (London: Methuen, 1985), p. 6.

to the Collective's productivity. According to John Fuegi: "Elisabeth Hauptmann's role as a collaborative writer in the twenties was absolutely indispensable, and long sections of Brecht plays were probably written by her. Later, in exile, Margarete Steffin and Ruth Berlau made contributions to 'Brecht's' major exile plays. After Brecht's return to Berlin, Hauptmann again became enormously important."[3] In a personal communication Fuegi outlined his findings on the contributions of Hauptmann, Steffin, and Berlau:

> Of the three I consider the contribution of Hauptmann to have been the greatest between 1925 and 1931 and then again from circa 1948 until Brecht's death in 1956. Steffin's contributions were made between 1931 when she first met Brecht and her untimely death in Moscow in 1941. Ruth Berlau's contributions, though they began shortly after she met Brecht in 1933, were mainly made after Steffin's death. Whereas Hauptmann and Steffin, so I am convinced, often wrote the actual words and scenes used, I believe that Berlau's contribution was more in the more general area of scene structuring and in the actual staging of the plays.[4]

The Collective began work on *Good Person* in the late 1920s and did not complete it until 1942—or 1943 if the American version is taken into consideration. John Willett credits both Steffin and Berlau as collaborators on the script, and Berlau's memoirs attest to her daily discussions with Brecht during the period of its creation.[5] Willett also asserts that Elisabeth Hauptmann "had clearly not only done a lot of the spadework for those plays, finished or unfinished, to which [Brecht] put his name between 1924 and 1933; she had actually written parts of them. . . . If she could so collaborate with him without seeming to want credit for it, might she not in the same

3. John Fuegi, *Bertolt Brecht: Chaos, According to Plan* (Cambridge: Cambridge University Press, 1987), p. 50.

4. In a personal letter dated August 6, 1990. See also Fuegi's book on the Brecht Collective, *Brecht & Co.* (New York: Grove/Weidenfeld, 1993). I am grateful for his permission to cite the results of his research.

5. See John Willett, *The Theatre of Bertolt Brecht* (New York: New Directions, 1975), p. 51, and Ruth Berlau, *Living for Brecht: The Memoir of Ruth Berlau*, ed. Hans Bunge, trans. Geoffrey Skelton (New York: Fromm International, 1987), pp. 93–94.

retiring way have done rather more?"[6] Willett thereby suggests (in what seems a very understated way) that Hauptmann also worked on the early versions of *The Good Person of Szechwan*. Since Brecht began this play as a short story at a time when he and Hauptmann were co-writing a series of stories, it is likely that Hauptmann also co-authored the prototype for *Good Person*. This reconstructive process of determining how much and what Brecht's collaborators wrote is, of course, still in process and presents a complex research problem, but one thing seems clear: the issue of how the idea of woman and man are constructed is central to an understanding of the performance codes of many of the parables and reflects the tensions within the Brecht Collective, whether or not the women actually put pen to paper.

In *Good Person* the gods' commandments to be good cannot finally be met, dictating within Shen Te a feeling of failure, just as Brecht's call to collaboration also dictated a certain sense of failure for his female collaborators. At first Shen Te, like the members of the Brecht Collective, seems to accept the rules laid down by the gods; but as the narrative unfolds, the gender constructions reproduced in the play become more and more complicated. Shen Te stretches the rules regarding gender, finally turning over to the audience the responsibility for inventing new guidelines based on her critique. As the actor playing Shen Te/Shui Ta moves between and rejects two interwoven constructions of character, bipolar opposites labeled "woman" and "man" respectively, she refuses fixity and reveals the untenability of existing at either pole. In so doing the actor reminds us that the First God's project fails precisely because Shen Te/Shui Ta, like herself, must finally be viewed as an unstable, ever-changing subject. The actor transforms the simple parable into a parabolic gesture toward the audience, a call to carry on the action beyond the curtain.

The exploration of gender issues within the script begins shortly after the play opens. Shen Te, a young Chinese prostitute, opens her

6. John Willett, "Bacon ohne Shakespeare?—The Problem of Mitarbeit," in *Brecht: Women and Politics/Frauen und Politik, The Brecht Yearbook*, vol. 12, ed. John Fuegi, Gisela Bahr, and John Willett (Detroit: Wayne State University Press, 1983), p. 122.

home to the three visiting gods, whose mission is to find a good person so that the world may remain as it is, thus vindicating their rule. In their relief at finding such a good person, the gods reward the young girl with a gift of money, which she uses as collateral to rent a tobacco shop. She invents an imaginary male cousin named Shui Ta to protect herself from creditors and to secure a lease. In scene two she actually dons the disguise of Shui Ta to hold off the demands of those who want to cash in on her good fortune from the gods. Typically Shen Te and Shui Ta are played as opposites: the ultrafeminine, selfless woman, and the macho, conniving man. Katrin Reichel's 1957 Berliner Ensemble portrayal exemplifies this tradition. (See figure 5).

The power that Shen Te enjoys as a result of disguising herself as Shui Ta derives in part from her construction as a man, of course, but onstage she is never *simply* a man: she is a female actor playing a woman playing a man (and who, on occasion, forgets that she/he is a man). According to Sara Lennox: "Since it is Shen Te herself who incorporates this male self-interest, Brecht seems to be indicating that such sex-related differences are tied more to the social expectations accompanying gender than to any natural differentiation by sex in psychological characteristics."[7] The representation of gender becomes even more complicated when Shen Te, now pregnant, refuses to relinquish the power that resides in the mask of the male Shui Ta even as her body reveals the fact that she is expecting a baby, one of the potentialities traditionally associated with matriarchal power. (Except for Mrs. Shin, who becomes Shen Te's confidant, the other characters in the play believe that Shui Ta, the successful factory owner, is gaining weight as a result of his new wealth). The actor playing Shen Te/Shui Ta thus simultaneously reproduces and critiques a construction that embodies both patriarchal and matriarchal power. In the final scene the actor is asked to present Shen Te as both a powerless woman shouting "Help!" and a powerful female revolutionary demanding assistance in the process of revising society.

These considerations of the Collective's writing process and the representation of gender in the script prompt a rethinking of the

7. Sara Lennox, "Women in Brecht's Works," *New German Critique* 14 (1978): 92.

Figure 5. Poster showing Katrin Reichel as Shen Te and Shui Ta in *Der Gute Mensch von Sezuan* (1957), courtesy Berliner Ensemble

play's structure. Brecht called *Good Person,* like many of his later plays, a parable. These parables have come to be regarded as straightforward pedagogical exercises, simple stories that illustrate a lesson, such as—in the case of *Good Person*—the fact that goodness cannot survive in a capitalistic world.[8] When the Deutsches Theater director Friedo Solter was asked about his reasons for choosing to produce the pre-Marxist Brecht plays rather than the later parables, he replied: "We in this society have outdone ourselves in terms of enlightenment, in terms of dogma, in terms of reducing everything to one simple message. . . . Brecht's later plays were written at a time . . . when one needed a few solid slogans and dogmas . . . but when you've done that sort of thing year after year the way we have, then you need a new lever."[9] Brecht's Marxist parables, by contrast, are now seen as "closed, narrative-centered, overly didactic"— ironically, the very qualities Brecht originally tried to oppose. But, as Solter is quick to point out, "the binary opposition of the early vs. the late Brecht is *itself* a construction which sublimates the very real contradictions and inconsistencies of even the later Brecht."[10] In this chapter I examine some of these inconsistencies in light of an alternative reading of the notion of parable, one that incorporates the newly recognized sources within the Collective.

In *The Genesis of Secrecy* Frank Kermode discusses the parable in terms of the hermeneutics of biblical scholarship, exploring the interpretive act engendered by the parable as one that creates mystery rather than disclosure, excess rather than didacticism. Parables by their very nature offer different readings to different audiences— an insight that challenges us to revise our notions of narrative closure in the Collective's parables. Kermode notes that Jesus regarded his parables as stories expressly designed to hide from outsiders a mystery that was meant to be comprehended only by insiders: "Jesus said, 'To you has been given the secret of the kingdom of God, but for those outside everything is in parables; so that they may indeed

8. John Willett, for example, identifies the moral of the script thus: "In a competitive society goodness is often suicidal." Willett, *Theatre of Bertolt Brecht,* p. 85.

9. Quoted in David Bathrick, "Patricide or Re-Generation: Brecht's *Baal* and *Roundheads* in the GDR," *Theatre Journal* 39, 4 (December 1987): 437.

10. Ibid., p. 443.

see but not perceive, and may indeed hear but not understand; lest they should turn again and be forgiven' [Mark 4:11–12]."[11]

Parables do not make a simple story clear; they hide a complex truth. The act of creating meaning is not easy even for those insiders familiar with the codes of any given discourse; even the disciples, for example, have some difficulty interpreting the parable of the sower of seeds. The nature of interpretive change also complicates the issue in a process that applies to the present analysis as well: "Our acts of divination—for the acts that determine undetected latent sense are properly so called—our divinations are made necessary by the fact of our occupying, inescapably, a position in history which is not the position of the text we cultivate and not a position of which we have much objective understanding, though it helps to constitute the complex of prejudices we bring to the task of discovering a sense, for us, in the text we value (another element of prejudice)."[12] As I "perform" *The Good Person of Szechwan*, then, I am divining tensions that I understand to be implicit in the originary collaboration of the Brecht Collective (tensions that open up the supposedly closed narrative of the parable), and I am simultaneously (and necessarily) transgressing the script. Just as Strindberg's transformational performance style has only recently become visible because of technological advances and the audience's familiarity with a plethora of acting styles, the particular means of interpreting this rereading of parables has only just become accessible, largely because of the work of contemporary feminist theorists and those researching the Brecht Collective itself.[13]

Walter Benjamin reports Brecht's definition of parable, one that resembles Kermode's rather than Solter's reading of the form. Imagining himself to be the defendant in a court proceeding, Brecht

11. Frank Kermode, *The Genesis of Secrecy* (Cambridge: Harvard University Press, 1979), pp. 2–3.

12. Ibid., p. 4.

13. I am especially indebted to theorists Elin Diamond, Sue-Ellen Case, Jill Dolan, and Janelle Reinelt, whose Association for Theatre in Higher Education conference presentations, along with their publications, noted in this chapter, prompted my renewed interest in Brecht and helped me consider a new element in the discussion already in process. I also thank John Fuegi for his insights into the contributions of the women writers of the Brecht Collective.

(during the course of his discussion with Benjamin) considers the question "Are you really in earnest?" His somewhat surprising negative answer leads him to posit two distinct types of writers: "the visionary artist, who is in earnest, and the cool-headed thinking man, who is not completely in earnest."[14] Benjamin records Brecht's conversation as he explicates these phrases:

> To explain this thought he proceeds from the hypothesis that Confucius might once have written a tragedy, or Lenin a novel. That, he thinks, would be felt as improper, unworthy behaviour. "Suppose you read a very good historical novel and later you discover that it is by Lenin. You would change your opinion of both, to the detriment of both. Likewise it would be wrong for Confucius to have written a tragedy, say one of Euripides's tragedies; it would be felt as unworthy. Yet his parables are not." . . . Kafka's starting point is really the parable, which is governed by reason and which, therefore, so far as its actual wording is concerned, cannot be entirely in earnest.[15]

Parable, then, for Brecht is associated with rationality and a lack of earnestness, with clarity, coolness, and a complexity of thought that resists closure. Here Brecht presages Kermode: a parable hides and proliferates meaning.

What does it mean to read *Good Person* as a parable hiding secrets? Is there any sense in which it raises questions other than those customarily addressed? To begin with, let us reconsider the question of authority in the script in light of the women writers who collaborated with Brecht.

The Brecht Collective made possible and yet limited female creativity. Steffin, Berlau, and Hauptmann obviously contributed, but because of the nature of their sexual relations with Brecht, none of the women was ever able to feel sufficient and irreplaceable. Fuegi writes: "Each woman in each period was periodically required to adjust to Brecht's sexual and professional needs and to sometimes serve as lover as well as secretary and collaborator but to be ready to be displaced as lover (without rancour) and continue as co-worker as

14. Walter Benjamin, "Conversations with Brecht," in *Understanding Brecht*, trans. Anna Bostock (London: NLB, 1973), p. 107.
15. Ibid.

though nothing had changed."[16] By the time Brecht began work on *The Good Person of Szechwan,* he was married to his second wife, Marianne Zoff. He had had children by three different women (by Zoff; by his first wife, Bie Banholzer; and by his mistress, later his third wife, Helene Weigel). And he was collaborating with another mistress, Elisabeth Hauptmann, on a number of projects. Brecht's profound ambivalence toward women, reflecting both attraction and fear, is echoed in *Good Person* in the gods' flimsy excuses and deliberate flights, and in Yang Sun's fecklessness. Brecht's pattern of behavior was thoroughly predictable, but as Fuegi reports, his collaborators were nonetheless powerfully drawn to him: "To be involved with Brecht was to give up virtually all independence. By sheer force of personality and with a superb sense of theatre and of business Brecht drew people to him, used those people to the utmost and then felt free to reject them when they were no longer useful. . . . As Marieluise Fleisser, one of his lover/collaborators, said of him: 'The man undermined and the man fascinated.'"[17] Part of the reason why the members of the Collective stayed with Brecht was that they were able to contribute in a substantive way to the joint projects despite his cruelty. The alternative, work in the traditional "culinary" theatre, offered even fewer opportunities for women writers.

But how, precisely, are these tensions embedded in Brecht's parables, and how might they inform performance? One of the linguistic correlatives of the term *parable*—parabola—may pry loose some important issues here. A parabola is a plane curve created by a point moving so that its distance from a fixed point is equal to its distance from a fixed line. Parable, its literary equivalent, may be viewed as a narrative that turns back on itself, shaped by the relation between two fixed times outside itself: the time of writing (of "sowing"), and audience time. Audience time refers not only to the presence of any particular audience (the moment of the creation of meaning) but also to the time of the transformed world or order that would come about if the audience grasped (and therefore acted on and through) the parable. The parable is not that future, just as it is not the "present" of the audience, nor even the original words at the mo-

16. Fuegi, *Bertolt Brecht,* p. 50.
17. Ibid.

ment of dissemination. It is a mediating time—a time between—
which opens up the possibility of moving from that past to this
present to that future, or in any desired fashion along the line. This
is where the element of concealment is introduced. The message or
meaning of the parable lies in the way it gestures to a time before or
after.[18]

What does this mean for a performance of *The Good Person of
Szechwan?* It means that we may restore the lack of earnestness to the
script, acknowledging the fictionalized moral tale of the failure of a
good person to flourish in a capitalistic world (a tale that a fiction
writer might very well have fashioned in earnest) as well as the parabolic gestures toward the originary moment of the parable (toward
the Brecht Collective), toward the present audience viewing the play,
and toward a point in time when an audience might fully act on the
feminist concerns woven into the parable. A parabola is formed only
when a *moving* point generates a curved line. I am not trying to
suggest that my reading is in any way definitive. Rather, to usurp
Brecht's phrase, I believe it is permissible, and perhaps useful at this
particular juncture.

To perform the Collective script one needs to reconsider even the
title of the play, *Der Gute Mensch von Sezuan.* Perhaps the most widely
produced and anthologized American translation of the script is
Eric Bentley's "revised English version, in which translation becomes
"adaptation," to use Bentley's own term.[19] Bentley begins his adaptation with his translation of the title of the script, which becomes "the
good *woman* of Setzuan." In effect, this translation throws the emphasis within the play on the female figure of Shen Te, erasing the
parabolic process by which the moving point (which is the heart of
the audience's creation of Shen Te/Shui Ta) keeps moving while
remaining equidistant from the genderized polarities of Shen Te
and Shui Ta. John Willett, among others, offers a better solution to
the problem, translating the title as *The Good Person of Szechwan,*
thereby retaining the non–gender-specific quality of the character
Shen Te/Shui Ta, as well as of the noun *Mensch.* Another translation

18. To John Glavin and George Kimmich Beach, who helped me think through the
implications of parables, I offer my warmest thanks.

19. Bertolt Brecht, *The Good Woman of Setzuan,* trans. Eric Bentley, in *Two Plays by
Bertolt Brecht* (New York: New American Library, 1983), p. xvii.

is *The Good Soul of Sezuan,* offered by Frederic Ewen.[20] This translation evokes a disembodied soul, a spirit without a gendered body. Despite the aptness of Ewen's translation, I have adopted Willett's, largely for reasons of positionality: that is, to clarify the ways in which ideologies shape bodies, there must be a body, a person, as the focus of the play.

In fact, the long history of work on the script complicates the issue of the title even further. Brecht, and probably Hauptmann, initially envisioned it as a short story, set in Berlin in the late 1920s, about a prostitute who disguises herself as a man to act as her own pimp because she realizes "that she cannot be both commodity and retailer at the same time."[21] That is, she cannot easily play the roles of lover and worker simultaneously (no more than the women in the Brecht Collective could). Projected as an economic study of the relationship between prostitution and capitalism, the story was provisionally titled "Die Ware Liebe," with a play on the noun *Ware* (which means goods for sale) and its near-homonym *wahr* (which means true).[22] The original title of the germinal story that Brecht and Elisabeth Hauptmann probably worked on together thus evokes the idea of both "True Love" and "Love for Sale" (or "Commodity Love"). It was not until Brecht was in exile, a decade or more later, that the locale was changed to China and the three gods began to play a pivotal role.[23]

What began as a Marxist analysis of love as commodity within the institution of prostitution, then, later develops into an exploration of love as commodity within the divided self, within romance, and within religion. From scene two on, Shen Te is divided into two constructions, each part packaged for a particular audience: Shen Te is shown to be a useful object of exchange among gods and men, while Shui Ta becomes a valuable commodity in the business world. Within the romance story line, Shen Te is valued both as a source of economic power to generate a pilot's career for Sun and as a vessel

20. Frederic Ewen, *Bertolt Brecht: His Life, His Art, and His Times* (New York: Citadel Press, 1967), p. 364.

21. Quoted in Klaus Volker, *Brecht: A Biography,* trans. John Nowell (New York: Seabury Press, 1978), p. 181.

22. Fuegi, *The Essential Brecht,* pp. 129–30.

23. Ibid., p. 130.

for the potential reproduction of other sons, other flyers. And of course, within religion the gods commodify her as a good person. Shui Ta, in contrast, acts as a vessel for the promotion of capitalism. In addition, both Shen Te and Shui Ta are shown to hold access to certain kinds of matriarchal and patriarchal power.

What concerns the performer here is that these two constructions do not exist separately on stage: Shui Ta is never simply Shui Ta, nor is Shen Te solely Shen Te from scene two on. The fact that Shui Ta is visibly pregnant militates against the character's being viewed as simply male, so every time Shui Ta appears onstage, the cultural constructs of "womanly" and "manly" functions are simultaneously on view, and our preconceived notions of gender collapse. In performance, then, the character Shen Te/Shui Ta emerges as a parabolic character, moving between the two fixed gender poles of man and woman, but refusing to be subsumed by either polarity.

Brecht, as one of several incompetent and impotent gods, searches for a good woman and ends up with Shen Te/Shui Ta, a constantly moving self-creation that not only rejects his narrative search for godhead but even refuses the two diametrically opposed gender poles which he takes for granted. This Collective Shen Te/Shui Ta confuses our notions of man and woman, first as Shen Te, but especially as Shui Ta. She is, onstage, visibly expectant. She carries strong power in this combination. She represents at one and the same time the creator as man, in the business world, and the creator as woman, with (the potential) child but also—and this is important—as the self-progenitor, the virtual author of another (cross-dressed) version of herself. Because of this twofold threat she presents to traditional views, some actors and directors may prefer to focus instead on the romance plot of Shen Te and Yang Sun and the salvation plot of the gods. Such a choice, despite the very real framing critique of the capitalist mode of production, erases the fact that Shen Te/Shui Ta quite usefully breaks two important taboos. First, the pregnant female body in this script is the site of sexuality and power as well as nurturance. This image exists in direct contrast to Mrs. Shin, whose power is linked to her barren commodification of Yang Sun as a sexual object. (Nor is nurturance solely associated with Shen Te. Shui Ta's business, for all its despicable exploitation of the workers, attempts to redeem Yang Sun through work, and to provide for a family.) Second, the parabolic actor challenges the taboo against staging the figure of the self-authored female who refuses easy gender categories, quoting but not being subsumed by the traditional roles of man and woman.

This approach to *Good Person* gains support from Brecht's notes on the script. After settling in Finland in April 1940, Brecht and Steffin worked on the project for some weeks. In June Brecht wrote: "li gung [the prototype for Shen Te] . . . is not wholly and invariably good, not even when she is being li gung. nor is lao go [Shui Ta] conventionally bad, etc. the continual fusion and dissolution of the two characters, and so on, comes off reasonably well, i think. the god's great experiment of extending love of one's neighbor to embrace love of one's self, adding 'be good to thyself' to 'be good to others,' needed to stand apart from the story and at the same time to dominate it."[24] Here Brecht embraces the idea of the "fusion and dissolution of the two characters," while at the same time he states his wish to confuse the issues of good and bad within each character. He also suggests the necessity, presumably for Shen Te in particular, of self-love.

One of the reasons why the Collective production approach I have sketched here has only recently become realizable may be the cultural taboo against representing a pregnant woman as a powerful businessperson. In *Good Person* the female is presented as the author not only of a subverted romance plot and a potential new life in the domestic sphere but also of a freshly invented and powerful plot in the public sphere. Shen Te/Shui Ta may be regarded, in part, as an expression of a sexually desiring pregnant woman who tries to retrain her lover so that he might learn to be worthy of her desire. As a potential single parent she also commands our attention as a major controlling factor in her own life as well as that of her unborn child. (The fact that the child is represented as a boy, a recreation of Yang Sun the flyer-father, of course complicates this issue, and reveals the way in which women are used to promote patriarchal ideology at the very moment when they have the power to envision giving birth to a daughter, teaching a son a new ideology, or rejecting motherhood altogether.) But most important, the character conflates the private

24. Quoted in Willett and Manheim, *Collected Plays*, p. 128.

image of the expectant mother with the public figure of the woman/man as business magnate, drawing to the character a double-edged power, breaking a deeply entrenched taboo, and critiquing conventional gender polarities.

Another reason why this reading has only recently become possible is the taboo against representing the female who—like the actor playing the self-authoring, cross-dressed Shen Te/Shui Ta—refuses easy gender categorization and frustrates attempts at pigeonholing. Sarah Hoagland writes: "In the conceptual schemes of phallocracies there is no category of woman-identified-woman, woman-loving-woman, or woman-centered-woman."[25] But this position of supposed "invisibility" masks the power of the stagehands, who, as Marilyn Frye has suggested, act as seers, clarifying the boundaries of the competing gender ideologies.[26] The actor performing in *Good Person* virtually invents herself as a moving point, rejecting the fixed definitions promulgated by the patriarchy.

Instead of viewing the characters Shen Te and Shui Ta as entirely separate entities associated with need-oriented naïveté and goal-oriented evil, respectively, we may perceive them as two characters in one, refusing to accept either gender choice. As in a parabola, they act jointly as a moving point between two fixed choices. Shen Te moves between the two poles of motherhood: between the self-effacing, desexed figuration of the parent and the self-authoring, sexually desiring mother. She also clarifies the differences between her role as a commodified woman and her cross-dressed self-authorship. She marks the boundaries between romantic love for a man (and devotion to the gods) and a rejection or subversion of the romance and "angel of the slums" plots. Shen Te's counterpart Shui Ta, pregnant-woman-as-man, moves between an oppressive capitalism and a pragmatic, necessary self-love leading to the creation of self. Shen Te constantly "looks at" Shui Ta, as Shui Ta "looks at" Shen Te, and both confront the audience as it views them.[27] These complex contradictions within each character, and between the two

25. Sarah Hoagland, "Lesbian Epistemology," paper delivered at a meeting of the Midwestern Division of the Society for Women in Philosophy, quoted in Marilyn Frye, "To Be and Be Seen: The Politics of Reality," in *The Politics of Reality: Essays in Feminist Theory* (Trumansburg, N.Y.: Crossing Press, 1983), p. 152.

26. Frye, *Politics of Reality*, p. 170.

27. I am indebted here to Elin Diamond, "Brechtian Theory/Feminist Theory: Toward a Gestic Feminist Criticism," *The Drama Review* 32, 1 (Spring 1988): 86.

characters, complicate an understanding of the parable. Mother-hood does not have to be the antithesis of sexuality, nor does it have to relegate the female figure to selflessness. Authoring the self does not have to mean choosing between bipolar opposites; it can mean moving between them, refusing fixedness.

In her response to Laura Mulvey's articulation of the function of the male gaze in the cinema, Naomi Scheman suggests that one of the tactics, among many, that can be employed to disarm the male gaze at the female performer is to embrace the representation of the mother as a potential site of power. This tactic is useful to the Collective actor in breaking the first taboo. But the focus on the representation of motherhood is decidedly not the sole source of power for women; in fact, glorification of motherhood is a customary means through which the patriarchy controls women's bodies. I am not espousing a monolithic cultural feminist approach. The image of a powerful mother-as-businesswoman, however, can be a useful source of power in certain situations for certain women. Shen Te/Shui Ta, the woman-as-businessperson is clearly pregnant: she has authored herself as Shui Ta and at the same time holds onto herself as Shen Te. That is very different from the more customary representation of the unattached woman-as-business-person, for example Mrs. Mi Tzu, in whom childlessness and power seem to go hand in hand. Scheman discusses in some detail the taboo against conflating matriarchal and patriarchal power:

> The requisite virginity of Athena and of other women—mortal and divine—who play her role of mediating between the worlds of maternal and paternal power (for example, the modern stereotype of the spinster schoolteacher) is, I am beginning to suspect, less a matter of avoiding sex than of avoiding maternity, which, as [Stanley] Cavell points out in a related discussion, used to require (hetero)sexual abstinence. The difficulties women encounter today when they attempt to combine motherhood and career are rooted in part in their violating a long-standing taboo against combining the symbolically loaded power of maternity with power as constituted in the extradomestic world. To be allowed to exercise that second sort of power, to act like a man, has generally meant thinking of oneself as a genetic fluke—parthenogenetically fathered and sterile.

Cavell's guess from the region of myth about the absence of

heroines' mothers makes reference to this tradition: "Mythically, the absence of the mother continues the idea that the creation of the woman is the business of men; even, paradoxically, when the creation is that of the so-called new woman, the woman of equality." Beyond the obvious paradox, a deeper one appears in the claim that only as fathered can a woman claim *either* public empowerment *or* feminine sexual identity.[28]

In *The Good Person of Szechwan* matriarchal and patriarchal power are conflated onstage in the image of Shen Te/Shui Ta, an image that subverts the traditional notion that "the creation of the woman is the business of men" by positing the possibility that the creation of the fluid woman/man who rejects traditional gender categories is the business of women. In assuming her role as Shui Ta, and especially in maintaining it throughout her pregnancy, Shen Te not only produces another version of herself but also simultaneously acknowledges herself as a mother, breaking the taboo which mandates that powerful women must be childless.

In a set of undated notes on *Good Person* under the heading "it is bad," Brecht lists "to neglect oneself," proof that Brecht at least did not consider Shen Te's supposed selflessness to be unmitigated goodness.[29] In fact, Brecht's journal at that time reveals that "he had begun holding discussions about Marxist ethics with the actor Hermann Greid and other friends. In the *Flüchtlingsgesprache* or *Conversations between Exiles,* which he was writing in Finland around the same time, he deals with the concepts of good and evil in a comic-paradoxical way, showing in a long 'Parade of the Vices and Virtues' how both these opposites can 'identify themselves as the servants of *Oppression.'"[30] One cannot draw up a simple list of virtues and vices, any more than one can accept customary gender polarities.

Whereas in Ibsen's plays the character—Hedda Gabler, for example—sees the ironies of the plot through which she moves (in

28. Naomi Scheman, "Missing Mothers/Desiring Daughters," *Critical Inquiry* 15, 1 (Autumn 1988): 72–73. This essay is in part a response to Laura Mulvey, "Visual Pleasure and Narrative Cinema," *Screen* 16 (Autumn 1975): 6–18, reprinted in *Movies and Methods: An Anthology,* ed. Bill Nichols, 2 vols. (Berkeley: University of California Press, 1976–85), 2: 303–15.

29. Quoted in Willett and Manheim, *Collected Plays,* p. 119.

30. Ibid., p. x.

Hedda's case the intertwining of the romantic melodrama plot with the realistic plot), in the Brecht Collective's parables the character is designed to demonstrate clearly the *choices* she moves between, selecting or rejecting. That is one of the reasons why her subjectivity resists fixity, resting in the audience's determination of the nature of her choice. The Collective actor represents Shen Te/Shui Ta not as someone locked in an ideology but rather as someone who clarifies the boundaries of competing ideologies while inviting the audience to imagine a third, better choice. This approach builds on Janelle Reinelt's articulation of the Brechtian subject as a middle ground between the ever-receding definition of Derridean playfulness and the ever-channeled ideological definition of Althusser:

> The implicit theory of the subject in Brecht's work is the subject in process, criss-crossed by the contradictions of competing practices. Brecht's split characters like Puntila and Shen Te or Mother Courage . . . are the sites of ideological struggle through competing social practices which may not resolve into unified subjectivity, but which do provide grounds for dialectical change. . . . In that Brecht's theatre always requires the representation of agency implicated in historical and material processes, it refuses and critiques Althusser's interpellation theory as well as deconstruction's dispersed and infinitely deferred self.[31]

Through the characterization of Shen Te/Shui Ta, the Brecht Collective actor may reveal competing codes regarding gender, prompting the audience to recognize new possibilities for performing the self.

Many critics have identified the appearance of the powerful woman in the Brecht Collective's plays with the emergence of Marxist concerns in Brecht's work, arguing that as the women gain prominence as revolutionaries fighting capitalism, they lose their sexuality as well as their access to daily life.[32] They become moral mothers

31. Janelle Reinelt, "Rethinking Brecht: Deconstruction, Feminism, and the Politics of Form," in *Essays on Brecht: The Brecht Yearbook 15*, ed. Marc Silberman et al. (College Park, Md.: International Brecht Society, 1990), pp. 103–4.

32. As Sara Lennox notes, for example: "In the Marxist works the women are abstract, 'model' figures. . . . The disappearance of the woman as sex object in the mature works occurs, as Fritz Raddatz pointed out several years ago, at the cost of a

devoted to large social concerns, a figuration that is perhaps most apparent in *The Mother*, in which Pelagea Vlassova acts as the ethical barometer of an entire revolutionary movement.[33] But readings that characterize Shen Te as a sexless, selfless mother in the tradition of Pelagea Vlassova ignore the traces of Shui Ta in Shen Te and of Shen Te in Shui Ta, traces that signal the insufficiency of the representations of woman as moral mother and man as slick capitalist, and which make problematical the traditional polarities of woman-man, good-evil, in the play.

This mysterious parable prompts us to explore subversive feminist readings of other Brecht Collective scripts, including *The Mother*. Cross-gender casting, casting against expected types: these are tactics Brecht himself discussed, and they may be very useful to contemporary directors and actors seeking to explore the "lack of earnestness" in all the parables. The one major tenet that pervades all of Brecht's writing about the theatre is, after all, the importance of contradictions.[34] Breaking the taboo against representing joint matriarchal and patriarchal power necessitates a fuller exploration of the opportunities for contradictions within character in these late plays.

Lennox tries to redeem the moral mother in Brecht's scripts by exploring the subversive nature of her activities and even the potential utopia that might arise from her alternative mode of behavior. Like Ulrike Prokop, she identifies typically female production

---

deeroticization of women altogether." Lennox, "Women in Brecht's Works," pp. 85–86. Sue-Ellen Case, among others, agrees: "I concluded that the rise of this stable, asexual, instrumental mother figure suppressed the earlier experiments in discourse and desire and brought with it the material cleanliness, extreme assiduity of language, asexual, political commitment, etc., of the Epic style as a compensation for what had come before." Sue-Ellen Case, in the introduction to her essay "Homosexuality and the Mother," in Fuegi et al., *Brecht: Women and Politics*, p. 62. In her analysis of transvestism in Brecht, Anne Herrmann agrees that Brecht "desexualizes" Shen Te. Anne Herrmann, "Travesty and Transgression: Transvestism in Shakespeare, Brecht, and Churchill," *Theatre Journal* 41, 2 (May 1989): 146.

33. Nancy Chodorow discusses the American genesis of the myth of the moral mother in "Mothering, Male Dominance, and Capitalism," in *Capitalist Patriarchy and the Case for Socialist Feminism*, ed. Zillah R. Eisenstein (New York: Monthly Review Press, 1979), pp. 91–92.

34. "The coherence of character is in fact shown by the way in which its individual qualities contradict one another." Bertolt Brecht, "A Short Organum for the Theatre," in *Brecht on Theatre*, ed. and trans. John Willett (London: Methuen, 1987), p. 196.

(which she associates with child care and housework) as "expressive," "noninstrumental," need-oriented behavior, in contrast to the goal-oriented production commonly associated with men. She posits the possibility that this need-based form of labor, expressed most obviously in the mother-child relationship, may provide a model of protest and power "despite the repressive forms it assumes in the present society."[35]

Although I agree that the Collective's parables contain subversive feminist possibilities, I locate these possibilities at a different place in the scripts. It seems unnecessary to identify "need-oriented" work as specifically female, or more valuable than supposedly male "goal-oriented" work. Both seem to be potentially useful and necessary for men and for women. The issue becomes, then, not just one of patriarchy versus matriarchy but rather a matter of how men as well as women can adopt useful tactics from both camps to reformulate ideas of gender and social relations. For feminists an orientation toward goals, toward the exercise of power, is not necessarily bad, nor must it be irrevocably linked to maleness. To quote Nancy Hartsock: "There is, after all, a certain dangerous irony in the fact that both feminists and antifeminists agree that the exercise of power is a masculine activity and preoccupation, inappropriate to women or feminists, and not a subject to which attention should be directed."[36] In fact, the Collective actor of *The Good Person of Szechwan* might envision Shen Te/Shui Ta as a figure who refuses to separate matriarchal from patriarchal power. And in the present explorations of the other parables new possibilities can be discovered, too. For example, Grusha in *Caucasian Chalk Circle* is not simply a moral mother; she is a construction illustrating the factions warring for control over her life. Her impulse to save the child and her desire for Simon fight with her need for independence in an imbricated action that complicates the relationship between actor and character. Pelagea Vlassova may also be played to reveal not only her revolutionary fervor but also the way in which, as she gains public power, she pays the price of losing her private life with her son. Both actor and director can find ways to suggest the complexities of the situation.

35. Lennox, "Women in Brecht's Works," pp. 95–96.
36. Nancy Hartsock, *Money, Sex, and Power: Toward a Feminist Historical Materialism* (New York: Longman, 1983), p. 2.

More than any other playwright discussed in this book, Brecht sought to articulate and promote his view of the relationship between the actor and the character, disseminating his ideas in his own playwriting and direction and also in his writings about acting and directing. Brecht exploded the old metaphor of the actor as sleepwalker, subordinated to character, moving as if in a trance. He detested actors who approach their work "by means of hypnosis. . . . If the seance is successful it ends up with nobody seeing anything further, nobody learning any lessons, at best everyone recollecting. In short, everybody feels."[37] The trance metaphor as a means of describing the actor-character relationship is inscribed in a theatre that pretends that the audience is the subject of the play, when in fact the real subject is the playwright's particular ideological bent.

From its first attempts to supplant that late nineteenth-century metaphor of the actor's art with the image of the actor as an athlete, the Brecht Collective engaged in sport. Brecht bemoans the fact that "all those establishments with their excellent heating systems, their pretty lighting, their appetite for large sums of money, their imposing exteriors, together with the entire business that goes on inside them: all this doesn't contain five pennyworth of *fun*. . . . There is no sport. . . . *And nobody who fails to get fun out of his activities can expect them to be fun for anybody else.*"[38] Part of the source of this fun is the way the actor presents the character to the audience. Brecht likens the Chinese acting he so admired to the theatrical performances at the German popular fairs of his youth, recalling how the clowns and hand-painted panoramas illustrated the familiar in an unfamiliar way. In making the character (and thereby the staged event) seem strange and surprising, the clown/actor plays with the audience, enjoying the carnival atmosphere and the sport of the theatre in the scientific age. "The Chinese performer," says Brecht, "is in no trance. He can be interrupted at any moment. He won't have to 'come round.' After an interruption he will go on with his exposition from that point. We are not disturbing him at the 'mystic moment of creation'; when he steps on to the stage before us the process of creation is already over."[39] Demonstrating an awareness of being

37. Brecht, *Brecht on Theatre*, p. 26.
38. Ibid., p. 7.
39. Ibid., p. 95.

viewed, the Chinese actor, like the Collective actor, is an acrobat, observing the self while turning occasionally to the audience "as if to say: isn't it just like that?"[40]

Responding to the challenge of the Collective script, the actor approaching *The Good Person of Szechwan* may delight in showing the limitations of the representation of both Shen Te and Shui Ta, adopting a circuslike technique to demonstrate the customary "feminine" or "masculine" traits as unfamiliar or awkward for the characters and for herself. The actor can also reject these binary oppositions, instead experimenting with nongendered movement, so that the actor is not signifying "reality" but rather exploring the very process of perceiving and representing reality. By gesturing toward the relationship between actor and character—at the moment of the playwrights' conception, at the moment of actual performance, and at the moment when character and audience are liberated in a parabolic movement away from the actor—the Brecht Collective actor resists the trance as she creates her strangely unfamiliar experiment in examining the process of representation.[41]

Typically the Brecht actor focuses on what the playwright calls the "not-but," in both the preparation and the execution of the character:

> When he appears on the stage, besides what he actually is doing he will at all essential points discover, specify, imply what he is not doing; that is to say he will act in such a way that the alternative emerges as clearly as possible, that his acting allows the other possibilities to be inferred and only represents one out of the possible variants. He will say for instance "You'll pay for that," and not say "I forgive you." He detests his children; it is not the case that he loves them. He moves down stage left and not up stage right. Whatever he doesn't do must be contained and conserved in what he does. In this way every sentence and every gesture signi-

40. Ibid., p. 92.

41. "It is with reference to the portrayed character's actual inscription in the narration and in society, that the discourse (gestures included) of the character is defined as a discourse revealing the mode of social integration and class appurtenence, but it is with reference to a *future* society that the actor and the character become dissociated, and that a new subject of enunciation emerges." Josette Féral, "Alienation Theory in Multi-Media Performance," trans. Ron Bermingham, *Theatre Journal* 39, 4 (December 1987): 467.

fies a decision; the character remains under observation and is
tested. The technical term for this procedure is "fixing the
"not . . . but."[42]

Thus Brecht expected his actors to show clearly the points at which
their characters make choices, revealing not only the path taken but
also the path rejected. Elin Diamond analyzes the usefulness of
Brecht's "not-but" for feminist theatre by noting that "each action
must contain the trace of the action it represses, thus the meaning of
each action contains difference. The audience is invited to look beyond representation—beyond what is authoritatively put in view—
to the possibilities of as yet unarticulated actions or judgments. . . .
The Brechtian 'not, but' is the theatrical and theoretical analog

42. Brecht, *Brecht on Theatre*, p. 137. As John Willett and Marjorie Hoover have
pointed out, the concept of alienation as a means of thinking about the relationship
between the actor and the character, and the actor and the audience, did not originate
with Brecht. See John Willett, *The Theatre of Bertolt Brecht: A Study from Eight Aspects*
(London: Methuen, 1959), p. 208, and Marjorie Hoover, "Brecht's Soviet Connection:
Tretiakov," *Brecht Heute—Brecht Today* 3 (1973–74): 39–56. Josette Féral gives a useful
and very perceptive summary of the genesis and various manifestations of the process
of alienation; see Féral, "Alienation Theory in Multi-Media Performance," pp. 463–
66. In the discussion that follows, I use her translations of the V. V. Chklovski articles.
The Russian formalist Chklovski employed the term *priem ostrannenija* to describe the
operations of art as a process of foregrounding in which "the form of the object is
obscured," so that the act of perception is made more difficult and is thereby pro-
longed. The poet or playwright "operates by semantic displacement. He removes the
notion from the semantic series in which he finds it, and, by associating it with other
words (a trope), places it in a different semantic series. Such a displacement creates a
new way of perceiving the object." V. V. Chklovski, "La construction de la nouvelle et
du roman," quoted in Féral, "Alienation Theory in Multi-Media Performance," p.
464. Féral argues that Brecht's *Verfremdungseffekt* "functions to promote mastery—
mastery of the realities to which words refer, of sought-after truths, of extra-
theatrical truths to which words are linked, and of discourse" (pp. 466–67). I do not
deny the validity of Féral's conclusions as they pertain to readings that focus only on
Brecht's "fixed" narrative, but I invite into consideration a competing "fixed" narrative and then suggest that the actor moves, with the audience, between the two,
rejecting both as indicators of reality. The issue of mastery in Brecht, then, as I
understand it, is complicated by the inclusion of the second "fixed point" and the
refusal of the Brecht Collective actor to embed the character in one narrative or the
other. Brecht encountered Chklovski's theory on his trip to Russia in the spring of
1935, and articulated his concept of alienation as it applies to the actor-character
relationship shortly thereafter, although his work in the theatre had from the first
employed the techniques Chklovski discussed, not only in terms of the actor-character
(and actor-audience) relationship but also in terms of the other production elements.

to the subversiveness of sexual difference, because it allows us to imagine the deconstruction of gender—and all other—representations."[43] Diamond's insight is crucial to an understanding of how the Collective actor might explore Brechtian scripts, particularly in terms of sex and class issues and gender construction. It also provides the basis for a redefinition of the "not-but."

In "A Short Organum for the Theatre," Brecht contended that epic actors must join in the Marxist struggle against the class system outside the theatre. That engagement would, in turn, enable them to make thoughtful, class-conscious performance choices onstage.[44] In the present context this requirement of political awareness translates into a need for actors conversant with feminist theories. Brecht's urgent call echoes Shaw's assertion decades earlier that Ibsen actors require special intellectual gifts, including an awareness of current trends of thought. This demand for social engagement contrasts with Strindberg's focus on the naive actor, and reinforces the characterization of Ibsen and Brecht as iconoclasts potentially useful to feminist actors. But whereas Ibsen worked to hide the trappings of the theatre, perfecting the retrospective method to help avoid exposition and employing a box set so as to submerge the audience's subjectivity, Brecht and his collaborators foreground the theatricality of the theatre, calling attention to exposition *as* exposition through the use of titles, for example, and to the operations of the stage and auditorium by means of various well-known alienation devices. They also emphasize the relationship between the actor and the character through the *Verfremdungseffekt*—the alienation effect.

What Brecht does not foreground in his theoretical writing or his explications of his plays is the way in which the traces of Berlau, Steffin, and Hauptmann in his work expand his consideration of class issues to sexual issues of which he was largely unaware. The hypothetical Brecht Collective performer envisioned in this chapter

43. Diamond, "Brechtian Theory/Feminist Theory," p. 86.
44. Brecht wrote: "Unless the actor is satisfied to be a parrot or a monkey he must master our period's knowledge of human social life by himself joining in the war of the classes. . . . For art to be 'unpolitical' means only to ally oneself with the 'ruling' group. So the choice of viewpoint is also a major element of the actor's art, and it has to be decided outside the theatre. Like the transformation of nature, that of society is a liberating act; and it is the joys of liberation which the theatre of a scientific age has got to convey." Brecht, *Brecht on Theatre*, p. 196.

reclaims these issues by building on Diamond's understanding of the relationship between the alienation effect and sexual difference, and by complicating the "not-but." This imagined performer goes one step further than the Brecht actor. The latter demonstrates *one* narrative, showing how the contradictory character decides to do "not *this* but *that*." The Collective actor, by contrast, displays *two* competing narratives—one Brecht's, one the collaborators'. This actor shows her character moving between two fixed points (the "this" and the "that") and rejecting both in favor of charting a third arc— the moving point of the parabola.

The Collective actor, then, illustrates the character's rejection of fixed bipolarity. Instead of delineating carefully the differences in the characterization of Shen Te and of Shui Ta, as in Benno Besson's 1957 Berliner Ensemble production or Andre Serban's 1987 American Repertory Theatre production of *The Good Woman of Setzuan*, thereby revealing "the exhausted and broken woman under the harsh male exterior," the parabolic actor plays the differences, the liminal zone between the two characters, demonstrating contradictions within each character as well as contradictions within those contradictions—finally enabling the audience to join her in drawing a line equidistant from these two equally disabling choices called Shen Te and Shui Ta.[45] The parabolic actor, then, refuses the bipolarity inscribed by Brecht's dialectical strategy and substitutes for it a demonstration of its limitations.

Brecht, in his casting note on Shen Te recorded in his journal in 1939, writes: "The girl must be a big powerful person."[46] This instruction has been ignored in many productions. Traditionally Shen Te/Shui Ta has been played by a pretty, petite actor with a strong alto voice, a performer who demonstrates clearly the differences between a very "feminine" Shen Te and a macho Shui Ta. Exploding this tradition, the Collective actor adopts strategies similar to those employed by the feminist performance artist Rachel Rosenthal, whose approach illustrates how the Collective actor may present parabolic characters onstage. An impressive actor who resists easy gender categories, Rosenthal suggests a constantly shifting ground,

45. See Sam Abel's review of the American Repertory Theatre production in *Theatre Journal* 39, 4 (December 1987): 506.
46. Quoted in Willett and Manheim, *Collected Plays*, p. v.

defying either polarity as she simultaneously indicates them. In *L.O.W. in Gaia,* her blue eyeshadow and dangling earrings contradict her camouflage gear and her shaved head. (See figure 6.) Her movements are difficult to categorize as "masculine" or "feminine"; instead they suggest an alternative, freer mode of movement. The work of other performance artists might also be invoked here (Laurie Anderson's experiments with gender confusion, for example, especially her use of an amplifying system that transforms her voice into a deep bass, or Peggy Shaw's cross-dressed constructions for the New York–based Split Britches), but Rosenthal's larger physical type is more to the point.

Although Rosenthal is committed to lesbian and environmental concerns in her own performance pieces, her strategy of creating a liminal zone between gender polarities functions in a manner similar to that of the hypothetical parabolic actor, who must walk the tightrope between Shen Te and Shui Ta as well as between the two aspects of Shen Te and the two aspects of Shui Ta. This Collective actor would acknowledge Nancy Hartsock's exhortation to "understand sexuality as culturally and historically defined and constructed. Anything can become eroticized. . . . Sexuality must be understood as a series of cultural and social practices and meanings that both structure and are in turn structured by social relations more generally."[47] Building on this premise, feminists have shown how female sexuality and desire have traditionally been constructed to serve male (as well as capitalist) ends, a point that is apparent in Shen Te's relationship with Yang Sun, the full consummation of which depends on Shen Te's willingness to hand over the cash that will enable him to enter the labor force. By playing the parabola, the Collective actor demonstrates the "not this and not that," calling into play what Roland Barthes identifies in Brecht as "this presence of *all* the absences (memories, lessons, promises) to whose rhythm History becomes both intelligible and desirable."[48] The parabolic actor might play the moment when Shen Te realizes that she is pregnant with Yang Sun's son so as to suggest not just the joy of the "moral mother" in the making but also her awareness that the patriarchy

47. Hartsock, *Money, Sex, and Power,* p. 156.
48. Roland Barthes, "Diderot, Brecht, Eisenstein," in *Image, Music, Text,* trans. Stephen Heath (New York: Hill and Wang, 1977), p. 73.

Figure 6. Rachel Rosenthal in *L.O.W. in Gaia* (1986), photo by Jan Deen

has shaped that emotion, gesturing toward the audience to posit alternative behaviors.

Instead of attempting to master the Brechtian fable, and through it the character and the audience, the Collective actor, then, tries to avoid mastery by tightrope walking a line that reveals the contradictions that are staged at any given moment, inviting the audience to invent a different, more liberating fable. This process of studying the entire dramatic action to gain access to the character reverses the intellectual process of the Ibsen actor, who first explores the spine of the character, then tries to determine how it connects with the spine of other characters to create the superobjective of the play. The Collective actors' approach to the script also differs from that of the melodramatic actor, for whom the fable is implicit in the conventions of the drama itself and in the traditional lines of business of the acting company. By contrast, the Strindberg actor learns the fable in its entirety by the end of the first scene and plays it over and over again, in telescoped fashion, throughout the production. Although the Strindberg actor, like the Collective actor, must frequently make clear the breaks in the scenic action, these breaks do not mark a new stage in the story line or a new focus for the actor involved in moving the character through time; rather, they denote a return to the beginning of the fable, which must be played from the start once again, although frequently in a different performance style.

The Collective actors' challenge, consequently, is not to illustrate, indicate, or express specific emotions, as the melodramatic actor strove to do, nor is it to gesture autistically toward the divided self, as the Ibsen actor did, or toward a shifting illusion, as the Strindberg actor did. Instead the challenge is to demonstrate contradictory, historically specific and culturally bound choices and suggest the limitations of those choices. The seeds of this focus on the social and political context of the actors' art were sown with the Ibsen actor's attempt to attune herself to the movements of the times, but the full flowering of the idea of social gest emerges, of course, with the Brecht Collective. From the gesture as illustration in the melodramatic theatre, to the autistic gesture as communication with self in the Ibsen theatre, and then to the gesture as illusion in the Strindberg theatre, we move in the Brecht Collective theatre to the gesture as a critique of the limitations of bipolar social attitudes (not simply, as in Brecht's theatre, to gesture as the explication of social relationships existing at a given moment in time).

Rehearsal strategies employed by the Collective may include cross-gender casting, transposing speeches into the third person or past tense, or speaking stage directions out loud.[49] The parabolic actor can implement these strategies in actual performance, accompanied, perhaps, by an acrobatic feat such as juggling. For instance, when Shen Te (dressed as Shui Ta), discovering that Yang Sun has sold her shop, laments "I'm lost," the actor might stand still and juggle, speaking aloud the stage directions: "He begins to rush around like a captive animal, continually repeating, 'The business has gone!'" By reciting stage directions, the actor reveals that in the love story Shen Te is represented as a "captive animal," trapped to finance Sun's career. By standing still, in contradiction to the stage directions, the actor also acknowledges that Shen Te is not merely Shen Te but also Shui Ta, a part of her own self represented as capable of acting out of self-love (thus the woman is not limited to her figuration in the romance plot). And through the gest of juggling the actor suggests an awareness that in this situation both of the contradictory representations are to be rejected. Or perhaps later in the scene, when Shen Te says that she wants to go with the man she loves, without counting the cost, the actor might employ the device of speaking as a woman other than herself reading a case for the patriarchy, "prepared at some quite different period, without understanding what it meant as she did so."[50] Another technique that might achieve a similar end is the use of dialect for particularly poetic passages, such as the sequence in which Shen Te introduces the audience to her unborn son, or, in *Caucasian Chalk Circle,* the sentimental reunion across the river between Grusha and Simon.

Central to all this thinking, of course, is the retrieval of women's bodies—those of Brecht's collaborators as well as of the contemporary actors—all potentially trapped by the playwright's inscriptions. It is not enough just to expand the fable or suggest the "not this and not that." The Collective actor also needs to explore liberating processes through movement. Women's bodies are traditionally the site for promoting the dominant ideology, but they also provide an op-

49. Brecht, *Brecht on Theatre,* p. 138.
50. Ibid., p. 54.

portunity for subverting that ideology.[51] One of the primary reasons why the Brecht Collective's scripts are particularly useful in constructing an underground subject is that the alienation effect acts as a catalyst to disassociate the actors' body from the character's body, allowing the actor to demonstrate how the character's body is being employed by the dominant value systems and the ways in which those systems might be critiqued. As Elin Diamond remarks: "Verfremdungseffekt also challenges the mimetic property of acting that semioticians call iconicity, the fact that the performer's body conventionally resembles the object (or character) to which it refers. This is why gender critique in the theatre can be so powerful."[52]

In performance the actor playing Shen Te/Shui Ta can deconstruct traditional bodily sign systems used to designate gender. The feminist performance artist Marianne Goldberg articulates the first step in this process of reclaiming the body: "If the body is to become subversive in gender terms, it must exceed the representational frame of the patriarchal stage: The insistence on binary physical differences—male/female—can give way to a fluid spectrum of oppositions that have meanings other than 'masculine' and 'feminine': The body redefines itself in relation to others: Those others, whether male or female, need to allow shifts in the potential meanings of touch/initiation/response/strength/subtlety: The male body moves

51. Sarah Bryant-Bertail writes: "Brecht uses women as didactic objects most notably in *Die Mutter, Die Heilige Johanna der Schlachthofe, Der kaukasische Kreidekreis, Der gute Mensch von Sezuan* and *Mutter Courage und ihre Kinder*. . . . The plight of women in these plays is significant if looked at from a contemporary feminist perspective, because the role assigned to them by society and aesthetics is always strategically designed to harmonize the ideologically disharmonious and to conceal the ruptures between those ideologies and the real conditions they attempt to justify. At the same time that women characters are disenfranchised and exiled from power, they are, as didactic objects, accorded the double task of veiling society's seams and reflecting its values. In the didacticism of Brecht as in that of the Enlightenment, the woman's body as object, whether she is mother, lover, or deity, is the favorite medium through which ideologies are displayed, disguised and appropriated. In *Kabale und Liebe*, for instance, the eyes of the female figure are supposed to function metaphorically as a mirror in which the hero can verify his ideal selfhood as this is defined by bourgeois market-place values. But since these eyes also belong to a character with her own narrative, they are an unstable sign. They can be used to constitute an 'underground subject,' from whose viewpoint the dominant ideologies of the text can be criticized." Sarah Bryant-Bertail, "Women, Space, and Ideology: *Mutter Courage und ihre Kinder*," in Fuegi et al., *Brecht: Women and Politics*, pp. 44–45.
52. Diamond, "Brechtian Theory/Feminist Theory," p. 84.

beyond the 'masculine' as patriarchally defined, just as the female body is not limited by the 'feminine.'"[53] In an effort to explore how to accomplish this process onstage, Goldberg asks questions that might serve as a basis for a physical characterization of Shen Te/Shui Ta, or any other Brecht Collective character. She writes: "If gestures are broken down into small units, how miniscule [*sic*] must they become before they lose gender definition? Is the relation of gesture to its gendered meaning as distant or as arbitrary as the relation between a word and its meaning? (Wide stance = male / delicate articulation = female) Is it possible to suppress the defined meaning of even the smallest units long enough to discover a unit of movement that has the requisite ambiguity to shift meaning in multiple directions / to disrupt conventional movement phrasings / to assert gender non-sequiturs that might allow different meanings to arise?"[54] Goldberg's hope that this nongendered movement will build a new root language, untrammeled by its gender-bound precedents, prompts her to position her body at a point reminiscent of the moving point of the parabola: "I place myself at the middle of meaning—at the point of contradiction where meanings are formed in the body. I am not a sculptured landscape, a surface for projected meanings. At the middle point: intense changes of perception redefining my body, strands of information, desire for motion."[55]

This work on nongendered movement, so important to the Brecht Collective actor whom I envision, has also been explored by the lesbian actors and theorists Monique Wittig and Sande Zeig. They have devoted themselves to introducing actors to the problems of gender-bound movement and have tried to help them distance themselves from that social patterning through classes in topics such as the dynamics of language and the semiotics of gesture.[56] They write: "Lesbians' task is to change the form of the actors' movement and gestures. . . . Through gestures, lesbians are able to radically influence the direction of contemporary theatre."[57]

53. Marianne Goldberg, "Ballerinas and Ball Passing," *Women and Performance* 3, 2 (1988): 27.
54. Ibid., p. 20.
55. Ibid., p. 21.
56. See Sue-Ellen Case, *Feminism and Theatre* (New York: Methuen, 1988), p. 80.
57. Quoted ibid., p. 80.

The Brecht Collective director concentrates on the specifics of a given historical moment. Brecht contrasts this approach with that of the bourgeois theatre associated with Ibsen: "The bourgeois theatre emphasized the timelessness of its objects. Its representation of people is bound by the alleged 'eternally human.' Its story is arranged in such a way to create 'universal' situations that allow Man with a capital M to express himself: man of every period and every colour. All its incidents are just one enormous cue, and this cue is followed by the 'eternal' response: the inevitable, usual, natural, purely human response."[58] But the Collective director must historicize and critique the incidents of the plot, encouraging actors to respond, "That's how I would act . . . if I had lived under those circumstances," and revealing the limitations of the bipolar choices presented to the character.[59] For example, the director might situate the events in *Good Person* by casting a Brecht look-alike as Yang Sun as well as First God, and by casting several female actors as Shen Te, modeling the character on Brecht's collaborators, who were inexorably drawn to the playwright, despite his callous behavior. Shortly after Brecht, and doubtless Hauptmann, had worked on the seed story for *Good Person*, Brecht,

> simultaneously conducting, as usual, a number of love affairs . . . arranged a discount system with his tailor who provided the prescribed costume for his women. Those having an affair with Brecht were required to wear a close-fitting woolen coat that reached almost to the ankles. The coat was never to be buttoned, but was to be held closed with one's elbow across the stomach. Thus all of Brecht's mistresses were highly visible to one another and to every one else in Berlin. In April 1929 Brecht suddenly married Helene Weigel but on the same day attended a rendezvous with Carola Neher at a Berlin train station. He handed Neher a bouquet (was it the wedding bouquet being recycled?) and announced of the marriage; "It couldn't be avoided, but it doesn't mean anything." Neher threw away the bouquet. For Elisabeth Hauptmann the shock of the marriage was so great that she attempted suicide. For Marieluise Fleisser the shock was almost equally severe.[60]

58. Brecht, *Brecht on Theatre*, pp. 96–97.
59. Ibid., p. 190.
60. Fuegi, *Bertolt Brecht: Chaos, According to Plan*, p. 66.

Imagine that the romance scenes between Shen Te and Yang Sun
were played with four or five Shen Tes, all dressed in the prescribed
garb of Brecht's mistresses, a costume, furthermore, too small to
contain the powerful bodies of the women. Such a conception would
historicize the action in a way that would speak directly to the issue
of representation within the Brecht Collective while also indicating
the prevailing winds of our own time.

In addition to commenting on the imbricated fable and using
contemporary issues to fuel the production, the Collective director
might wish to assume control of the means of production, or failing
that, to acknowledge within the performance text the limitations
presented by the theatrical system itself. Brecht holds that by its
nature the theatre undermines any attempt at revolutionary thinking: "This apparatus is conditioned by the society of the day and
only accepts what can keep it going in that society. Society absorbs via
the apparatus whatever it needs in order to reproduce itself. This
means that an innovation will pass if it is calculated to rejuvenate
existing society, but not if it is going to change it—irrespective of
whether the form of the society in question is good or bad."[61] For
the opera *Mahagonny* Brecht, Elisabeth Hauptmann, Carola Neher,
and Kurt Weill collaborated in finding ways to demonstrate "the
commercial character both of the entertainment and of the persons
entertained."[62] But the Collective, because of its devotion to the
"godlike" Brecht, was ill suited to reveal the truth about the economic basis of his work: that Brecht was in fact utterly dependent on the
unacknowledged labor of women, not only in the home but also in
the study and the theatre itself. To reveal the context of the representation, to take control of the ensemble, was impossible for the
women who collaborated in writing, translating, directing, and acting in his plays. Thus the hidden aspects of the parable, the "foreign
bodies" within the fable, were swallowed up by the theatre apparatus
itself.

The Brecht Collective director now has the opportunity not only
to highlight the nature of the revised fable but also to stage the
workings of the Collective production unit. One of the reasons why

61. Brecht, *Brecht on Theatre*, pp. 34–35.
62. Ibid., p. 41.

British and American actors felt that they had so much freedom in working on Ibsen's plays is that they themselves frequently owned the means of production, whether by pawning their jewels, as in Elizabeth Robins's production of *Hedda Gabler*, or through the relative autonomy of the subscription series. Contrast this with Strindberg's Intimate Theatre, operated by the playwright, with his former wife in the starring roles, and with Brecht's final theatre, the home of the tightly controlled Berliner Ensemble, featuring Helene Weigel as one of the leading actors.

The relationship that the Collective director forges between the actor and the audience differs radically from that promoted in the theatre of Ibsen or Strindberg. For Ibsen's audience the pleasure emerged from discovering keys to the plot, from considering which key to choose (should Mrs. Alving give Oswald the morphine or not?), and then basking in the universal realization: "That's how it is." Strindberg's audience took pleasure in acknowledging the pain of the illusions enacted before them, for by contrast their reality seemed joyful. But for the Brecht Collective's audience the sport comes from observing the process through which choices are selected and rejected, from understanding the plot as a construction, the character as a representation, the actor as an athlete. The audience apprehends the imbricated fable and acts on it instead of being mastered by it. Whereas Ibsen hid the plot within the structure of retrospective action to create a sense of inexorable fate and moral responsibility, the Brecht Collective foregrounds the plot, allowing actor, director, and audience to make genuine choices.

Directors of Ibsen and Strindberg assumed a unified audience. By contrast, the Brecht Collective director works to separate the audience members from one another, to make them aware of their differences. As Brecht noted:

> Plays of the aristotelian type still manage to flatten out class conflicts . . . although the individuals themselves are becoming increasingly aware of class differences. The same result is achieved even when class conflicts are the subject of such plays, and even in cases where they take sides for a particular class. A collective entity is created in the auditorium for the duration of the entertainment . . . the basis of the "common humanity" shared by all spec-

tators alike. Non-aristotelian drama of *Die Mutter's* sort is not interested in the establishment of such an entity. It divides its audience.[63]

The actor addresses different members of the audience differently, widening the gaps, making enemies as well as friends. She can manipulate the divisions within the audience which are caused by the class and cultural bases of emotions. To help the audience experience and establish a critical attitude toward culturally molded emotions, the Collective director aims for a complex response from spectators, one that leads them into action.

Far from being disengaged from the actor, then, viewers are moved to examine the social catalyst that has prompted their emotion. As a result of this action of historicization, the divided audiences may be prompted to alter their behavior. Elin Diamond writes:

> The crux of "historicization" is change: through A-effects [that is, alienation effects] spectators observe the potential movement in class relations, discover the limitations and strengths of their own perceptions, and begin to change their lives. There is a double movement in Brechtian historicization of preserving the "distinguishing marks" of the past and acknowledging, even foregrounding, the audience's present perspective. . . . When Brecht says that spectators should become historians, he refers both to the spectator's detachment, her "critical" position, and to the fact that she is writing her own history even as she absorbs messages from the stage. Historicization is, then, a way of seeing and the enemy of recuperation and appropriation. . . . In historicized performance, gaps are not to be filled in, seams and contradictions show in all their roughness, and therein lies one aspect of spectatorial pleasure—when our differences from the past and within the present are palpable, graspable, applicable.[64]

These differences, of course, help the actor and the audience dismantle the idea that truth and emotion are universal by revealing the way in which audiences create their own disparate meanings to maintain or to break down certain kinds of power relations. For the

63. Ibid., p. 60.
64. Diamond, "Brechtian Theory/Feminist Theory," p. 87.

Collective audience this focus encompasses sexual as well as class difference.

The Collective's adoption of the alienation effect allows the actor to reveal the ideological underpinnings of the character, thereby disrupting in the audience what Naomi Scheman calls "the specular economy of patriarchy." As Scheman writes: "Culturally normative male arrogance demands that women look, but as [Marilyn] Frye argues, the maintenance of phallocratic reality requires that we not be the authors of what we see. . . . We also are to be seen, but only as the beautiful objects we can make ourselves up to resemble."[65] But in Collective productions, for example in *Good Person*, the actor playing Shen Te refuses to be seen simply as an object of commodified love. She illustrates for the audience the limitations as well as the pleasures of constructions such as the self-sacrificing mother and the heterosexual woman in love. And as Shui Ta she also shows how men are shaped by ideology. We see the actor quoting the character's potential lines of action.

The Collective's structural strategies and performance codes allow us to discover ways of subverting the customary workings of spectatorial pleasure in the theatre. Instead of placing the female body in the position of the object of the audience's desire, as often happens in the naturalistic theatre, the Collective theatre sets up a triangular relationship between the actor, the character, and the audience, thereby complicating the nature of the audience's pleasure. As Elin Diamond describes the dynamic:

> Sitting not in the dark, but in the Brechtian semi-lit smoker's theatre, the spectator still has the possibility of pleasurable identification. This is effected not through imaginary projection onto an ideal but through a triangular structure of actor/subject—character—spectator. Looking at the character, the spectator is constantly intercepted by the actor/subject, and the latter, heeding no fourth wall, is theoretically free to look back. The difference, then, between this triangle and the familiar oedipal one is that no one side signifies authority, knowledge, or the law. Brechtian theatre depends on a structure of representation, on exposing and

65. Scheman, "Missing Mothers," p. 89. See also Frye, *The Politics of Reality*, pp. 165–66.

making visible, but what appears even in the Gestus can only be provisional, indeterminate, nonauthoritative.[66]

Because of the special nature of the Brecht Collective's parables in performance—because of the structural strategies that brought about a new relationship between the actor and the character, the director, and the audience—this playwrights' theatre offers unique opportunities for exploring the condition of women, and for changing that condition.

Berlau, Steffin, Hauptmann, and Brecht created a revolutionary, socially aware theatre in which the actor and the audience actively collaborate with the playwright in the creation of meaning. That meaning is always historicized, always in process, always culturally constructed. For the Brecht Collective actor, director, and audience, meaning is embedded in a parable, a parabola, created by a point moving between and critiquing two fixed entities. The women in the Brecht Collective challenge their collaborators to keep moving.

66. Diamond, "Brechtian Theory/Feminist Theory," p. 90.

Chapter Four

Pinter and the Cinematic Actor

Just as Henrik Ibsen's seemingly obscure dramas baffled and infuriated many critics and audiences a century ago, Harold Pinter's plays confused theatregoers in the early 1960s. Reid Douglas, for example, writing in 1962, and echoing the Ibsen critics of the 1890s, remarked that a Pinter play was "complex enough to be interpreted in a dozen ways—always a suspicious indicator, suggesting as it does that the commentator has little idea of the real purpose of the script."[1] Whereas the difficulty with Ibsen's plays stemmed from his use of retrospective action, his characters' complex motivations, and his use of symbols, the initial confusion about Pinter's work emerged primarily from his treating the stage as if it were a film screen. For several decades Pinter has worked as a screenwriter, adapting many novels, as well as his own scripts, for television and film.[2] His screenwriting career has affected his playwriting methodology, perhaps most clearly in *Old Times*. In it he depends heavily on various cinematic approaches to narrative structure, exploring onstage what Christian Metz once called the "new syntactical regions" of films.[3] He breaks away from the grammar of exposition, conflict, dénoue-

---

1. Reid Douglas, "The Failure of English Realism," *Tulane Drama Review* 7, 2 (Winter 1962): 181.
2. See Steven H. Gale, *Harold Pinter* (Boston: G. K. Hall, 1978), pp. 4–6.
3. Christian Metz, *Film Language*, trans. Michael Taylor (New York: Oxford University Press, 1974), p. 211.

ment of the well-made play, creating a structural system closer to the principles of film. Consequently, Pinter's scripts promote a cinematic relationship between actor and character, and between actor and audience. As an examination of *Old Times* reveals, Pinter's filmic structural method leads actors and directors to abandon Stanislavsky's approach to acting, which germinated with the emergence of realistic dramas by playwrights such as Ibsen and Chekhov, for a subtle acting style more typical of film. This performance style, in turn, affects the nature of the audience's gaze, and presents challenges and opportunities for the female actor and spectator in particular.

As early as 1966 Pinter chafed at what he saw as the major drawback of playscripts, their tendency to foster the smoothly flowing motivational sequences of cause and effect: "I do so hate the because of drama. Who are we to say that this happens because that happened, that one thing is the consequence of another? . . . Life is more mysterious than plays make it out to be."[4] In an effort to capture that mystery in *Old Times,* Pinter transposes, edits, and interlaces scenes. In keeping with concepts such as Sergei Eisenstein's montage theory and Christian Metz's perception that the cinematic shot is "not comparable to the word in a lexicon; rather it resembles a complete statement (of one or more sentences),"[5] Pinter treats each dramatic scene as a shot or statement that may be placed in various ways against a competing statement. In so doing he abandons the Ibsenian tradition of lining up each scene as if it were a word demanding a particular placement within an individual sentence. He reinvents Ibsen's retrospective action by confusing reality and illusion, but in a way different from Strindberg's plays. In Ibsen the past is a given: all of the characters accept an actual, communal past, though they may or may not be aware of previous events at the outset. Frequently the secret of the past is disclosed in the present, providing the driving force of the dramatic action. Nora's forged signature in *A Doll's House,* Mr. Alving's profligacy in *Ghosts,* Rebecca's past sins in *Rosmersholm:* each of these past occurrences is brought to light, examined, and shown to affect the present in Ibsen's dramas of metatheatrical double action.

    4. Interview with John Russell Taylor, *Sight and Sound* (Autumn 1966), quoted in Arnold P. Hinchliffe, *Harold Pinter,* rev. ed. (Boston: Twayne, 1981), p. 131.
    5. Metz, *Film Language,* p. 100.

By contrast, Pinter's characters appear in control of the nature and function of the past through their use of language and silence in the present: each creates a different past in the present. Each character, consequently, represents a different present, pitting various realities against one another and suggesting conflicting retrospective actions. As a result of these conflicts, the very nature of reality is brought into question. Which character's story is the true one? Which past is real and which illusion? Reality and illusion merge, not because reality seems like a waking dream as in Strindberg, but because the competing realities all seem real as they are being voiced. Together the actor and audience engage in a juggling act, considering several versions of a past reality simultaneously. At stake is each character's present.

This present differs from the present in the work of the Brecht Collective. The Collective's characters also face a world in contention, but its actors and audience feel certain that there is a controlling and controllable material reality being played out onstage. Pinter's actors and directors do not have that luxury, that sense that things can be changed given the proper social perspective. The characters in *Old Times* move within a world constantly in flux, but one as fiercely subject to a heterosexist male gaze as the mainstream Hollywood movie whose title—*Odd Man Out*—gives shape to the game they play. Pinter establishes Deeley, the in-house film director, as the character whose sensibilities supposedly most clearly reflect the presumed audience viewpoint. When Anna assumes the camera lens in act two, for example, momentarily creating an erotic scene of her intimacy with and mastery over Kate ("And so she listened and I watched her listening"), Deeley blurts out a rejoinder that typically draws a titter from the audience: "I mean I'd like to ask a question. Am I alone in beginning to find all this distasteful?"[6] To create this treatment of character in relation to actor and audience, Pinter relies on what might be called the grammar of film, a structural system explored in Metz's early studies of the cinema.

In his examination of cinematographic syntax, Metz identifies a passage in *Pierrot le fou* in which Jean-Luc Godard "is able to suggest with a great deal of truth, but without determining the outcome,

6. Harold Pinter, *Old Times* (New York: Grove Press, 1971), p. 66. All subsequent references to *Old Times* are to this edition, and are cited by page in the text.

several possibilities at the same time. So he gives us a sort of *potential sequence*—an undetermined sequence—that represents a new type of syntagma, a novel form of the 'logic of montage,' but [one] that remains entirely a figure of *narrativity*."[7] The sequence follows the two protagonists of the film as they flee a Paris apartment by sliding down a drainpipe and then racing off in a red Peugot. This passage "freely alternates shots taken from the sidewalk in front of the building . . . with other images that, from the diegetic point of view, occur several minutes later in another location."[8] Godard freely intertwines times and places, presenting several versions of the car emerging from the apartment building. Pinter splinters his narrative in a similar manner; but instead of alternating several possible versions of a scene as Godard did in *Pierrot le fou*, he complicates the process even further by presenting various potential scenes simultaneously. For example, at the opening of act one in *Old Times*, the movie director Deeley and his wife, Kate, anticipate the arrival of Kate's former roommate—and possibly former lover—Anna. But Anna already stands upstage, as if Pinter had merged film shots of the scenes before and after dinner. For the audience Anna is at once *there*, by virtue of the fact that she is physically present onstage, and *not there*, since Kate and Deeley ignore her as they discuss her imminent arrival. Pinter merges these two shots to present several possible perceptions of the moment. Foremost in Kate and Deeley's minds, Anna upstages them in the audience's mind as well. And since Anna suddenly emerges as a "given" in the married couple's life, she poses a dangerous threat—one to be ignored. As a woman who possesses sexual desires independent of Deeley's, indeed as a woman who may very well prefer Kate or her own husband over Deeley, Anna embodies the fear that terrifies the insecure, homophobic Deeley.

Anna's presence onstage creates a double action unlike Ibsen's, for Ibsen's scenes do not posit two *different* and *simultaneous* realities. Hedda Gabler focuses on two sets of listeners actually present onstage (Løvborg as well as Brack and Tesman in the album scene, for example), just as Kate attends to two sets of listeners actually present onstage; but only one of them—Deeley—is present to *her*. Anna's

7. Metz, *Film Language*, p. 219.
8. Ibid., p. 218.

presence certainly must be taken into consideration in the way Kate and Deeley play the opening scene; but the script does not indicate that either of them sees or acknowledges Anna. She exists concretely, but in another frame, as if two shots had been superimposed. Deeley's initial reluctance to acknowledge Anna may be viewed as his attempt to ignore his fear of losing possession of Kate, his fear of castration, which he eventually works through by fetishizing both Anna and Kate. When Anna does burst out of her initial silence to converse with Deeley and Kate, Pinter uses the cinematic trick of skipping over time to a crucial moment. It is not important for us to see how Anna has entered, so we simply witness her *being* there. Pinter might have been discussing this moment in *Old Times* when he described his screenplay for *Accident* in 1966: "In this film everything happens, nothing is explained. It has been pared down and down, all unnecessary words and actions are eliminated. If it is interesting to see a man cross a room, then we see him do it; if not, then we leave out the insignificant stages of the action."[9]

This structural strategy contrasts markedly with the Brecht Collective's parable structure, in which the import of each segment may be announced by a title preceding the scene, and the objective of the scene is to make clear beyond a doubt the social implications of each gest, the choices that are and are not made, and the significant results of each. Pinter as a playwright seems absent compared to the Brecht Collective, but in both cases there is an attempt at tight control, a marshaling of forces to create a unique dramatic situation.

The suddenness of Anna's entrance into the dialogue in scene one of *Old Times* augments her initial chatter, crafted so that it drastically alters the slow, steady editing pace that opens the play. Her speed strikes an even more shocking note because of the almost slow-motion coffee and brandy rituals that follow. First Kate offers coffee to Anna (and reluctantly to Deeley), and then, as if in retaliation, Deeley immediately pours brandy for them all. These rituals force the audience to see a closeup of the coffee cups and the brandy snifters, as if calling attention to their importance as objects or weapons. Indeed, the ritualistic cups and snifters assume a magnified significance of their own, for Pinter cuts out the "footage" that shows the characters actually drinking their coffee. By creating this at-

9. Quoted in Martin Esslin, *Pinter*, rev. ed. (London: Eyre Methuen, 1973), p. 193.

tempt at a closeup shot in the theatre, Pinter's script combats the
static nature of the distance between the stage actor and the audience, attempting to substitute for it the more variable relationship
between the movie character and the film audience, whose point of
view can be altered at will through the movement of the camera. As
Keith Cohen writes in *Film and Fiction,* customarily in the theatre
"subject and object are part of the same living and playing space; the
distance, as well as the angle of vision, between the two [actor and
spectator] remains static, while in film these spatial relations are
extremely dynamic."[10] This characteristic distinguishes Pinter's dramaturgy from that of all of his predecessors.

The cinema itself acts as a central metaphor in *Old Times.* Deeley is
not only a filmmaker of sorts but also a movie buff and a fan of the
actor Robert Newton. Sometimes Pinter splinters the narrative of
Old Times by presenting a retake of the action, as he does with the
Odd Man Out incident: Deeley's version of his movie outing with Kate
is later repeated, supposedly from Anna's point of view. She contends that it was she, not Deeley, who shared the movie *Odd Man Out*
with Kate. Unlike Ibsen's dramas, with their keys to the past;
Strindberg's, with their certainty that life is a painful dream; or the
Brecht Collective's, with their absolute belief in the power to know
and change reality, Pinter's dramas do not let the actors, the director,
or the audience know the precise reality of the story. Only Pinter as
the master playwright holds the key, if indeed there is one.

And perhaps there is. While the characters manipulate the minute
realities of their shared pasts to suit their own desires in the present,
Pinter formulates those desires in a heterosexist fashion, thereby
framing the minor, competing realities within a larger reality in
which the possible lesbianism of Kate and Anna cannot survive. In
her analysis of lesbian representation, Teresa de Lauretis quotes
Luce Irigaray's critique of psychoanalytic discourse, in which, she
says, "*the feminine occurs only within models and laws devised by male
subjects.* Which implies that there are not really two sexes, but only
one. A single practice and representation of the sexual."[11] De Lau-

10. Keith Cohen, *Film and Fiction* (New Haven: Yale University Press, 1979), p. 73.
11. In Teresa de Lauretis, "Sexual Indifference and Lesbian Representation," in
Performing Feminisms: Feminist Critical Theory and Theatre, ed. Sue-Ellen Case (Baltimore: Johns Hopkins University Press, 1990), p. 18.

retis's exploration of this psychoanalytic theory illuminates Pinter's final positioning of Anna as the "odd 'man' out" in *Old Times,* the character whom Kate must finally "kill." As de Lauretis remarks, again quoting Irigaray: "Within the conceptual frame of that *sexual indifference,* female desire for the self-same, an other female self, cannot be recognized. That a woman might desire a woman "like" herself, someone of the "same" sex, that she might also have auto- and homosexual appetites, is simply incomprehensible' in the phallic regime of an asserted sexual difference between man and woman which is predicated on the contrary, on a complete indifference for the 'other' sex, woman's."[12]

Not only is Kate and Anna's desire for each other—for the "self-same"—outlawed in the script, but it is also used as a means to eroticize and energize Deeley's desire. Pinter represents Anna's passion as a "masculinized" reflection of Deeley's own urge to do battle, to duel verbally, to earn sole possession of Kate, the floating Other. "You have a wonderful casserole," Anna tells Deeley. "I mean wife. So sorry. A wonderful wife" (p. 20). Anna's slip, if it is one, reveals her complicity in the system of ownership and objectification of women. Like Deeley, she gazes at Kate, fetishizing her, claiming her as if she were a lost object or "found art": "I found her" (p. 69). She takes up the weapons of 1940s songs and movies with ease, is an old pro at sports competitions, represented as enjoying them as much as Deeley. Kate recognizes that both Deeley and Anna objectify her: "You talk of me as if I were dead," she protests (p. 34). Pinter roots Anna's characterization firmly in heterosexist reality. Again, De Lauretis quoting Irigaray: "'The object choice of the homosexual woman is [understood to be] determined by a *masculine* desire and tropism'—that is, precisely, the turn of so-called sexual difference into sexual indifference, a single practice and representation of the sexual."[13]

Jill Dolan has explored the way in which realistic structures erase lesbian experience, but the same can be true of nonrealistic narrative structures such as that in *Old Times.*[14] If the actors playing Anna

12. Ibid.
13. Ibid.
14. See Jill Dolan, "'Lesbian' Subjectivity in Realism: Dragging at the Margins of Structure and Ideology," in Case, *Performing Feminisms,* pp. 40–54.

and Kate follow the cues Pinter gives them for performance, if they move and speak as if in a filmic space, they end up "either dead or aping heterosexual behavior."[15] Pinter constructs Anna as driven by "masculine" desire, so Kate perceives her intent as similar to Deeley's: they both want to frame her, to "gaze" at her when she is "quite unaware," to subject her to their camera lenses. Herself watchful, she floats from one to the other, finally shattering both their views, rejecting them (almost) equally.

Deeley contributes to this process by collapsing Anna into Kate, creating Anna's desire for him as a double of Kate's own. "I'll be watching you," he cautions Kate ambiguously in act one, "to see if she's the same person" (pp. 11–12). Toward the end of act two he confides that Anna and he have met before, picturing himself as "slim-hipped. . . . Pretty nifty" (p. 69). Anna "was pretending to be [Kate] at the time," and "took a fancy" to him. "Maybe she was you," he concludes hopefully, "Maybe it was you, having coffee with me, saying little, so little" (p. 69). Having transformed Anna into a conduit for the playing out of masculine desire, that is, having neutralized the threat of a female desire independent of him, Deeley conflates Anna with Kate, transforming them both into the interchangeable object of his desire.

To combat this strategy Kate must therefore do away with Anna: first, to preserve her own separateness, her position as the sole object of Deeley's desire; and second, simultaneously, to reject Anna's masculinized attempt to possess her. Such a gesture is the logical conclusion to the triangular "odd man out" game played in this heterosexist script: "By dying alone and dirty you had acted with proper decorum," Kate concludes of Anna (p. 72). Interestingly, Kate achieves this rout by surreptitiously usurping the camera lens: "You didn't know I was watching you," she responds to Anna's account of voyeurism (p. 71). Even after Anna's "death" Kate cleanses herself and sits naked beside Anna to watch again. Suddenly stripped down to the "truth," figured as the "real," Kate presides over the demise of her own desire for the supposed "self-same."[16]

15. Ibid., p. 44.
16. Yann Lardeau, discussing pornographic films, says that "the naked woman has always been, in our society, the allegorical representation of Truth." Quoted in de Lauretis, "Sexual Indifference," p. 26.

She maintains that apparent position of power to bring Deeley back in, "a male body behaving quite differently," one who "resisted . . . with force" her attempts to dirty his face. He suggests, instead, a wedding and a change of environment, though "neither mattered" to Kate (pp. 72–73).

Even though (or perhaps because) the final tableau presents Deeley slumped in the armchair and Kate sitting triumphantly on the divan, it is Deeley with whom Pinter, finally, asks the audience to empathize. The threat of Anna is gone now: she is lying "dead" on the divan. But this is only a posture, part of the game, the end of round one, as the reenactment tableau suggests. Deeley is supposedly the underdog in this sporting contest, and the audience should, after all, root for him—although, in fact, his heterosexist ideology has already won.

This reading of *Old Times* reverberates with a special resonance when examined within the production history of the script. Vivien Merchant (at that time Pinter's wife) played Anna in the Royal Shakespeare Company's premiere at London's Aldwych Theatre on June 1, 1971, with Colin Blakely as Deeley and Dorothy Tutin as Kate. A confident, resourceful actor, Merchant had portrayed many of Pinter's independent characters over the years. In October 1985 (after their 1980 divorce, his marriage to Lady Antonia Fraser, and Merchant's subsequent death in 1982), Pinter himself played Deeley in a touring company with Liv Ullman as Anna and Nicola Pagett as Kate. Opening at the American Theatre in St. Louis, with David Jones directing, the production toured to Los Angeles and San Francisco. Pinter's assumption of the role of Deeley seems an extraordinary risk after a seventeen-year hiatus from acting, and must have been propelled by a powerful desire. But instead of being tempted into attributing psychological motivations to Pinter, let us examine the record of his performance. Comparing Pinter's rendering of the character with Anthony Hopkins's 1983 Roundabout Theatre performance in the role, Steven H. Gale felt that "with Pinter as Deeley, the emotional undercurrents were even stronger, and the relationships between the characters were more obvious from the very beginning. . . . Pinter plays a Pinter character surely and with understanding. He is quiet and sensitive, knowing the essence of his character and underplaying the part naturally so that the strong,

emotional outbursts are heightened by comparison. In this play
Deeley's actions fall neatly between the outward softness of Kate and
the exuberance of Anna and thus serve to define all three characters
simultaneously."[17] Already a defining agent, Pinter's Deeley assumed special power for this particular viewer as a result of Pinter's
authority as dramatist. Liv Ullman, who had never before acted
onstage in a script written by a living playwright, commented that
having the author as a co-actor helped guide her work. She joked
that "when Pinter cut a pause short no one could 'accuse him of
misunderstanding' the author's intent," thereby voicing a deference
shared by the director, who also acknowledged to Gale his gratitude
for Pinter's assistance. Gale describes a specific moment of Ullman's
performance that verifies the montage effect I have described: "The
pause, a glance, and the intonation of Anna's next words, 'This man
crying in our room,' simultaneously cause the imaginative concept
described, the image of the crying man, and the person of Deeley to
coalesce in the audience's mind."[18]

In fact, this competition between Deeley and Anna over Kate, and
Kate's final revenge, was sharpened in this production that Pinter
helped shape. The second-act setting, for example, was "obviously a
bedroom." This choice of setting erases the tension created by a
simultaneously public and private space, the space suggested by the
script's stage directions, and wrests power from Anna, who can better play with and hold off the satisfaction of Deeley's desire when
she is in a more equivocal space. In another move that flattens out
the possibilities for contradiction, for feminist countersparring, the
director opted to employ a sound track of sorts, opening each act
with the sound of waves and closing the show with "the sound of a
heartbeat growing steadily louder."[19] These sounds emphasized the
supposedly universal, natural cycles being represented onstage and
asserted the "rightness" of the battle, its passion and elemental re-
currence. By framing the action with things beyond human
control—the endlessly moving ocean, the heart that beats without

17. Steven H. Gale, "Observations on Two Productions of Harold Pinter's *Old
Times*," *Pinter Review* 1, 1 (1987): 41.
18. Ibid., pp. 41, 42.
19. Ibid., pp. 42, 43.

any voluntary effort on our part—Jones defined the contest as "natural," this heterosexist male fantasy that crushes a woman's right to desire herself or her "self-same."

The staging of the final scene in this production reflects my earlier contention that this dumb show is only a posturing, "part of the game, the end of round one." As I have noted, Deeley is figured as the underdog in a sporting contest, and the audience is invited to root for him—to watch as his heterosexist agenda wins again. Gale writes: "There was more posturing among the characters as they created the dumb-show scene. . . . It lessened the moment a bit" (p. 42). In my view, however, this final scene prompted the audience to see in it yet another round in the ritualized contest in which the "best man" wins. Some members of Pinter's midwestern audience may have understood the competitive nature and subtext of this ritual in a curious and unexpected way. The production opened during the World Series between the St. Louis Cardinals and the Kansas City Royals. "Miss Ullman admitted to being a bit *non-plussed* at seeing all of the earphones being worn in the audience."[20] There is a possibility that these particular viewers, simultaneously wired to a major sporting event, saw the play at a distance, as they might the second of two televised sports events they were watching in tandem; and yet they remained close enough to take pleasure in *Old Times* as another manifestation of the "ultimate" male contest. The three characters' battle over possession "proves" the ascendancy of heterosexist manhood just as surely as the World Series does.

As feminist film theorists have pointed out, however, even Hollywood movies offer sites of resistance to the heterosexist male gaze, and the script of *Old Times* itself reveals the tensions of various conflicting gazes, each subject to a process of negotiation.[21] Structurally, Pinter builds a nonrealistic narrative with characters who alternate possession of the lens onto reality, so that spectators viewing act one may glimpse at times what might be called a female gaze, a feminist critique of Deeley's possession of Kate which can change their un-

20. Ibid., pp. 42, 43.
21. A useful summary of recent feminist film criticism may be found in Tania Modleski, *The Woman Who Knew Too Much: Hitchcock and Feminist Theory* (New York: Routledge, 1989), pp. 1–15.

derstanding of the entire play. When Anna pretends to praise the couple's courage in remaining "permanently in such a silence," for example, she may be viewed as criticizing them both for their heterosexual union, born of the silencing of Kate, who had previously enjoyed a lively life with Anna (p. 19). If the actors playing Anna and Kate share a look at that precise moment, if their costumes are reinvented to suggest their connection with each other, the critique becomes palpable. Instead of the coy exchange between Vivien Merchant as Anna and Dorothy Tutin as Kate in full view of Colin Blakely's Deeley (under Peter Hall's direction in the 1971 Royal Shakespeare Company production of *Old Times*), the two actors playing Kate and Anna can acknowledge, through any number of alternative performance choices, the primacy of their relationship with each other and its independence from a more marginalized onstage representation of Deeley. (See figure 7.) And Anna's story—about the man crying in the room that she shared with Kate—enables her to reject the male lover totally: "I would have absolutely nothing to do with him, nothing" (p. 32). But perhaps the most intriguing possibility for a feminist rendering of character materializes at the end of the first act, with the segment that opens with Kate's questioning Anna about her home in Sicily: "Do you have marble floors?" she asks (p. 41). Suddenly the two women for the moment play in a duet rather than a triangle of desire, a duet in which Deeley is completely ignored. They playfully "quote" the question-and-answer format which normally indicates mastery, but which signals here an equilibrium of desire. That equilibrium collapses the minute Anna seduces Kate back into their girlhood past with "Don't let's go out tonight." Anna returns to her masculinized effort to enclose and domesticate Kate, even suggesting that they invite men over (p. 43). The act-two slip into the past continues this heterosexist ascendancy, opening with a representation of Kate's desire for men: "Is Charley coming?" and ending at Deeley's, not Kate's request: "Christy," Deeley interjects, "can't make it. He's out of town." This time Kate welcomes Deeley into the conversation with her reply, "Oh, what a pity" (pp. 62–63).

By letting his characters change the frames of reference at will, Pinter creates a new theatrical form and allows for a new approach to performance. According to John Bury, the set designer for Peter

Figure 7. Vivien Merchant as Anna, Dorothy Tutin as Kate, and Colin Blakely as Deeley in *Old Times* (1971), photo by Zoë Dominic, London

Hall's Royal Shakespeare Company premiere of *The Homecoming*,
Pinter

> absolutely throws out the whole of the Stanislavski school of pro-
> duction and acting. Under the old rule you all sit down and you
> decide. And you decide imaginatively a set of given circumstances.
> You invent your granny and your mother and your whole life
> history, and everybody's got to know the mother and everybody's
> got to agree to the same image of mother. Then when you all act,
> you'll put mother on stage. And usually with Stanislavski one's
> working with a dead author or a translation, so you and the direc-
> tor have to establish a given set of circumstances. This is the thing
> with Harold—there are no given circumstances.[22]

This lack of definition irritated certain American actors of the
1960s, accustomed to Ibsen-style retrospective action and Stanislavsky's method. Patrick Henry, after directing a 1963 Goodman
Theatre production of *The Birthday Party*, explained the difficulty
actors faced if they used a Stanislavsky-based approach to playing
Pinter: "Each actor was frustrated by his inability to determine why
and how his character performed as it did within the framework of
the play." But "Pinter provides no past or future," so discerning a
"logical line of development in each character's behavior from the
past to the time of the play" is impossible.[23] Complicating this process is the fact that Pinter's characters often exist in two time frames
simultaneously, as in Kate and Anna's "girlhood" conversations pep-
pered with Deeley's attempts to cajole the women back to the present. At these times a precise identification of "beats," or minute-to-
minute motivational changes, to borrow Stanislavsky's term, becomes difficult because for each woman there are two sets of motivations, one for the past scene and one for the present. Within a given
scene the Pinter actor may well play a double action similar to that of
an Ibsen actor, but without the firm grounding in a logical cause-
and-effect sequencing of events or the inexorable past of Ibsen's
world.

But what is an appropriate alternative to the Method for the Pin-

22. Quoted in John Lahr and Anthea Lahr, *A Casebook on Harold Pinter's 'The
Homecoming'* (London: Davis Poynter, 1974), p. 34.
23. Patrick Henry, "Acting the Absurd," *Drama Critique* 6 (Winter 1963): 13.

ter performer? Pinter demands that the actor study the character. In his often quoted speech to the Student Drama Festival in 1962, he said, "Between my lack of biographical data about [my characters] and the ambiguity of what they say there lies a territory which is not only worthy of exploration but which it is compulsory to explore."[24] In examining this territory, Pinter's actors are prompted to avoid a preoccupation with the sort of character definition found in Ibsen, and to focus instead on the script as a "kind of shorthand, like a painting by Ben Nicholson . . . suggestions of meaning."[25] Instead of searching for the superobjective of the plot or the spine of the character, the actor can follow Sir John Gielgud's advice to Pinter audiences and substitute "a lot of concentration, and a certain attitude of mind" for the more traditional performance methodology and set of expectations.[26]

Pinter's cinematic approach asks that actors determine not the cause-and-effect narrative of the script but the reality of the events in the plot. Unlike in Strindberg's world, all of the events are taken to be real, even those that may initially seem impossible. The Pinter actor cannot assume that everything is true, however, since Pinter draws characters whose memories distort or merge occurrences and whose will creates past events. A future event may even become a present reality for a Pinter character, as Anna's death becomes real at the end of *Old Times*. The problem of how to perceive a real or imagined event in time is therefore central to the actor's study of a Pinter script. Each actor may arrive at a different conclusion about various events in the story line. For example, the actors playing Anna and Deeley may secretly disagree about the nature of their past encounters. Instead of clarifying the one "true" reading of the characters' relationships, the director may wish to help each actor decide what "camera angle" to take on each event, with the character's circumstances changing with every alteration in point of view. The feminist director can expand the subversive potential of the gaps in the heterosexist gaze of *Old Times* by affirming the female gaze in moments of alternative framing.

24. Quoted in Hinchliffe, *Harold Pinter,* p. 34.
25. Sir Ralph Richardson, quoted in Robert Berkvist, "What Does Pinter Mean? Don't Ask!" *New York Times,* November 7, 1976, sec. 2. p. 22.
26. Sir John Gielgud, quoted ibid.

In *Old Times* the actor encounters a character created in the moment only. Austin Quigley maintains that Pinter's linguistic usage creates this world "primarily as a means of dictating and reinforcing relationships," which "thus become major battlegrounds as characters attempt to negotiate a mutual reality."[27] Although Pinter's language certainly contributes to the fluctuating reality of his world, his cinematic stage directions, acting as nonverbal signs in the script, are an equally important means through which the characters fashion their contradictory truths. In his effort to dissuade Pinter critics from concentrating exclusively on the referential function of language, Quigley calls attention to Ferdinand de Saussure's statement that any two linguistic signs "are not different but distinct. Between them there is only opposition."[28]

Pinter, however, uses not only linguistic signs in opposition to one another but also verbal signs in opposition to nonverbal ones. For example, when Kate says, "You talk of me as if I were dead," the dialogue itself (the linguistic signs) may seem to indicate a peevishness on Kate's part, but the stage directions (the visual signs) that precede the line drastically alter the tone of the speech itself: "Kate stands. She goes to a small table, takes a cigarette from a box and lights it. She *looks down* at Anna" (p. 64; emphasis added). The stage directions indicate that Kate dollies around the set to establish her down-shot on Anna, demolishing Anna's importance at a moment of what might otherwise seem like defensiveness.

Whereas the actions of a character in a well-made play by Ibsen or a parable play by Brecht generally line up in an orderly and somewhat predictable fashion, actors working on *Old Times* may notice that the characters jump from one motivation to the next without a smooth cause-and-effect transition. During the silences there may be no visible stage business, only a flurry of actions or desires for the actors to hint at. These motivations are often linked by association, dream, or memory rather than chronological time or rational

27. Austin E. Quigley, *The Pinter Problem* (Princeton: Princeton University Press, 1975), pp. 52, 54.
28. Ferdinand de Saussure, *Course in General Linguistics*, trans. W. Baskin, ed. Charles Bally and Albert Sechehaye, in collaboration with Albert Reidlinger (New York: McGraw-Hill, 1966), pp. 121–22, quoted in Quigley, *The Pinter Problem*, pp. 58–59.

thought processes; actors must thus present characters who suddenly age or shed years, or even seem to exist outside of time as the past or future becomes the present in their desires. But unlike Strindberg's characters (the Officer or Victoria, for example) who also shed years or transform at will, Pinter's characters are not jumping into a new performance style, nor are they leaping into a fantastic or absurd revision. For example, Anna's sudden motivation to lure Kate to the past with her line "Don't let's go out tonight" is not so much a simple reversion in time as an attempt to hide from time, and from Deeley's observation—to replace Deeley (p. 43). As the scene develops, Kate ignores her husband and focuses on Anna, asking, for a second time, "Do you like the Sicilian people?" Anna abandons her position of shared power with Kate, assuming the more aggressive stance of someone with a secret. Attempting to mystify Kate, Anna refuses to answer. Instead she stares at Kate, ignoring Deeley's attempt to distract her. During the silence that follows, Anna, imposing her camera eye on the scene, is finally powerful enough to lure Kate toward her on the line "Don't let's go out tonight." Anna's motivation—to hide additional information about her life in Sicily—jumps by association to the motivation to hide *with* Kate, as Anna attempts to eclipse Deeley.

The apparently obscure connections between one motivation and the next created by cinematic editing principles in *Old Times* provide actors, particularly female actors, with rich territory to explore. In these moments they can perhaps most clearly see their characters. The film critic Tom Milne might have been discussing *Old Times* when he wrote of Pinter's screenplay for *Accident:* "The characters refuse to be limited by what we are shown of them. The whole film is put together virtually without transitions, using only direct cuts, and as with Resnais, it is in the gaps that the real story is told."[29]

Because these jumps in motivation are central to the play's syntax and vision, the actor's job is to clarify that each character may choose any one of several particular motivations at any given moment. Paul Rogers, who played Max in the Royal Shakespeare Company's *Homecoming,* supported this idea in an interview with John Lahr:

29. Quoted in Katherine H. Burkman, *The Dramatic World of Harold Pinter: Its Basis in Ritual* (Columbus: Ohio State University Press, 1971), p. 126.

[Lahr]: I get the feeling as a member of the audience that you're making up your mind as you go along at every point, that you could go one of four or five ways.

Rogers: That's a good observation. Because, of course, that's what the characters are doing to each other.[30]

The female actor can also permit the audience to see a collage of conflicting and potentially subversive motivations, then clarify which precise choice the character makes at each juncture. In addition, she must find an analogue for the sudden changes in point of view in Pinter's dialogue. For instance, during much of act one Deeley and Anna refer to Kate in the third person, indicating their observation of her from a safe distance, as if to discern her reaction to their battle without getting burned themselves. This use of third-person discourse allows Pinter's characters to protect themselves from one another and to gaze at the objects of their desire. By contrast, its use in Brecht enables his actors to demonstrate clearly to the audience the choices made by their characters: a similar device, but with very different functions.

Walter Kerr's comments on Pinter's structure in *The Dumb Waiter* calls attention to yet another important task for the actor in a Pinter play. Kerr writes: "Whatever action is taking place must have no clear beginning. . . . Similarly, [it] must have no foreseeable future."[31] Although the actor should, of course, avoid anticipating cues in any production, Pinter asks that his actors maintain their concentration on the present moment to avoid creating the sense of a closed narrative or shattering the character's seemingly cool exterior. Since in Pinter's *Old Times* the process of character *creation* replaces character *revelation*, actors constantly threaten to rewrite the script their acting partners initiate, aware that they are writing separate scenarios and competing for photographic accuracy in observation. This ambiguity can be especially useful for female actors seeking ways to undercut the patriarchal biases of the script. By "believing in something that's just air,"[32] by deciding something is true, Pinter actors

30. Lahr and Lahr, *Casebook*, p. 155.

31. Walter Kerr, *Harold Pinter* (New York: Columbia University Press, 1967), pp. 20–21.

32. John Normington, quoted in Lahr and Lahr, *Casebook*, pp. 149–50.

form their characters, in direct contrast with the method of Ibsen actors selecting their keys to performance, or Brecht Collective actors juggling competing parables. Pinter actors, particularly female actors, need not confine themselves to a single spine to create characters that may best be thought of in terms of "possibility, movement."[33] To convey character, these actors rely heavily on the moment and movement, or on the decision not to move. Because of Pinter's cinematic techniques, however, movement may be evidenced onstage as nothing more than an actor's shift in focus, as if the character were a camera lens.

Pinter's characters often perceive one another in terms of visual images. Notice the visually oriented diction and its relationship to character creation in this speech by Len in *The Dwarfs:*

> What you are, or *appear* to be to me, or *appear* to be to you, changes so quickly, so horrifyingly, I certainly can't keep up with it, and I'm damn sure you can't either. But who you are I can't even begin to *recognize,* and sometimes I *recognize* it so wholly, so forcibly, I can't *look* and how can I be certain of what I *see?* You have no number. Where am I to *look,* where am I to *look,* what is there to *locate,* so as to have some surety, to have some rest from this whole bloody racket? You're the sum of so many *reflections.*[34]

In *Old Times,* as in *The Dwarfs,* each character shares Pinter's penchant for being "the objective, meticulous recorder of the world around him" or her.[35] These attempts to see are inextricably linked to the ability to perceive or enforce another's identity. At the end of act one, for example, Anna behaves like a camera's eye as she "stares" at Kate, coaxes "Don't let's go out tonight," and thus prompts Kate's transformation into her girlhood lover. In accordance with cinematic principles, the nature of the person on whom Anna is focused—Kate in this instance—changes as she is observed. Utilizing the Heisenberg principle of indeterminacy, Pinter stresses the fact that neither Anna nor the audience can be certain of Kate's

33. Kerr, *Harold Pinter,* p. 32.

34. Harold Pinter, *The Dwarfs,* in *A Slight Ache and Other Plays* (London: Eyre Methuen, 1968), p. 112; emphasis added.

35. Martin Esslin, *Pinter: A Study of His Plays,* rev. ed. (London: Eyre Methuen, 1973), pp. 234–35.

nature, since the very act of observation alters its object. With Brecht and Ibsen the converse is true: observation clarifies character.

All too aware of the Heisenberg principle, the characters in *Old Times* attempt to impose their own photographic realities upon one another. At the close of act one, after Kate's exit, Pinter dictates:

> Deeley stands looking at Anna.
> Anna turns her head towards him.
> They look at each other.
> FADE (p. 46)

Calmly they monitor each other, as if the very act of looking might allow them to overpower or perhaps possess the other. Rather than catalogue the countless times this same action occurs during the course of the play, however, let us examine two central uses of it toward the end of act two. Anna reveals that, on returning home from an evening out when she and Kate roomed together, she would tell Kate "anything of interest" that had occurred during her outing (p. 65). When Deeley asks, "Did she blush then?" to determine the accuracy of Anna's picture of Kate, she responds: "I could never see then. I would come in late and find her reading under the lamp, and begin to tell her, but she would say no, turn off the light, and I would tell her in the dark. She preferred to be told in the dark, what with the light from the gasfire or the light through the curtains, and what she didn't know was that, knowing her preference, I would choose a position in the room from which I could see her face, although she could not see mine. She could hear my voice only. And so she listened and I watched her listening" (pp. 65–66). Anna forces Kate, unwilling and unknowing, into a spotlight so that she can observe her and thus fetishize and control her. Aware of the power of the gaze, Kate so prefers the dark that Anna's disclosure triggers her desire for revenge: "I remember you lying dead. You didn't know I was watching you" (p. 71). Thus, in one stroke, with nothing more effortful than a new camera angle on the scene just past, with the sole change that Kate discloses that she also acted as an observer, Kate wins the battle with Anna.

Pinter's conception of his characters as objective cameras prompts many critics to call them dispassionate, when in fact they feel deep-seated emotions. Arnold Hinchliffe, for example, cites a *Homecoming* review in which Pinter is "accused of the same emotional coldness that is charged against Alain Resnais."[36] But the playwright's appropriation of the supposedly objective film vision provides for a unique emotional exchange among performers. According to Pinter's favorite director, Peter Hall, "The personal involvement of the actor in Pinter has to be deeper and more passionate and more instinctive at a certain time in rehearsal, and then one has to cool it" by opening night.[37] The actor playing Kate, for instance, may attain her power through evasion, silently panning the events as they transpire, applying all her energy toward remaining emotionally uninvolved.[38] Similarly, the actors portraying Deeley and Anna must be careful not to allow a blow to register.[39] Playing a self-assured character may be a deplorably uncommon experience for female actors, accustomed to mainstream misrepresentations of women; even male actors, accustomed to playing strong-willed characters, find the level of haughtiness unusual. Asked if he had learned anything about acting from his work on *The Homecoming*, Paul Rogers replied: "*Arrogance*. Plain, bloody arrogance. I've played kings and tyrants, Lear, Macbeth, Hamlet, and God knows what. But never in a play was it essential in one's relationship to the audience to come and *be*, relentlessly, without a thought of playing for any kind of sympathy, to be utterly arrogant and sure of the play, of yourself, and your own skill as a player." This self-possession lends a knife-edge clarity to the stylized naturalism which the actor John Normington describes as Pinter's performance mode.[40]

In effect, Pinter asks for film acting onstage: the ability to undertake a number of different scenes, not necessarily in chronological order, on one evening's "shoot"; and, more important, the ability to maintain a distance from the audience and an awareness that economy and precision are essential. Rogers agrees that Pinter's scripts call for "comma accuracy." Peter Hall cites this need to avoid even the

36. Hinchliffe, *Harold Pinter*, pp. 138–39.
37. Quoted in Lahr and Lahr, *Casebook*, p. 22.
38. After directing *The Homecoming*, Peter Hall observed of Teddy: "The amount of force he has to apply to keeping uninvolved—that's the main thing." Quoted in Lahr and Lahr, *Casebook*, p. 165.
39. Paul Rogers, quoted in Lahr and Lahr, *Casebook*, p. 21.
40. Ibid., pp. 153, 138.

smallest irrelevant gestures as a return to style, though it may also be compared to the need for film actors to avoid any inappropriate small gestures, since they are magnified a hundred times on the screen.[41] As in Robert Wilson's operas, inspired also by the slow-motion possibilities of film, movement is enlarged and tone amplified, and therefore both must be even more tightly controlled than in a more traditionally realistic play, such as, for example, *Hedda Gabler*, with its customary abundance of nonverbal signs.

In Pinter, acting is *behaving*. As Vincent Canby wrote in a *New York Times* review: "Because of the nature of the camera and its ability to crawl into an actor's eyeball if required, a lot of movie acting isn't acting at all in the ordinary sense. It's what Alexander Knox once called 'behaving,' the simulation of being natural, of being devoid of irrelevant mannerisms that, if magnified a couple of hundred times on the screen, could suggest psychosis rather than an incipient sneeze."[42] Like film actors, Pinter actors hone their movements to a cutting edge, carefully granting import and urgency to those moments when they do choose to move. The female actor exploring *Old Times* achieves success when moving—behaving, if you will—with complete confidence and absolute control in a performance that would make an Ibsen actor appear baroque. With characteristic bluntness Pinter says: "I think what has to be done is just to play the damn lines and *stop, start, and move* and do it all very clearly and economically."[43] Pinter might almost be talking about something as mechanically controlled as a camera, signaling his insistence on movement as movement rather than as the outer manifestation of a deeper meaning. As Walter Kerr notes in his study of Pinter, the playwright has "accepted, for practical dramatic purposes, the post-Greek proposition that the lip moves first and that its nature as lip comes later—after the utterance and because of it."[44] Gesture and movement in Pinter are not a revelation of an inner motive so much as acts of momentary definition. And in *Old Times* Pinter goes far-

41. Ibid., pp. 153, 16.
42. Vincent Canby, "In Film, Acting Is Behavior," *New York Times*, December 12, 1976, sec. 2, p. 1.
43. Michael Dean, "Late Night Line-up: Harold Pinter Talks to Michael Dean," *Listener*, March 6, 1969, p. 312.
44. Kerr, *Harold Pinter*, pp. 44–45.

ther than in any of his other dramas to establish that fact, as is proven by the final scene, in which silent movement offers us our last glimpse of the characters.

As Patrick Henry discovered in directing *The Birthday Party,* it may be difficult for actors to consider motivation and movement in this way. The actor playing Meg in his production tried to make her business of darning socks "dramatically valid" rather than "devoting her entire attention to such trivialities and then making this increased focus seem completely natural."[45] Oddly enough, however, this reliance on behavior does not mean that the Pinter actor is doomed to being undramatic. As Pinter himself remarked in a 1968 television interview, in some ways the impact of his characters' movements resembles the theatrical effects engineered by a barnstorming actor such as Donald Wolfit, with whom Pinter acted in *King Lear:*

> I was playing one of Lear's knights, and I remember we were pretty much in the shadows, with Wolfit standing on a very high rostrum with his back to the audience, with his cloak. There was a spotlight on him. And at a certain moment—it was the most tingling experience to be on stage with him and watching this happen every night—the cloak would *fling* right around. It was quite a shattering moment. It's that *taking* of dramatic moments that was unparalleled. One doesn't see anything like that these days, except for Sir Laurence Olivier. And so far as I'm concerned, there are comparable moments in what I seem to write. The moments are very exact and even very small, perhaps even trivial—as when a glass is moved from there to there. Now, in my terms I feel that this is a very big moment, a very important moment. You haven't got the cloak, but you do have the glass.[46]

Actors making a dramatic gesture with the glass, however, cannot allow themselves to be surrounded by a flurry of activity, nor can their movement be just part of a string of illustrative gests, as they might well be in a Brecht production. The gestures must customarily be not only precise and controlled but also infrequent or sometimes half restrained, so that the pivotal moments will be accentuated. "Experts have long recognized," writes Walter Benjamin, "that

45. Henry, "Acting the Absurd," p. 14.
46. Quoted in Lahr and Lahr, *Casebook,* p. 39.

in the film 'the greatest effects are almost always obtained by "act-ing" as little as possible.'"[47] Kate's initial immobility emphasizes her later courtship of Anna through the mere offer of coffee, just as Deeley's stillness is shattered when he dramatically upstages her with the nuanced brandy ritual. Like the cigar-lighting and tea ceremo-nies in *The Homecoming*, these ritualistic movements derive their meaning from the *doing*.

By using such a cinematic approach, Pinter forges a new relation-ship between audience and actor as he invites spectators to view his *Old Times* not from a single vantage point, as they might a more conventionally structured play, but from any number of camera angles. Sometimes the spectators watch from their own point of view outside, sometimes from the continuously changing points of view of the three characters. As Walter Kerr writes, the audience begins to "share the anxiety of the characters whose lives we can observe but cannot chart. We no longer judge their collective state of mind. We inhabit it."[48] Instead of presenting one given set of circumstances (the crystal clear "who, what, when, where, and why" of melodrama), or even one slowly revealed, shifting set of circumstances (as in Ibsen), Pinter seems to allow the characters in *Old Times* to govern the circumstances of their backgrounds and their relationships with one another. But, of course, even within themselves these characters do not experience life in a unified fashion. They constantly renego-tiate the scenes they remember from their past, using what Jurij Lotman identifies as the second type of film narration: "the trans-formation of one and the same shot."[49] Anna, for example, first describes Deeley's movements as "quick" when she recalls (or cre-ates) her encounter with him in the bedroom. But she immediately offers a revised image, reporting that "he didn't move quickly . . . that's quite wrong . . . he moved . . . very slowly" (p. 32). As Anna's speech reveals, the given circumstances of Pinter's dramas are dis-cernible only from moment to moment, as the characters review and edit their own scenes. Even the setting transforms, or rather splits,

47. Walter Benjamin, "The Work of Art in the Age of Mechanical Reproduction," in *Illuminations* (New York: Harcourt, Brace and World, 1968), p. 232.

48. Kerr, *Harold Pinter*, pp. 20–21.

49. Jurij Lotman, *Semiotics of Cinema*, trans. Mark E. Suino (Ann Arbor: University of Michigan Press, 1976), p. 63.

during the scenes of Kate and Anna's past, as Deeley and Kate's country house becomes simultaneously the girls' London flat. In *No Man's Land* the characters also reformulate the setting through their dialogue. Pinter actors must help the audience discern these crucial shifts.

Pinter's Eisenstein-style approach requires actors to cue in their viewers' minds a forward motion (or sometimes a reverse motion) during the apparent stop action of a pause or silence, getting them to sort, edit, and replay certain moments, reflect on past scenes, make their own syntheses of individual stage images or bits of dialogue. Pinter often posits situation A, allows for a pause or silence, then presents situation B, at which time the actor must signal that the audience is to create situation C, a synthesis of A and B which does not necessarily exist onstage. For example, in act one of *Old Times*, Deeley blurts out, "Yes, you need good food in the country, substantial food, to keep you going, all the air . . . you know" (p. 21). Then there is a pause, after which Kate states, "Yes, I quite like those kind of things, doing it." This moment derives its interest from the dialectic Pinter sets up in his montage.

Situation A.   Deeley pretends to make polite conversation with Anna about the sustaining power of food.
Pause

Situation B.   Kate voices that she enjoys "those kind of things."

Though the narrative impulse and the linguistic sign "those" lead toward Deeley's later line, "Do you mean cooking?" the montage device demands that the audience synthesize the focus of situation A (sustenance) and B (the sexual suggestiveness of the phrase "doing it") to create C: Kate muses on the sustaining power of sex.

Pinter's method of engaging the audience differs from Brecht's. Pinter uses montage to create irony, and to frustrate the audience's effort to identify a single "because." He invites the audience to reconsider earlier shots or scenes to forge a meaningful narrative, but when they do, they frequently confront the menace of uncertainty. In contrast, Brecht hopes that his audience of experts will "check the footnotes," rethink the preceding scenes, and find not just "an" answer but "the" answer to the questions raised in the script. His collaborators' work may question his conclusions and suggest others, but even with the Brecht Collective there is never any confusion about the nature of causality or its function in the theatre or in life. In Pinter, causality itself is questioned, partly through the use of cinematic devices such as montage. Female actors and spectators can use this to their advantage.

Pinter's filmic experimentation complements his efforts to alter the distance between the actors and the audience. Stanley Cavell, in *The World Viewed,* argues that "the audience in a theatre can be defined as those to whom the actors are present while they are not present to the actors. But movies allow the audience to be mechanically absent. The fact that I am invisible and inaudible to the actors, and fixed in position, no longer needs accounting for; it is not part of a convention I have to comply with; the proceedings do not have to make good the fact that I do nothing in the face of tragedy, or that I laugh at the follies of others."[50] Pinter's structures promote a performance situation that departs radically from the playwriting traditions of the late nineteenth and early twentieth centuries: he uses several techniques that seem to place the spectator in the "mechanically absent" position of a person viewing a film or a photograph. He concentrates on filmic economy and polish in paring down stage business and demanding of his actors a tight control of movement, thus approximating the closed quality of film performances. John Normington might be speaking for any successful Pinter performer when he says of the Royal Shakespeare Company production of *The Homecoming:* "Economy is the thing. . . . We felt like a string quartet. That we were very proficient. We could all play the score. We knew the tempos and we had our conductor. We all knew exactly what we were going to do. There was no 'we'll try this tonight.'"[51]

This refined, precise performance style minimizes the actor's on-stage presence, a presence that contradicts the audience's temptation "to perceive him [or her] as a protagonist in a fictional universe."[52] Instead, Pinter actors often create an impression of reality closer to that offered by film, which substitutes the presence of the character for the presence of the actor. As Christian Metz says of

50. Stanley Cavell, *The World Viewed* (New York: Viking, 1971), pp. 25–26.
51. Quoted in Lahr and Lahr, *Casebook,* pp. 145–47.
52. Metz, *Film Language,* pp. 9–10.

Jean Leirens's theory, film "does not depend at all on the strong presence of an actor but, rather, on the low degree of existence possessed by those ghostly creatures moving on the screen . . . [which] are, therefore, unable to resist our constant impulse to invest them with the 'reality' of fiction (the concept of diegesis), a reality that comes only from within us, from the projections and identifications that are mixed in with our perceptions of the film."[53] Perhaps the clearest example of Pinter's enhancing the fiction of a character in this cinematic way arises when he leaves Anna onstage, mobile and very much alive to the subversive possibilities of the scene, even after Kate's act-two statement, "I remember you dead" (p. 71). As in the opening scene, Anna becomes at that moment a felt presence, a distanced fiction whose reality the audience itself creates through reflection.

Another facet of Pinter's playwriting strategy which "mechanically" distances the audience is his handling of motivation. Instead of directly addressing the objects of their desires, the characters in *Old Times* drive their actions through one character to another.[54] This oblique approach to interaction places the spectator at a remove from the third actor, the object of the action at any given moment. For example, the actor portraying Kate may recognize that the stage direction calling for her to offer Anna a cigarette does not necessarily indicate her desire to please Anna but may rather illustrate her wish to punish as well as attract Deeley, the odd man out at the time. And with her gesture she distances Deeley not only from herself but from the audience as well. Just before Anna's arrival, Deeley puts this distancing into a filmic context as he admits to Kate that he plans to frame her and use her as a camera lens during Anna's visit, to monitor his rival Anna through Kate: "I'll be watching you. . . . To see if she's the same person" (pp. 11–12).

By using pauses and silences to arrest the motion of the visual image onstage, Pinter creates, in those stock-still stage "photographs," a holographic effect, furthering his attempt to distance the audience and create a more autonomous and therefore more "real" stage fiction. As a result, the audience may experience what Roland

53. Ibid., p. 10.
54. David Savran, "The Girardian Economy of Desire: *Old Times* Recaptured," *Theatre Journal* 34, 1 (March 1982): 40–54.

Barthes calls spectatorial awareness, or the feeling that "this has been real."[55] By creating filmic spaces in his silences, expanding the space-time in which his actors remain still, Pinter makes his actors momentarily resemble holograms, three-dimensional images, especially in the final tableau. The playwright seems to remove his spectators temporally as well as spatially from the unfolding action, thereby, paradoxically, allowing them to perceive more fully its apparent reality.

Pinter's alteration of modes of perception is further complicated by the fact that his structural model triggers a merging of the linear process of perception (the syntagmatic step in the spectator's creative process when he or she perceives a succession of images) with the nonlinear process of reflection (the paradigmatic step in the creative process when the viewer links images that are not placed in a sequence).[56] Let us reexamine the scene at the end of the first act when Anna prompts Kate to return with her to their girlhood. The two women suddenly drop into the past:

> Anna: (*Quietly*) Don't let's go out tonight, don't let's go anywhere tonight, let's stay in. I'll cook something, you can wash your hair, we can relax, we'll put on some records.
>
> Kate: Oh, I don't know. We could go out. (p. 43)

Instead of simply providing a flashback, however, Pinter leaves the husband, Deeley, onstage, fighting to reestablish the "present" and his dominance over Kate. The audience, if it is to perceive the reality of either fiction, must try to determine how the two competing scenes fit together. (It must also, of course, eventually place both in the narrative that has thus far been disclosed.) This mode of structuring the dramatic action is one of Pinter's trademarks, distinguishing his method from that of Ibsen, Strindberg, and Brecht. His dramaturgy posits a filmic spectator, complicating the relationship between actor and audience. And, like the Hollywood movies it evokes, *Old Times* invites the spectator to subject Kate and Anna to

55. Roland Barthes, *Communications* 4 (1964): 40–51; see discussion in Metz, *Film Language*, pp. 5–6.
56. Here I utilize Keith Cohen's explanation of the two processes in *Film and Fiction*, p. 76.

the heterosexist male gaze which denies, finally, not only their desire for each other but also their existence independent of Deeley's use of them as interchangeable erotic possessions. Nonetheless, this truth about the relationship between the actor and the audience in Pinter is not the only truth. The female gaze which may be discovered within the script and explored by the actors in creating their characters is also available to female spectators actively negotiating meaning in the performance text.

To examine this process I must complicate the analysis of Pinter's dramaturgy with which I opened this chapter, for in its reliance on the grammar of film, it necessarily mutes the role played by spectators, particularly female spectators, in creating meaning. As Teresa de Lauretis writes: "The hypothesis of classical semiology that cinema, like language, is a formal organization of codes, specific and non-specific, but functioning according to a logic internal to the system (cinema or film), apparently does not address me, woman, spectator."[57] She proceeds to critique the way in which both Metz's early semiological study of cinema and his later shift toward psychoanalytical models fail to allow for the subjecthood of either fictional woman or real women. Both semiology and psychoanalysis, she contends, erase this possibility by arguing that woman's difference (and therefore her inferiority) is founded in nature: "To say that woman is a sign (Lévi-Strauss) or the phallus (Lacan) is to equate woman with representation; but to say that woman is an object of exchange (Lévi-Strauss) or that she is the real, or Truth (Lacan), implies that her sexual difference is a value founded in nature, that it preexists or exceeds symbolization and culture. That this inconsistency is a fundamental contradiction of both semiology and psychoanalysis, due to their common structural heritage, is confirmed by Metz's recent work."[58] As de Lauretis concludes, then: "Going back to the cinema, [woman] finds herself in the place of the female spectator, between the look of the camera (the masculine representation) and the image on screen (the specular fixity of the feminine representation), not one or the other but both and neither."[59] In other words,

57. Teresa de Lauretis, *Alice Doesn't: Feminism, Semiotics, Cinema* (Bloomington: Indiana University Press, 1984), p. 18.
58. Ibid., p. 24.
59. Ibid., p. 35.

female spectators of *Old Times* may find themselves positioned as film viewers, asked to choose between the "look" of the camera (so frequently controlled by a masculine representation of desire) and the images of Kate and Anna as "screens" for that desire. But Pinter's viewers are not, like de Lauretis's, filmic spectators but rather theatregoers asked to view the operations of the stage as if it were a film screen—and therein lies a potential source of subversion.

As a film, *Old Times* must fail, precisely because it is a play. Its spectators certainly watch women trapped within a filmic rerun of masculine desire, but they also can perceive the mechanics of Pinter's performance style: they can *see* the cinematic techniques that attempt to "mechanically distance" the audience, and that conflate the two women into the object of Deeley's desire. These cinematic methods ultimately fail to transform the theatre into Deeley's movie because the audience is aware of the female actors themselves, aware of the peculiarly sculptured, cinematic style of the performance. Especially because of our ability to perceive the shifts in "camera movement" from character to character, we are continually reminded of the playwright and his investment in the ongoing action. Female audience members can therefore actively recognize and reject the male gaze and stage alternatives to it.

With *Old Times* Pinter forged a new theatrical form, borrowing from the art of the cinema to reconceive the stage. His incorporation of film techniques challenges actors to respond in kind, to fashion an approach to performance that centers on movement instead of on the Stanislavsky "spine." His reliance on nonlinguistic signs and counternarrative inspires actors, directors, and audiences alike to explore new ways of interpreting his plays. Critics often depend on metaphors to elucidate Pinter's work. Those metaphors, however, ought to share the visual orientation of the scripts themselves, as the film metaphor that erupts in *Old Times* surely does. In *Old Times* Pinter attempts to tell his critics and his actors how to behave, but his gaze can be redirected.

Chapter Five

Shepard and the Improvisational Actor

Shortly before Sam Shepard moved to New York in the early 1960s, the artist Robert Rauschenberg had attracted the attention of the art world with his "combines," constructions that merged painting and sculpture in an attempt to push beyond the collages of Braque and Picasso. By juxtaposing real, usually "found" objects with his abstract canvases, Rauschenberg tried to maintain in his work the improvisational quality he later explored in his theatrical happenings. John Cage remarked that these combines, by virtue of linking two or more disparate elements and complicating the idea of framing, offered the viewer "at least the possibility of looking anywhere, not just where someone arranged he should."[1] The combines allowed Rauschenberg to call into question the nature of representation as well as the idea of the constant frame. He incorporated real objects in their entirety into his work (not just fragments of objects, as in cubist collages), thereby allowing the objects to remain completely themselves while he re-presented them in new and startling contexts that denied the "*trompe l'oeil* illusionism of traditional realism."[2] By disrupting the viewer's expectations with regard to the nature and

1. John Cage, "On Robert Rauschenberg, Artist, and His Work," *Metro* 1, 2 (1961): 37.
2. Gregory L. Ulmer, discussing collage in "The Object of Post-Criticism, in *The Anti-Aesthetic: Essays on Postmodern Culture* (Port Townsend, Wash.: Bay Press, 1983), p. 84.

significance of his work, and by constantly frustrating the spectator's search for a definitive frame, Rauschenberg invited his viewers to consider his combines playfully, and to enjoy the constant delayed satisfaction of their desire for meaning.

Sam Shepard invites a similar kind of response by structuring his work like Rauschenberg's combines. Joining two or more unlikely and contradictory dramatic actions in a seemingly spontaneous fashion, Shepard complicates traditional notions of framing and representational characterization and calls for an improvisational actor and director who can prompt the audience to respond to dramatic art as casually as Rauschenberg encourages his viewer to respond to visual art. By comparing Shepard's structural method to Rauschenberg's, I hope to suggest an alternative way of considering his scripts, one that complicates the traditional feminist critique of his narratives. Feminist actors and directors can take advantage of the combine-like jamming together of real and not-real actions in Shepard, driving a thicker wedge between the two lines of action rather than conflating them, thereby increasing the subversive potential of his female characters. Although Shepard's scripts have been widely and justifiably criticized as patriarchal, oddly enough they invite an improvisational style that allows the female actor to accomplish two useful tasks: to grant the audience the opportunity to piece together apparently disparate dramatic actions, and to focus on the woman's exit from the frame. Shepard's viewers, like Rauschenberg's, can renegotiate the relationship between the "real" and the "not-real."

Rauschenberg's combines exude a rough and unplanned air in their multiplicity of form. Cage calls Rauschenberg's approach "an entertainment in which to celebrate unfixity."[3] And indeed, Rauschenberg himself remarks that he seeks in his art the freshness and unpredictability he perceives in life: "I would substitute *anything* for preconception or deliberateness."[4] That is the painter from a small town in Texas talking, a transplanted cowboy who moved to New York City in his mid-twenties and befriended John Cage and Merce Cunningham. But we might just as easily be listening to Sam Shepard, the fledgling actor from the Bishop's company and rock musi-

3. Cage, "Robert Rauschenberg," p. 37.
4. Robert Rauschenberg, interviewed by Michael Blackwood in *American Art in the Sixties,* a film written and narrated by Barbara Rose (Blackwood Productions, 1973).

cian from the Holy Modal Rounders, who, before coming to New York, had lived on an avocado farm and raised a 4-H prize ram. Shepard began writing plays because the artistic atmosphere in New York in the 1960s "was like a carnival, a mardi-gras—it made you feel you could do anything. Art wasn't a career or anything intellectual—it was a much more active, playful thing, a way to inhabit a life."[5] From Shepard's playing rock 'n' roll and writing Ginsberg imitations to his more recent screenwriting and acting careers, one senses a casualness that stems at least in part from the Manhattan scene that surrounded him when he began to seek his own voice. And the voice—or voices—in his plays, like the images in Rauschenberg's combines, are multifaceted.

Two of Rauschenberg's combines visually symbolize the way Shepard's plays operate structurally. In *Monogram,* perhaps his best-known work, Rauschenberg chooses objects drawn from the landscape of the city (the automobile tire) and from the fast-disappearing countryside of his youth (the goat), thus linking the two different worlds also found in Shepard's plays, (see figure 8.) The first impression that this combine gives is of odd juxtapositions: real objects are put into play with the almost abstract use of the picture plane, and the canvas itself has been toppled, curiously, to rest face up on the floor. The real tire around the real but stuffed Angora goat makes the goat seem unreal, especially with the added details painted on its face. The very same reality of the tire (and the goat), however, transforms the painted platform into a real field of play for the goat. The viewer's eye moves from one element of the work to another without being able to locate a definitive (physical or mental) frame for it, or to account for any given object in terms of all the other parts. Rauschenberg allows for the free play of several simultaneous structures in *Monogram* without establishing a fixed perspective within or on the work.

Another of Rauschenberg's pieces, *Canyon,* operates in a similar way. This is Lawrence Alloway's description of it:

A tied pillow hung from the bottom of the picture projects out into the room. A stuffed eagle is perched low in the picture, but its

5. Quoted in Michiko Kakutani, "Myths, Dreams, Realities—Sam Shepard's America," *New York Times,* January 29, 1984, sec. 2, p. 26.

Figure 8. Robert Rauschenberg's *Monogram* (1959), courtesy Statens Konstmuseer

outspread wings stay within the limits of the canvas. The eagle over the dangling pillow has the effect of lifting up the painted and collage elements above. That is to say, the eagle, for all its awkward three dimensionality, functions pictorially. That this was Rauschenberg's intention is suggested by three images in the collage that imply ascent: a photograph of the night sky, a reproduction of a child with a raised arm, and a sky blue image from a low angle view of the Statue of Liberty. This kind of logic by contiguity runs through the combine-paintings. The images are not as a rule designed to make a point. . . . Usually chains of relationship follow from the discovery of an object, such as the Angora goat, or from the rendezvous of different pieces. It is definitely not a situation in which anything goes, but neither is it planned ahead.[6]

Rauschenberg attempts in *Canyon*, as in *Monogram*, to link his structures of "real" and "not-real" very loosely, in the hope that each of us will be able to move into the gap, to experience the work in a unique way. The center of his structures, then, is seen to be a function of each viewers' participation in the artwork, an individuated series of substitutions rather than a fixed presence within the combine itself.

Although *Canyon* strives to escape the traditional frame enclosing the canvas and thereby encourages viewers to chose their own vantage points, its canvas nonetheless remains, just as powerful elements of the patriarchal stage endure in productions of Shepard's scripts. Furthermore, *Canyon* controls the spectator's framing process in part by seeming to suggest a possible narrative about flight (perhaps, for example, the American eagle's frustrated attempt to fly), while at the same time it also hints, through its spontaneous disjunctions, at the disruption of that narrative and at the spectator's own freedom to choose a way of seeing, a way of perceiving the "real" and "non-real" in the work. Despite remnants of framing reminiscent of the proscenium arch in the realistic theatre, then, *Canyon* forces a reconsideration of the very nature of representation: Is the stuffed eagle real in the same way that the pillow is? Does it "represent" something in the same way that the pictures related to flight may (or may not)?

In like fashion Sam Shepard combines realistic and nonrealistic

6. Lawrence Alloway, *Robert Rauschenberg* (Washington, D.C.: National Collection of Fine Arts, Smithsonian Institution, 1976), p. 13.

worlds, juxtaposing them in multiple dramatic actions, in a series of images or scenes, while refusing to give either world precedence or to resolve his artwork into a totally unified "representational" whole. Shepard's theatre derives its cohesiveness from the precise juxtapositions of various textures, with realistic moments of characterization or elements of the setting jammed up against contradictory and therefore often nonrealistic speeches and stage images. Even Shepard's most traditional plays, including the 1979 Pulitzer Prize-winning *Buried Child,* offer hints of the structural properties apparent in Rauschenberg's combines. In *Buried Child* Shepard links contradictory lines of action and builds his characters by juxtaposing what might be thought of as a series of "found" selves, sudden and sometimes puzzling transformations of different sides of a character. In the work of both Rauschenberg and Shepard, the artist seems to be not solely responsible for the artwork but rather engaged in a partnership with objects or words or characters "taken from life." Viewers are then invited to reconsider the elements of the works divorced from their customary contexts. Of course, these artists are manipulating their representations of reality as carefully as any playwright discussed in this book, but their structural strategy, unlike Pinter's or Ibsen's, promotes the illusion of spontaneity. And the female actor or director can employ that illusion to her advantage.

As Kenneth Chubb remarks, some Western audiences have yet to cultivate the ability to read this alternative text comfortably: "Instead of actions, characters, situations, and dialogue all working together to present a plot or central idea, [Shepard's] plays are mosaics of different colours and textures that present an abstract rather than a formal pattern. We have come to accept his basic theory in music and painting but not in the theatre. We expect to be entertained in a climactic way."[7] Because of that predilection for the logical progression of scenes toward a particular kind of climax, some see Shepard's multiple actions, frequently accompanied by unresolved endings, as ineptitude or, worse yet, an abandonment of the unspoken pact between the playwright and the audience. Certainly with melodrama and Ibsen, and in a different way with Strindberg, Pinter, and even Brecht, the audience is given what Frank Kermode has called "the

7. Kenneth Chubb, "Fruitful Difficulties of Directing Shepard," *Theatre Quarterly* 4, 15 (1974): 19–20.

sense of an ending." Audiences often respond to any departure from an artistic norm by lagging behind a bit, remaining attached to more traditional expectations. Bonnie Marranca's critical method, in the introduction to her scholarly study of Shepard, resembles Shepard's own playwriting strategy.[8] Yet she, too, attacks the unresolved endings of Shepard's plays, thereby suggesting that (despite her own experimentation) her critical stance is nonetheless founded on a desire for conventional framing.

Shepard revealed his own attitude toward dramatic structure most clearly in a 1977 essay for *Drama Review:* "I'm talking now about an open-ended structure where anything could happen as opposed to a carefully planned and regurgitated event which, for me, has always been as painful as pissing nickels. There are writers who work this way successfully, and I admire them and all that, but I don't see the point exactly. The reason I began writing plays was the hope of extending the sensation of *play* (as in 'kid') into adult life. If 'play' becomes 'labor,' why play?"[9] Like Rauschenberg, and unlike Ibsen, Shepard seeks unpredictability in his work. He associates his particular structuring process with the world of child's play, implying not a lack of seriousness or concentration but rather a willingness to embrace new rules; a readiness to adjust spontaneously if necessary to new stimuli. This shifting of perspectives allows Shepard, like Rauschenberg, to explore the chaos as well as the vitality of their world.

One of Shepard's directors, Robert Woodruff, focuses on the nature of the satisfaction the audience is offered through this kind of structure: "People hit some of the plays because there are no resolutions, but I think that's the strength of them, that they just raised things. They allow you to just *look,* in a context which is new. If you can pose the questions in ways that speak to people, that makes them see a reality in a new way, in a way they've not seen before, that's good enough."[10] By complicating the frame around his work, Shepard allows the audience the pleasure of its own desire for meaning.

8. Frank Kermode, *The Sense of an Ending: Studies in the Theory of Fiction* (London: Oxford University Press, 1967). Bonnie Marranca, ed., *American Dreams: The Imagination of Sam Shepard* (New York: Performing Arts Journal Publications, 1981), p. 106.

9. Sam Shepard, "Visualization, Language, and the Inner Library," *Drama Review* 21, 4 (1977): 50.

10. Robert Woodruff, quoted in Robert Coe, "Interview with Robert Woodruff," in Marranca, *American Dreams,* p. 157.

The frame, however, still exists, and, like Rauschenberg's canvas in *Monogram,* it at least in part circumscribes the apparent free play of the audience.

Shepard achieves this relationship with the audience by combining several disparate dramatic actions in much the same way that Rauschenberg jams a goat and a tire or a bird and a pillow together on a canvas. In their simplest form these actions seem at once to provide a possible frame and yet to call attention to the impossibility of any definitive frame. Let us examine how they operate in Shepard's best-known (and most traditionally structured) play, *Buried Child.* In this drama the young man Vince returns to his midwestern homestead with his unsentimental girlfriend Shelly, only to discover that his grandfather, Dodge, and his father, Tilden, do not recognize him. In fact, Dodge thinks Vince (his grandson) is Tilden (his son). The puzzled but agreeable prodigal son leaves to get his grandpa a bottle of liquor. He suddenly returns, however, as a Marine commando, cutting through the porch window screen as if to take over the house. Shelly exits in disgust. Then, almost as abruptly, Vince settles peaceably into his (now dead) grandfather's position on the family couch. Tilden returns from "out back," this time hugging the corpse of a buried child. From Tilden's and Dodge's earlier confessions, we guess this child to be Vince, the product of Tilden's incestuous relationship with his mother, Halie.

At the end of the play, then, there seem to be two Vinces and two contradictory but simultaneous dramatic actions involving him. One line of action follows the traditional patriarchal narrative frame of Ibsenian retrospective action, with its hidden secret revealed in the final act: the father, Tilden, discloses his son, Vince, is the buried child. But the framing suggested by that action, which might be formulated as the theme of salvaging the family line, is denied by the physical existence of two Vinces. Vince surely cannot be a child's corpse and at the same time a young man who is very much alive; and yet this impossibility is precisely what the script suggests. The grown son engages in a second, equally powerful action, which might be summarized as the theme of ignoring the father's attempt at "framing" him.[11] This action highlights Vince's sudden transfor-

---

11. One might want to explore the implications of this argument in terms of Derrida's association of God-author-father with the word and its attempted tyranny over the mise-en-scène in the theatre. Tilden then becomes the father who attempts to

mation from prodigal son to a "Midnight Strangler [who] . . . devours whole families" in his attempt to find himself.[12]

Ironically, Vince's lack of awareness of the interplay between the two actions of father and son—his ignorance of his own corpse—condemns him to the same anaesthetized state that the grandfather had assumed at the opening of the play. Because he literally cannot see the patriarchal narrative, he is forced to relive it. And that is what Shelly, a key female character, can show the audience—the deadliness of the narrative frame—in her escape from it, her look back in anger.

By keeping these actions in operation simultaneously throughout *Buried Child,* Shepard establishes a playwriting strategy different from traditional models of the well-made play and from the approaches taken by several of his contemporaries. His structuring of dramatic action contrasts in important ways with Ibsen's typical use of the retrospective mode. Like Shepard in *Buried Child,* Ibsen reveals the past through the present; but Ibsen confines the double line of action that emerges from that strategy to individual scenes, whereas Shepard divides the entire action of his play. As a result, Ibsen's plays present a unified action that asks a question and offers optional or ironic viewpoints. In contrast, Shepard creates two or more conflicting main actions, which enter the realm of the nonrealistic as they attempt, unsuccessfully, to cancel one another out. In *A Doll's House,* for example, the action consists of the disclosure of Nora's secret life and ends with the question: What can/should Nora do at the close of the play? But in *Buried Child,* though the play teases us with suggestions about Vince's hidden past, he (unlike Nora) remains unaware of the secret of his roots, even at the moment when his own corpse is carried onto the stage. By using a retrospective mode, Shepard might be said to "cite" Ibsen's structure. But by juxtaposing it with nonrealistic elements, he incorporates the citation into his own text in a combine-like fashion. In his plays he stages

---

salvage the traditional *literary* form and Vince the figural presence of the son who frustrates the search for a "representational" reading of the script and who suggests the possibility of a new theatre of images that would ignore the written text. See Jacques Derrida, "The Theatre of Cruelty and the Closure of Representation," in *Writing and Difference,* trans. Alan Bass (Chicago: University of Chicago Press, 1978), esp. pp. 235–40.

12. Sam Shepard, *Buried Child* (New York: Urizen Books, 1979), p. 67. All subsequent references are to this edition and are cited by page in the text.

both the power of and the destruction caused by the realistic, patri-archal narrative, and often gestures toward a third "exiting" action, usually carried out by a female character or characters who reject the narrative altogether and begin their own independent journey— one that provides opportunities for feminist directors and actors.

Shepard's structural modus operandi may also be distinguished from Pinter's, although Pinter, too, frequently employs nonrealistic strategies in his handling of dramatic action. Whereas Pinter, for example in *Old Times,* allows his characters to control his play's filmic, fluid action, Shepard wrenches his characters from one transforma-tion to another, clearly denying them the choice among options that Pinter's characters ponder during their pauses and silences.

In producing Shepard, directors may wish to explore this combine-like structure, replacing a closed, autocratic directorial vi-sion with a freer collaboration with the actors and a more flexible interpretation of the play's action. Directors need not try to hide a "flawed" structure, as Sydney Schubert Walter attempted to do in his production of *Fourteen Hundred Thousand,* or to tie every element of the play together in an opening lecture to the cast, as Michael Smith did with *Icarus' Mother.*[13] They may simply wish to draw initially from the actors' own free play, then discover the action of the play with them, experientially, through what Robert Woodruff calls "a strong physicalization of the text."[14] Woodruff's discussion of Shep-ard's directorial approach is especially helpful here: Shepard "draws from actors and allows them enormous freedom to come up with what they can, but there's not a sense of improvisation for its own sake: there's nothing outside the play. He respects them, gives them room, and gets a lot of joy from seeing what they do with his work. There's not a sense of sanctity around the words."[15] By concentrat-ing on Shepard's affirmation of the actor's playfulness and his com-plementary belief that there is no need to explain the actor's or character's life "outside the play," Woodruff asks the Shepard actor to abandon a Stanislavsky-based approach to the character's action.

There are ways, of course, that a director can encourage actors to

13. Sydney Schubert Walter, quoted in Chubb, "Fruitful Difficulties," p. 17; Mi-chael Smith, "Notes: *Icarus' Mother,*" in Marranca, *American Dreams,* p. 160.

14. Quoted in Coe, "Interview with Robert Woodruff," p. 152.

15. Ibid.

play, to avoid worrying about discovering the definitive spine that will answer all their questions about character. When Woodruff directed *Suicide in B Flat,* for example, he instructed the actors to play the two detectives as a series of comic pairs: Laurel and Hardy, Kramden and Norton, "two 1940s Hollywood gumshoes, and finally a beleaguered husband and wife."[16] By using this type of improvisation (borrowed from the early days of the Open Theatre) to transform the script, the director enabled the actors to explore the bizarre "breaks" in character as dramatic assets, as gaps that need not be explained away but are rather to be emphasized and celebrated precisely because of their absence of fixity. These jumps in character differ from those found in Strindberg, even though Shepard, like Strindberg, frequently adopts a new performance style when a new set of characters appears: in *Angel City,* for example, he mixes realism, expressionism, jazz, and Japanese war play as the characters leap from one world to another. But Shepard makes no effort to provide an overarching style, as Strindberg does with his emphasis on reality as illusion. Nor do Shepard's breaks in character resemble the Brecht Collective characters' "moments of choice," or Pinter's characters' choreographed cuts in time and space.

As a director Shepard approaches his scripts very openly, but his own playfulness in that capacity is undercut by his attitude toward other directors who produce his scripts. Despite his combine-like structure which invites improvisational collaboration, Shepard, like Samuel Beckett, wants to authorize productions of his scripts. In fact, as early as 1973 Shepard took Richard Schechner to task for directing an unorthodox production of *The Tooth of Crime,*[17] and has frequently directed his own premieres, as if to ensure his presence in the performance text, just as his characters repeatedly attempt to fix the American myths that they try to live by. But, finally, neither Shepard nor his characters can succeed in establishing a sense of security because of the nature of the structures—theatrical and mythical—that frame them. These structures threaten to contradict themselves, to erase themselves, to disappear as meaningful guide-

16. Michael Ver Meulen, "Sam Shepard: Yes Yes Yes," *Esquire* 93 (February 1980): 85.

17. Richard Schechner, "Drama, Script, Theatre, and Performance," *Drama Review* 17, 3 (1973): 12.

lines at the very moment of crisis. And, as Woodruff suggests, a director's best defense may be Shepard's own mode of working as a director: rely on a sense of play, of Rauschenbergian juxtaposition. Feminist directors may want to emphasize not only the two conflicting actions (and the men's blindness to the debilitating effects of the patriarchy) but also the women's powerful act of exiting.

To explain the kind of directorial (script) work prompted by this reading of Shepard's structural strategies, and to suggest its potential efficacy for female actors, allow me to graft my own reading of Shepard's *Action* onto David Savran's deconstructive analysis of that play.[18] Savran's directorial vision distinguishes sharply between the trapped male characters, Shooter and Jeep, and the female characters Lupe and Liza, who seem free by comparison. Focusing primarily on the men, Savran concludes that the action of the play remains within a traditional framework because the women are relegated to the background; therefore their potential for disrupting the rigid sphere of the males is effectively silenced. I envision a much more prominent and productive role for the female actors and characters, one that a careful reading of Shepard's stage directions oddly enough encourages. In Savran's interpretation the women "remain in the background," and he places them in the darkness upstage. But in fact Shepard has situated them in the same part of the stage Jeep occupies: that is, throughout most of the play all three characters are specifically placed down left center. And even though Shooter moves down right, Shepard eventually hides him behind a chair. The optimistic, fun-loving Lupe, by contrast, stands prominently on top of a chair at the end of the play. The freeing actions of the women, as represented in the script, are featured at least as much as the trapped actions associated with the men.

Furthermore, the actions of Lupe and Liza suggest that they refuse to acknowledge their supposed marginality, improvising a sense of community as they share their activity; for example, Lupe (the one who remembers the term "community") wears Liza's apron as they work together to hang the laundry. While they may be, as Savran states, "closed off in their activity," the women's sense of commu-

18. David Savran, "Sam Shepard's Conceptual Prison: *Action* and the Unseen Hand," *Theatrical Journal* 36, 1 (1984): 57–75.

nity suggests a refusal to allow the Other, the men who watch them, to destroy their fun. They have abandoned their attempt to find their place in the male script (the book onstage), exiting the patriarchal world, and therefore no longer see themselves as supplemental beings.[19]

Instead of focusing on the primacy of Shepard's presence in the text, thereby emphasizing the actions of the male characters and the patriarchal frame, my director works with the female and male actors in such a way that the women are at least equally prominent in their action and equally visible to the audience. Taking a cue from Rauschenberg's combines, this director juxtaposes the mutually disruptive elements represented by the female and male characters without resolving them into a hierarchy, without directing our gaze toward one at the cost of marginalizing the other. A feminist director of *Buried Child* may focus on the ironic fact that Vince is forced to assume his role in the patriarchal lineup precisely because he cannot perceive the double lines of action, the wedge between the real and the not-real. He cannot see himself as the child buried by the patriarchy, and therefore must enact over and over again the "lie of the mind." By emphasizing the split between the two lines of action in *Buried Child,* the feminist director can prompt the audience to want Vince to "devour" this dysfunctional family and find a new self rather than submit to its infantilizing anaesthesia.

Significantly, Shelly *does* escape, rejecting both of these framing lines of action. Her escape may, of course, be viewed as the necessary ejection of a sexual threat to the male transfer of power, but in fact she often voices the projected audience's viewpoint, thereby allowing spectators a means of rejecting the patriarchal narrative. She does "quote" the role of mother for a moment but, unlike Halie, she abandons it and leaves for good when violence erupts. As she exits, she mocks Vince: "You want to stay *here?*" and impatiently quizzes him about his fate, asking in disgust, "What happened to you Vince?

19. See Jacques Derrida, "The Supplement of Origin," in *Speech and Phenomena: And Other Essays on Husserl's Theory of Signs,* trans. David B. Allison (Evanston: Northwestern University Press, 1973), pp. 88–90, 150. This strategy unfortunately does not work to deconstruct gender issues in all of Shepard's scripts. In *Fool for Love,* for example, there are two actions jammed together, but both reside within the old man's mind, that is, within the patriarchal narrative.

You just disappeared" (p. 70). The audience may well agree. In the 1983 Arena Stage production directed by Gilbert Moses, Christina Moore played Shelly as a strong-willed woman whose initial hilarity at the very idea of family transforms into a wary and absolute disbelief in and rejection of the myth of patrilineage. Her portrayal usefully highlights the female character's powerful exit through the fluctuating frame, an action that colors and potentially controls the audience's perception of the family myths examined in the play. The production photo of Moore as Shelly exiting the stage is posed, and therefore somewhat stilted, but it nonetheless conveys the contemptuousness that marked Moore's performance in that moment, her disdain for and commentary on the ongoing action. (See figure 9.) Moore's characterization of Shelly's exit contrasts sharply with Betsy Scott's approach to Shelly's departure in the authorized San Francisco Magic Theatre premiere: Scott's Shelly left, as Lynda Hart remarks, and as the photographic evidence demonstrates, "despondently," saddened by her boyfriend's abandonment of her.[20]

Lorraine and Sally, the mother and daughter transformed into female friends in *A Lie of the Mind,* also subversively walk out on the world of men, a world in which women are brutally victimized. They torch the house where Lorraine waited for her profligate husband and her violent son to give meaning to her life. Although Sally is concerned that they are "not gonna have any place to come back to" after their trip to search for new roots in Ireland, Lorraine dispels her fears with the absolute finality of her rejection of the male-defined home: "Who's comin' back?" she retorts.[21]

Shepard's splintering of the dramatic action fragments many of his characters, particularly male characters, so that they act as signs *sous rature* (under erasure), to borrow a phrase from Derrida.[22] For example, the contradictory actions in *Buried Child* explode the possi-

20. See Lynda Hart, *Sam Shepard's Metaphorical Stages* (New York: Greenwood Press, 1987), p. 65, fig. 2.

21. Sam Shepard, *A Lie of the Mind* (New York: New American Library, 1986), p. 120.

22. See Jacques Derrida, *Of Grammatology,* trans. Gayatri Chakravorty Spivak (Baltimore: Johns Hopkins University Press, 1976), pp. 18–19, 60–61, 66–67, 75, for his various uses of *sous rature,* as well as his essay "Difference," in *Speech and Phenomena,* pp. 158–60, for his discussion of Heidegger's explanation of the concept in terms of Being.

Figure 9. Christina Moore as Shelly in *Buried Child* (1983), photo by George de Vincent, courtesy Arena Stage

bility of viewing Vince as a unified character and call into question the very notion of representational characters. (Is the corpse real in the same way that the grown son is? Which body "represents" the character Vince?) Gayatri Chakrovorty Spivak offers an explanation of the concept of erasure in terms of writing, an explanation that helps clarify Shepard's handling of character: "My predicament is an analogue for a certain philosophical exigency that drives Derrida to writing 'sous rature,' which I translate as 'under erasure.' This is to write a word, cross it out, and then print both word and deletion. (Since the word is inaccurate, it is crossed out. Since it is necessary, it remains legible.) . . . In examining familiar things we come to such unfamiliar conclusions that our very language is twisted and bent even as it guides us. Writing 'under erasure' is the mark of this contortion."[23] A similar impulse drives Shepard to place a question mark after the term "character" as he records this sequence of dramatic elements: "timing, rhythm, shape, flow, character (?), form, structure, etc."[24] The playwright must use the word "character," since it is the closest he can come to signifying his idea, but at the same time he seeks to indicate its inaccuracy: he suggests something by way of "character" that is different from what is customarily signified. (Notice also that "structure," presumably in its traditional sense, comes last for Shepard.) Like Strindberg, who associated character with the concept of soul, or Brecht, who discussed character in terms of *gestus,* Shepard is trying to articulate his own idea of character.

In the preface to his 1976 play *Angel City,* Shepard describes the concept of character he has in mind for that play, a useful concept for an actor approaching any Shepard character. The playwright advises performers to think of characters in a nontraditional way, abandoning the Stanislavsky method for a different creative strategy:

> Instead of the idea of a "whole character" with logical motives behind his behavior which the actor submerges himself into, he should consider instead a fractured whole with bits and pieces of character flying off the central theme. In other words, more in

23. Gayatri Chakravorty Spivak, "Translator's Preface," in Derrida, *Of Grammatology,* p. xiv.
24. Sam Shepard, "Time," in Marranca, *American Dreams,* p. 211.

terms of collage construction or jazz improvisation. This is not the same thing as one actor playing many different roles, each one distinct from the other (or "doubling up" as they call it), but more that he's mixing many different underlying elements and connecting them through his intuition and senses to make a kind of music or painting in space without having to feel the need to completely answer intellectually for the character's behavior.[25]

Shepard himself, then, encourages performers to avoid thinking of his characters as psychological entities in the tradition of Ibsen, with clearly demarcated, if contradictory, motivations. Instead he sees his characters as collages, "paintings in space," precisely the description of Robert Rauschenberg's combines.

But what elements are combined to create Shepard characters? How might we think about the particular brand of character the playwright seeks to create? Perhaps we can turn from the customary psychological and ethical associations of the term "character" to two other, equally important but perhaps less frequently discussed functions of the term: character as "figure" (the German term *dramatische Figur* emphasizes this pictorial facet of character), and character as "word" (as a Japanese or Chinese character is not just a drawing but also a word).

Relying on Joseph Chaikin's transformational improvisations, in which actors embraced wildly different characters in quick succession, Shepard constructs characters as if they were wrenched from other contexts, pasted together as collages of figures or words, "combines" of image and language. In *Angel City* the character-as-figure constantly shifts, as the characters assume new roles from moment to moment, transforming their physical appearance as well as their relationship to the play's action. The play, then, becomes a Rauschenbergian combine of these various pictures of the characters. These improvisational characterizations differ from Strindberg's transforming characters because they are represented not as the result of recurring cosmic forces or the manifestation of evasive illusions but as fully articulated, real, "found" characters suddenly, spontaneously, and unexpectedly appearing onstage.

A similar process occurs in *Buried Child*, but in a submerged and

25. Sam Shepard, *Angel City, Curse of the Starving Class, and Other Plays* (New York: Urizen Books, 1978), p. 6.

more complicated fashion. Feminist directors in particular may profit from attending to the combine construction of male characters within the patriarchal myth in Shepard because, by virtue of their very construction, these characters may be shown to be participating in a myth, a lie subject to the possibility of change. In *Buried Child* the figural presence of Vince as a character is slowly but carefully built as a combine construction, culminating in the final moments of the drama. When Vince's father, Tilden, finally tramps onto the stage cradling his baby son's corpse, the grown son is lying prone on the couch center stage as immobile as a corpse but with his averted eyes open. After Shelly's exit, then, and her claim that Vince has "disappeared," Shepard presents the audience with *two* figures, both of whom have been identified as Tilden's son and may be understood as the character Vince. The two Vinces coexist in a non-realistic "combined" rendering of the moment, as the audience attempts to place them, to find the proper perspective from which to view the character Vince, who exists, by virtue of the corpse onstage, "under erasure." Furthermore, Vince's character has already been split by his two very different entrances—in act two as prodigal son and in act three as commando. The audience must juxtapose those two images of Vince in an effort to make sense of them.

In fact, Shepard hints at Vince's splintered figural presence even earlier in the play. Before Vince arrives onstage in act two, Tilden returns from his search for the buried child armed with freshly picked corn and carrots. Since the family farm has not been tilled for four decades, these vegetables function as found objects. They are curiously unreal on the spare stage, just as the real stuffed goat in Rauschenberg's *Monogram* becomes unreal because of its juxtaposition with another plane of reality. In a move that compounds this unreality, Tilden carefully places the husks from the corn on top of Dodge's sleeping body. This action counterposes two seemingly unrelated elements, Dodge's body (which has become in part an object) and the corn husks which Tilden somehow found out back. But since the husks take the place of the buried child, they also prefigure Vince's character. Tilden is thus figuratively returning the son to the patriarch of the family, offering a gift as well as a burial.

Shepard even puts the character-as-figure under erasure: he goes so far as to question Vince's credibility as a figure with stage presence. Not only do his father and grandfather not recognize him, but in act two Dodge pretends, seconds after Vince leaves on an errand, that this young man on a quest to reconnect with his family never existed: "Recognize who?" he asks (p. 44). In contrast, Tilden seizes the opportunity created by Vince's presence to use him as a picture frame in which he can place the buried child: "I thought I recognized him. I thought I recognized something about him. . . . I thought I saw a face inside his face" (p. 44). Vince earlier has tried to fight this refusal to acknowledge his visible presence with visual tricks, childhood strategies through which he hopes to gain attention and so trigger his family's memories of him. He shows his father and grandfather how he can still bend his thumb behind his knuckles, drum on his teeth, and transform his belly button into a talking cartoon mouth, but all to no avail. In disgust Shelly chastises him: "Vince, don't be pathetic will ya'! . . . Jesus Christ. They're not gonna play" (p. 41). She reminds the audience, through her debunking, once again, of the family myth—through her awareness of its performative nature—that Vince is trying to enact a lie. When Vince returns later in act three, his family suddenly recognizes him, but now he cannot recognize himself, let alone his family. "Vincent who?" he calls in answer to Halie; "What is this! Who are you people? (p. 67). To maintain the disjointedness of his combine construction, Shepard calls into question the character as figure just as surely as he establishes it.

By juxtaposing these fragmented views of his characters, he tries to control audiences' reactions to his work in a manner different from that of Ibsen, for example, whose characters enact the melodramatic images that others have of them. In *A Doll's House* Ibsen builds a costume party into his script, placing Nora onstage as the Capri dancing doll that Helmer would like to believe she is. But unlike Vince in *Buried Child,* Nora is seen to assume that vision at another character's prompting, with an increasing awareness of its distortion of her fuller, more psychologically complicated self. Vince's visual transformation into the "Midnight Strangler," in contrast, seems to have been forced on him by the playwright or from within, and it turns his character into a figural fragment that explodes onto the stage like a shell fragment of an exploding patriarchy. Moreover, whereas the audience sees Nora again after she has changed her costume, we do not witness the peculiar double figuration presented by the final images of Vince as corpse and usurper.

Shepard's strategy of presenting the character as figure can also be distinguished from Pinter's filmic and holographic strategies, used, for example, in *Old Times*. Although Pinter's Kate and Anna might be read as two aspects of the same character (and thus compared to the two Vinces at the end of *Buried Child*), in production we see Kate and Anna as two separate characters, both fully alive, each with distinct motivations. Vince, by contrast, is split into a live figure and a dead figure, embodying the unreal quality that emerges in so much of Shepard's work, from *Cowboys #2* on.

As figures rather than psychologically realistic representations of whole selves, Shepard's characters use words primarily to create images of themselves, to discover visions that they can inhabit. Thus the idea of character-as-figure is supplemented in Shepard by the concept of character-as-word. But the promise of meaning, like Derrida's signified, is for the most part delayed, dependent on context. Even Tilden understands the crucial relation of word to character: he warns Dodge, "Well, you gotta talk or you'll die" (p. 25). Tilden survives by virtue of establishing his presence in his story about the buried child, whereas Dodge dies the moment he completes his spoken will. Vince, too, relies heavily on words to envision himself. In a typical Shepard aria, the long, syncopated visionary speech delivered "front" which appears in virtually every Shepard play, Vince creates in words his figural transformation from prodigal son to corpse. Having returned (in act three) from a lengthy drive, he says:

> I could see myself in the windshield. My face. My eyes. I studied my face. Studied everything about it. As though I was looking at another man. As though I could see his whole race behind him. Like a mummy's face. I saw him dead and alive. . . . And then his face changed. His face became his father's face. Same bones. Same eyes. Same nose. Same breath. And his father's face changed to his Grandfather's face. And it went on like that. Changing. Clear back to faces I'd never seen before but still recognized. Still recognized the bones underneath. The eyes. The breath. The mouth. I followed my family clear into Iowa. Every last one. Straight into the Corn Belt and further. Straight back as far as they'd take me. Then it all dissolved. Everything dissolved. (pp. 70–71)

In this seemingly improvised speech Vince first recognizes himself simply as his own picture in the windshield, the Vince that Shelly knows. But the words, like the images they describe, carry him away as he then envisions himself "dead and alive" at the same time, precisely as he is at the end of the play. Through words he merges his own image with those of his father and grandfather, until he disappears at the end of the aria, subsumed by the family line. Like many of Shepard's characters, he performs various ideas of himself as figure and as word, playing this game in the hope of finding himself. His manipulation of language, particularly in the aria, differs drastically from the way in which Pinter's characters employ words, for unlike them, he does not direct the words toward changing someone else's behavior, nor does he have absolute control over them. Like the characters in countless Shepard plays, Vince seems to be transported as well as created by the words, which themselves possess a driving force.

This mode of characterization again recalls the combine: Shepard's characters seize one self, then another, and juxtapose them, often without explanation but almost always with full intensity and complete commitment. They continually seek a locus where they are fully present, but they fail time and again, destined to rely on others and on the context in which they move for the very thing they seek: significance. As Shepard remarks, "People are starved for a way of life—they're hunting for a way to be or to act toward the world."[26]

So play—or more precisely performance—constitutes the very act of creation for Shepard's characters. Instead of surveying all their options, as, for example, Pinter's characters do, Shepard's characters jump first in one direction and then another, often in response to a force beyond them. Nor do they seem as focused on other characters as Pinter's are; everything seems to depend on their willingness to commit themselves spontaneously and totally, if only momentarily, to an intuitive language and to the visions they have of themselves at any particular moment: "The characters *act themselves out*, even *make themselves up*, through the transforming power of their imagination."[27] Furthermore, they do so publicly, unlike, say, Ibsen's furtive

26. Quoted in Kakutani, "Myths."
27. Bonnie Marranca and Gautam Dasgupta, *American Playwrights: A Critical Survey* (New York: Urizen Books, 1978), p. 83.

characters Hedda and Nora, who carry on unspoken dialogues within themselves, often seeking to hide their private selves. Shelly, like
Vince, speaks her story aloud; there is no reluctance to share the
process of self-discovery, though Shepard's arias are not directed to
anyone in particular.

In building this kind of character Shepard capitalizes on precisely
what it is that creates an actor: living fully in the moment, unaware
of what is to come, occupying the gaps between the self and the
other, whether that other is an aspect of a character or an acting
partner. And as a result of this concept of character and the combine
structure from which it emerges, Shepard invites to his stage a new
brand of actor: the improvisational actor. Since Shepard's plays often do not follow one cohesive superobjective or central action, the
actor may find the search for a spine or a unifying objective a frustrating and useless exercise. In fact, with Shepard, as Robert Woodruff suggests, "There's something about trying to motivate an action
that weakens it, not letting it be what it is itself."[28] But what is the
action "itself"? Perhaps in Shepard the action is play, and so the
actor may simply yield, as one director puts it, "to the idea of 'playing at doing a play.'"[29] The actors' own need to perform, to play, to
imagine, may be—more than is customarily the case—the actors'
starting point. The images that abound in Shepard's plays trigger
for the character the drive to elaborate, improvise, explore the experience of the image; and the actor (or, by extension, the reader) can
perhaps draw the character most fully by relying on the joy that
results from trying out new versions of oneself, without attempting
to explain away the curious transformations within the script.

Joyce Aaron, who performed in several of Shepard's early plays,
emphasizes the need to act as if there were no script, no preplanned
sequence to fix the center and therefore the significance of the
character:

> Very often, he provides you with no transitions. As an actor, you
> have to live the moment as his plays give it to you—and you have to
> live it as experience, not as history or chronicle. You have to trust
> that moment and the language which he has captured in sporadic

28. Quoted in Coe, "Interview with Robert Woodruff," p. 156.
29. Jim Sharman, quoted in Chubb, "Fruitful Difficulties," p. 24.

resonances and reverberations. Unless you trust the reality that he sets up, you can't play him as he demands to be played. And from the very second you enter into one of his moments, you have to give that moment the fullest state it calls for. . . . You can't impose some linear line on the chain of his moments for your own pleasure or satisfaction.[30]

Although an actor in any play must focus on the present to create a character successfully, with Shepard this task is especially difficult because the character—and the actor—is usually not in control within the moment. The characters' fragmented language, particularly in Shepard's typical monologues, or their physical excesses (such as Wesley's food binge in *Curse of the Starving Class*) threaten to sweep them, and hence the actors, into what Shepard (in *Suicide in B Flat*) calls a "new dimension." Unlike Pinter's arrogant characters, who exercise their power over fellow characters and audience alike by choosing their own roles at any given moment, Shepard's characters, like the audience, are powerless to halt the disjointed movements of their play, just as they cannot fix their ideas of themselves.

Female actors may permit themselves to be swept, along with their characters, into this "new dimension," or they may critique the process, as I witnessed Kathy Baker do in Shepard's own New York production of *Fool for Love*. Confronted with the stage direction "she pounds her thighs," Baker, improvising, instead alternately pounded on and clung to the walls of the set, at one point escaping around a corner of the set. In breaking the convention of the stage set, she reminded the audience that she was a female actor who was, like her character May, seeking a way out of a scripted self. Playing opposite her, Ed Harris extended this device by also pounding the walls, as if he (as an actor) wanted to escape the set as much as Eddie, his character, sought to flee the room.[31] Not surprisingly, Shepard recorded these improvisations, incorporating them in the published version of the script as stage directions.

Since Shepard's characters, like professional actors, live by performing various fragments of themselves, Shepard's improvisational

30. Joyce Aaron, "Clues in a Memory," in Marranca, *American Dreams*, p. 171.
31. See Eleanor Blau, "Stars of 'Fool for Love' Find Success Can Hurt," *New York Times*, June 10, 1983, sec. C, p. 3.

actor may gain a sense of immediacy by allowing the audience to become aware of the game of performing. But unlike the Brecht Collective's parabolic actor, who uses an alienation effect to comment on the character, Shepard's actors are commenting on the audience, the real performers of the text. These actors suggest not just the strangeness but also the familiarity of the process of play, the excitement as well as the terror of being forced to live in the present, and the tension we all sense between openness and closure in our own lives.

Audiences are likely to be divided in response to the work of Shepard's actors, primarily because so much depends on the perspective from which they view a given Shepard performance. Walter Kerr, among others, finds this phenomenon distressing, calling Shepard's audience a cult that is divided against itself "in an odd but unmistakable way. At every Shepard play I have seen, a portion of the audience—a minority perhaps, but a determined one—has treated the work as a comedy, forcing giggles and twitters regularly as though in support of their man. Another portion treats the work before it with entire sobriety. People whose opinions I respect are to be found in both camps. . . . I find *that* disconcerting. I can understand a cult, its causes and perhaps its consequences. What I cannot quite understand is a split cult, re-subdivided."[32]

But this divided response is to be expected from an audience that is asked to view a combine construction directed toward what Robert Woodruff calls a "polytheistic" audience: "We worship different ideals, gods, world views, myths at different moments."[33] Such a response allows viewers to react depending on the circumstances of the moment, on how they frame the action at hand. For example, directors and spectators who choose to focus on Shooter and Jeep instead of Lupe and Liza may rightly protest the patriarchal frame of that aspect of the script. But they have the power to negotiate meaning in an alternative fashion: to choose, for example, to highlight the women's interaction. Similarly, given some assistance from the actors and

32. Walter Kerr, "Where Has Sam Shepard Led His Audience?" *New York Times,* June 5, 1983, sec. 2, p. 16.

33. Robert Woodruff on David L. Miller, *The New Polytheism,* in Scott Cumming, "American Directors on Directing: The Second Generation," *Theater* (formerly *Yale/theatre*) 15, 2 (1984): 65.

directors, audiences of *Buried Child* or *A Lie of the Mind* can choose to frame the plays through Shelly or Sally and Lorraine's final viewpoint. In seeking to make his audience experience viewing as a kind of performing, Shepard ultimately seeks to place the audience in the position of the writer. For, like many of his contemporaries, Shepard believes that the writer, in the search for meaning, "has to come back to the point where he feels he knows nothing at all about the heart of what he's after."[34] In depriving the actor, director, and audience of a definitive frame for the actions he jumbles together, Shepard puts them in the place where he insists any writer must begin, and from there the female actor, director, or audience member may start to refashion the patriarchal script.

34. Shepard, "Time," p. 211. To invoke only one of his contemporaries who has much to say about writing, Derrida describes the goal of his search for meaning in strikingly similar terms: "I am trying, precisely, to put myself at a point so that I do not know any longer where I am going." Jacques Derrida, quoted in "Discussion" following "Structure, Sign, and Play in the Discourse of the Human Sciences," in *The Structuralist Controversy: The Languages of Criticism and the Science of Man,* ed. and trans. Richard Macksey and Eugenio Donato (Baltimore: Johns Hopkins University Press, 1970), p. 267.

Chapter Six

Beckett and the *Nō* Actor

In August 1982 the NOHO Theatre Group of Kyoto, Japan, produced the British premieres of Samuel Beckett's *Rockaby* and *Ohio Impromptu* at the Edinburgh Festival and at the National Theatre in London. Performing in Japanese, the troupe employed the acting style they had learned from their training in classical fourteenth-century *nō* and farcical *kyōgen* acting, fusing it with techniques and, of course, the Beckett scripts borrowed from the West.[1] It is no accident that they chose to explore Samuel Beckett's scripts rather than those of, say, Harold Pinter or Sam Shepard. Critics have commonly regarded Beckett as a major dramatist of the nuclear age, a playwright whose bleak world reflects this particular moment in Western civilization, but his last plays suggest that his vision, like that of his countrymen Yeats and Synge, encompasses the distant past as well as the present, the East as well as the West. Despite the playwright's self-confessed lack of training in Eastern theatrical traditions, Beckett's final work for the theatre uses structural properties and production techniques that encourage an acting and directing approach similar to that found in traditional Japanese *nō* drama and theatre.[2] In *Footfalls* and *Rockaby*, to cite the two primary examples

1. "Beckett and *Kyōgen:* NOHO Tours U.S.," *Theatre News* (May 1984): 7. In 1986 the NOHO troupe produced *Quad I & II* at the American Folk Theatre in New York City, and the following year Jonah Salz directed NOHO in *Theatre I.*
2. "I am not at all acquainted with Noh drama or Oriental Theatre in general and have made no attempt to use such techniques in my plays." Samuel Beckett, quoted in

under consideration here, Beckett utilizes novelistic narrative devices to create spiraling dramatic structures similar to those used by Zeami Motokiyo, the early fifteenth-century father of *nō* drama and acting theory. Through these devices Beckett moves toward creating a *nō*-like performance situation and style marked by paradox, mystery, and strict control.

Beckett's narratives, like Zeami's, frequently enable his characters to distance themselves from the unbearable but necessary pain of consciousness as they seek peace from their own unrelenting will. Both dramatists complement their narration with distinctive production techniques onstage: masks, dance, music. In Beckett's last scripts the characters' immobilized faces act as *nō* masks, and their carefully choreographed patterns of ritualized movements bear a striking resemblance to *nō* dances. Beckett's characters also accent their narratives with percussive sounds, providing a music akin to the customary *nō* drum accompaniment. Furthermore, the stylized acting required by the *nō*, based on restraint, presents a possible paradigm for those performing Beckett scripts (whether in their own minds or onstage). Zeami's concept of opposition in acting, the idea that every stage attitude must also convey its opposite, applies as well to the customary stance of Beckett actors, who often reveal characters' longing for oblivion—for the destruction of the voice— while at the same time hinting at their sometimes humorous determination to prolong the pain. Like *nō* masters, Beckett actors are prompted to crystallize their experience, to capture the essence of the human condition in a single economical and paradoxical gesture or turn of the head. And, like Zeami, Beckett attempted to maintain control over the staging of his scripts by directing them himself or by codifying the instructions for their performance, thereby trying to

---

Leonard Pronko, *Theatre for East and West: Perspectives Toward a Total Theatre* (Berkeley: University of California Press, 1967), p. 106. When Beckett was asked more than a decade later, in 1981, if *nō* had influenced his work, he replied more evasively: "Not consciously." Samuel Beckett, quoted in Yasunari Takahashi, "The Theatre of Mind: Samuel Beckett and the Noh," *Encounter* 58, 4 (1982): 68. Ed Menta illuminates this switch in Beckett's stance in "Samuel Beckett in a Noh Light: Selected Plays Read Through Critical Principles of the Noh Theatre," *Theatre Studies* 35 (1990): 51–63. Menta examines an early, a middle, and a late play in terms of various *nō* techniques. The work of Takahashi and Menta came to my attention after I was well launched on writing this chapter, and I was encouraged to discover that Takahashi, Beckett's Japanese translator, as well as Menta share my sense that Beckett is illuminated by an intertextual reading of the scripts through *nō*.

predetermine the role played by his directors, artists who, interestingly enough, are not required for the production of *nō* drama.

Both Zeami and Beckett wrote primarily one-act plays with small casts, minimal scenery, and few stage properties, which are generally produced with a couple of other works by the same author. They frequently focus on central characters who attempt to escape a purgatorial state by telling agonizing stories about themselves. There is a static quality to their dramas, as the stories are related in a spiraling fashion: told, retold, then retold yet again, as more details emerge and the voices that tell the stories multiply and divide in complex sequences.

A close examination of two specific scripts, the phantasmal *nō* play *Nonomiyo* by Zeami and *Footfalls* by Beckett, reveals particularly striking correspondences, and enables us to see more clearly the conventions of structure and performance that have emerged from Beckett's work and their implications for female actors. In both plays a ghostlike woman returns to what is (or appears to be) a sacred space in the hope of silencing her inner voice, a will or spirit that drives her to reconsider old passions and attachments. In *Nonomiyo* a priest (the *waki* or secondary character) arrives at the shrine of Nonomiyo at twilight to discover the ghost of the woman Miyasudokoro (the *shite* or principal character), who tells and retells, with the help of the *waki* and the chorus, the story of her jilting.[3] She eventually achieves a release from her torture through the priest's prayers. In *Footfalls* an offstage "Woman's Voice," figured in the opening dialogue as a ninety-year-old mother (the *waki*) oversees her daughter May (the *shite*), as the forty-year-old May paces methodically back and forth across the stage, telling and retelling, with the help of the Voice, the story of (possibly) another jilting. The prematurely aged, tattered May has been abandoned, however, not by a nobleman, as Miyasudokoro was, but by a vague and nonmaterial presence which some may be tempted to call the divine. Not yet born and not capable of a definitive death, May paces the stage, head bowed, in a tiny figure eight, a piece of infinity. Her stooped figure resembles Kom-

---

3. Zeami Motokiyo, *Nonomiyo*, trans. Stephen Comee, in Kunio Komparu, *The Noh Theater: Principles and Perspectives*, trans. Jane Corddry, rev. ed. (New York: Weatherhill/Tankosha, 1983), pp. 304–25. All subsequent references are to this edition and are cited by page in the text.

paru Zenchiku's illustration labeled "a dance appropriate for a Woman's role," as pictured in Zeami's *nō* treatise *Nikkyoku santai zu* ("Illustrations for the Two Basic Arts and Three Role Types").[4] (See figure 10.) Whereas Zeami's heroine achieves a tentative salvation in the closing scene of *Nonomiyo,* however, Beckett's May simply disappears. The offstage Voice cannot serve as a true *waki,* a priest to pacify May's spirit and lead her to nirvana. May has to rely on her own *waki,* her own inner voice, in her attempt—and I think it remains an attempt—to exorcise her own spirit in her search for nothingness.

In Beckett's *Footfalls,* as in Zeami's *Nonomiyo,* the main character is not fully alive but not yet dead; not there but, to the character's distress, nonetheless present through a voice, or, as in the case of *nō,* through a ghost. This voice or shadowy presence is simultaneously the "I" and the "Not I," "one's deepest self" and "the other," emerging from "an unknown 'sacred' country that Beckett, in *Ohio Impromptu,* calls the 'profounds of the mind.'"[5] As John Pilling notes, "Though far from being a Buddhist, [Beckett] can quote Gautama's 'mad wisdom' with such relish in his essay 'Henry Hayden; homme peintre': 'Gautama . . . said that one is fooling oneself if one says that the "I" exists, but that in saying it does not exist, one is fooling oneself no less.'"[6]

This paradox informs all of Beckett's work, certainly, but it seems especially prominent in his last plays, which frequently focus on women. If the voice or ghost could be silenced in the Beckett or *nō* dramas, all would be well: if May's consciousness could stop "revolving it all," as the Voice describes their ghostly pacing through the past, or if Miyasudokoro's ghost could be pacified, the women would be put out of their misery, as well as their only source of pleasure. The voices of the mother and the *waki,* and the third-person voices of the characters themselves, would no longer need to puzzle through or report their histories. This exorcism, however, can be

4. See J. Thomas Rimer and Yamazaki Masakazu, trans., *On the Art of the Nō Drama: The Major Treatises of Zeami* (Princeton: Princeton University Press, 1984), pp. li–lii.

5. Yasunari Takahashi, "Qu'est-ce qui arrive? Some Structural Comparisons of Beckett's Plays and Noh," in *Samuel Beckett: Humanist Perspectives,* ed. Morris Beja, S. E. Gontarski, and Pierre Astier (Columbus: Ohio State University Press, 1983), p. 106.

6. John Pilling, *Samuel Beckett* (London: Routledge and Kegan Paul, 1976), p. 122.

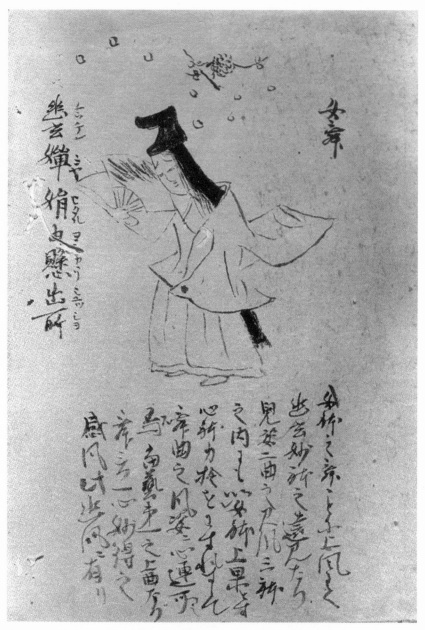

Figure 10. "A dance appropriate for a Woman's role," drawing by Komparu Zenchiku for Zeami's treatise *Nikkyoku santai zu* (Illustrations for the Two Basic Arts and Three Role Types), courtesy Hosei University Institute of Nohgaku Studies

accomplished only through the voices of the ghosts themselves relinquishing control, through the kind of will-lessness described by both Schopenhauer and the Buddha. As Pilling writes:

> Beckett is in profound agreement with many of [Schopenhauer's] ideas. . . . Schopenhauer's arguments . . . resolve themselves into one basic conclusion: the less we exercise the will, the less suffering we endure. And if we are fortunate enough to actually silence the will for good, we will be restored to the ineffable peaceful condition of effective non-existence. The conclusion to *The World as Will and Idea* is only the most resonant of many similar passages, and it is a passage Beckett and his characters would unhesitatingly endorse: "to those in whom the will has turned and has denied itself, this our world, which is so real, with all its suns and milling ways— is nothing . . . time and space . . . subject and object; all are abolished. No will: no idea, no world; before us there is certainly only nothingness."[7]

In Buddhism this idea is formulated in different terms, of course, but the interim goal (ending suffering), if not the final one (achieving nirvana), is similar. The Noble Truths can end misery and bring about a kind of salvation: if life is suffering, and suffering is caused by desires, then ending desires will end suffering. Beckett and Schopenhauer, of course, stop short of the fourth Noble Truth (that the Eightfold Path is the way to end desires), but Beckett's characters, like Zeami's, grope their way out of this world toward the center, or, in Buddhist terminology, the *an-ātman*, the no-self.

Beckett's and Zeami's characters find it just as difficult to relinquish their consciousness, however, as do Strindberg's characters, lost in their karmic transformations. The Beckett figures attempt to reach truth, to silence their voices, partially through what Fritz Mauthner, an Austrian logical positivist, calls a critique of language. Pilling writes:

> According to Mauthner, ordinary language, which we cannot go beyond, is of no use to us in our quest for truth. Only in language do these two words "mind" and "body" exist, in reality they cannot

7. Ibid., p. 127.

be separated, says Mauthner; as a result the so-called self-observation has no organ. Since for Mauthner there is "no thinking without speaking," and since, when we speak, there is no distinguishing between the report and that which it is supposed to be a report of . . . we are continually uttering meaningless statements. Only by transcending the limits of language (which Mauthner considers impossible) will we get to know things as they really are. And this can only be achieved by a critique of language. . . . The critique's success coincides with its own destruction. . . . The critique tries, as Beckett tries, to say the unsayable.[8]

In *nō*, as in Beckett, this critique consists of an exposé of the circularity of language and of the ability of a storytelling voice to move from one character to another, from *shite* to *waki* or from May to her mother and back. (And if this can happen, how can we say there is one voice, one self?) Beckett fragments sentences as he creates a precise indirectness, often paralleling the quality of the Japanese language, which is "ill-suited to the direct expression of will."[9] Beckett also tries to silence the voices of his characters, an ultimate critique of language, just as the *waki* tries (more optimistically) to pacify and silence the ghost at the end of *Nonomiyo*. Here Beckett's dramaturgy contrasts with Strindberg's, despite the apparent superficial similarity in its compatibility with Eastern philosophy. Whereas Strindberg posits a godhead that has abandoned his characters, locked in their repetitive transformations, Beckett does not. His approach rests more easily in Buddhist than in Hindu thinking: the attempt to abolish desire leads in Beckett toward the no-self, not, as in Strindberg, toward the hope for release into the godhead Brahma or into a Christian heaven.

This critique of language is accompanied, in Beckett as in *nō*, by another, more elemental critique. Both Beckett and Zeami suggest, through their reliance on carefully controlled stage movement, the centrality of the body as well as the mind in the search for truth through will-lessness. They explore the possibility that Mauthner is only partially right, that one can, in fact, think without speaking. An actor can do so somatically, through bodily movement—May's pac-

8. Ibid., p. 128.
9. Komparu, *Noh Theater*, p. 215.

ing or the ghost's dancing. And just as their voices (tied to language) are subject to a critique of language, so too are May's and Miyasudokoro's movements subject to a critique in a *nō* phenomenon called the *i-guse,* the "non-dance."

In *Nonomiyo* the seated and immobile *shite* Miyasudoko delivers her "non-dance" by focusing in her mind on the beauty of the dance that she would normally perform at a particular moment in the play: she concentrates on the movements she does *not* engage in as she and the chorus tell her story. In a similar manner, May at one point in *Footfalls* halts and faces front, straining to move, concentrating on her nonexistent pacing as she and the Voice tell her story. Both Zeami and Beckett attempt to critique, to go beyond, not just the limits of language as a vehicle for the creation of meaning but also our customary perceptions of what the actor's body can do to create significant meaning within what might be called still movement. Like the Brecht Collective's hidden mandate to explore the body onstage in new ways, Beckett's *i-guse* asks his actors to reinvent the very idea of stage movement. As a playwright he exercised exacting control over actors' bodies, prompting through his structural strategies a unique performance style that required actors to internalize a technology of the body more rigorous, perhaps, than that demanded by any playwright preceding him.

Beckett's *Footfalls* resembles Zeami's *Nonomiyo* in more than just its story line and philosophical underpinnings. The plays are structurally similar as well. Both are loosely divided into five sections, each part telling the story of the play in miniature, so the plays encompass, in effect, a series of five spirals, each adding details but not changing the essence. Both playwrights vary the story just before the resolution through a metaphorical episode, and both employ unusual narrative devices within their circular structures, as if to distance their characters from their own voices and thus from their suffering.

The traditional introductory (*jo* and *ha*) sections of Zeami's *Nonomiyo* find no counterpart in Beckett: these scenes allow the priest (the *waki*) and Miyasudokoro (the *shite*) to introduce themselves in what would doubtless be too leisurely a fashion for Western audiences. Beckett's script opens instead with a section corresponding to the first half of the third (developmental *ha*) part of Zeami's work, the opening dialogue between the *waki* and the *shite*. Just as Miyasudokoro begins conversing with the priest in that segment, May talks with her mother, each work considering at that point who the women are and why they are "revolving it all." The second half of this section corresponds to the second part of Beckett's script: in *Nonomiyo* the priest and the chorus gradually assume many of Miyasudokoro's lines, telling her story just as the Voice discloses the tale of May's past in *Footfalls*. Here May launches into her own *third-person* narrative about her pacing: "Sequel. . . . A little later, when she was quite forgotten."[10] At a corresponding moment in the fourth (concluding *ha*) section of *Nonomiyo*, Miyasudokoro also employs the third-person pronoun, calling herself a "nonexistent one" as she and the chorus retell her story (p. 314).

The next traditional section of the *nō*, the interlude, is missing from Beckett: there is no one to verify the identity of the ghost in *Footfalls* as the *ai* performer does Miyasudokoro's in the *nō*, nor is there anyone to ask the priest to pray for her, as there is in Zeami or in Strindberg. In the fifth and final *nō* movement, the *kyū*, Miyasudokoro tells a metaphorical story (the coach episode) which illustrates the belief that "nothing can escape the balancing of Karma,"[11] as the priest prays for and then delivers her salvation. Beckett's May also tells the "reader" her metaphorical story in the fourth section of *Footfalls* (casting herself, perhaps, as Amy and her mother as Mrs. Winter). In the fifth and final section of *Footfalls*, however, there is no salvation awaiting May. She is simply "not there." A strip of light promptly disappears, leaving nothing. The resolutions of the two plays differ, then, but not their basic structure: the women's stories are repeated within each of the five main sections of both dramas.

Like Zeami, Beckett achieves this spiraling structure at least in part by embedding complicated narrative patterns in his dramatic scenes: he links the "dead" past (the story told) to the "live" present (the story enacted), thereby staging the simultaneous nonexistence and existence of the story and the character's telling or reenacting of

10. Samuel Beckett, *Footfalls*, in *Collected Shorter Plays* (New York: Grove Press, 1984), p. 242. All subsequent references are to this edition and are cited by page in the text.

11. Komparu, *Noh Theater*, p. 323.

it. Beckett's May, like Zeami's Miyasudokoro, tries to distance herself from the agony of her situation by narrating her own story in the third person, sometimes finding her voice taken over by others (her mother, Mrs. Winter, Amy) who keep talking when she wants to disappear into oblivion. Frequently in Beckett these takeover voices are on tape, and are represented onstage only by a shaft of light or a megaphone, as in *Footfalls* and *What Where*. Zeami's ghosts also try to create a history for themselves while at the same time they desperately want to destroy that history. In *Footfalls* May initially refers to herself, naturally enough, in the first person, as she directs at least part of her consciousness outside herself: "Would you like me to inject you again?" she asks her aged mother (p. 240). Gradually, however, she addresses herself in the third person and then finally connects her identity to that of Amy, daughter of a fictional Mrs. Winter, whom the reader (one step removed from the present audience), she assures us, "will remember" (p. 243). In a similar manner, Miyasudokoro identifies herself: "*Nonexistent one . . .* that is *I* so *she* says" (pp. 314–15). Like May, she speaks of herself paradoxically in both the first and the third person, regarding herself as alive and dead at the same time. This narrative consciousness, a female voice that is not yet fully born but that refuses to die, forms the heart of more than one Beckett character. This unborn but overripe quality sets Beckett's characters apart from the characters that people the plays of the other writers I have considered. Beckett's fusion of first- and third-person narrative devices differs considerably from the Brecht Collective's employment of the third person. In Beckett the character speaks of herself as alive and dead, whereas the Brecht Collective actor speaks of the character as a creature capable of choice. Beckett's use of third-person narrative functions not to demonstrate a social gest and enable the audience to envision revolutionary change but rather to explore a philosophical, existential question and allow the audience to peer into a gap, a mystery.

Complicated storytelling strategies allow Beckett, like Zeami, to interweave the narrative past and the dramatic present. The action of Zeami's *Nonomiyo* may be summarized as retelling the story until one achieves nirvana, whereas the action of Beckett's *Footfalls* may be conceived as "revolving it all" until it stops or perhaps striving to tell (destroy) the story until one achieves nothingness. In both plays, then, the story is a self-destructing spiral, a critique of itself.[12] Even the conclusions of these stories (and their corresponding actions) may not be as different as they initially seem. The *shite* in a dream *nō* play would normally achieve salvation through the *waki*'s prayers, but Zeami closes *Nonomiyo* with the chorus's lines: "So once more into the / Flower coach [Miyasudokoro] steps, / Through the gate of the burning house, / As if about to leave / The burning house" (p. 325). As Kunio Komparu notes, Zeami concludes this particular script not with the traditional compulsory adjective but with a noun, *kataku* (burning house), which is "a Buddhist image for this earthly world."[13] He leaves us with the picture of Miyasudokoro frozen in the gateway between life and death, "as if about to leave" the earth but not, in fact, doing so. And, in another unusual break with tradition, Zeami refuses to repeat the final line of the play exactly, a device that normally serves "to bring the action to a final close."[14] He thus undercuts the certainty of Miyasudokoro's salvation, bringing her closer to Beckett's vision of May's end.

May cannot complete the action of her play, either: she cannot sufficiently "revolve it all"; she disappears without offering a solution to or final comment on the mystery of human consciousness in the universe.[15] No matter how many narrative voices she assumes, she cannot tell her whole story, any more than she can destroy it. She has to continue to circle around it, to pace out its measures, until she is no longer there. The audience leaves, still hearing the hauntingly precise voice of her will. In Beckett, then, the action repeats a tightly circumscribed dramatic ground with an intensification of the stakes at each tightening of the nooselike spiral. A strong will conflicts with

12. One of Beckett's favorite actors, Billie Whitelaw, recalls that she started work on the role of May by tapping out the lines of *Footfalls* "like a robot," but that "gradually something happens whereby my spine starts to spiral down as though I am disappearing. . . . That's the shape my body wants to take, of somebody who's spiraling inward." Quoted in Jonathan Kalb, *Beckett in Performance* (Cambridge: Cambridge University Press, 1989), p. 236.

13. Komparu, *Noh Theater*, p. 325.

14. Ibid.

15. When Billie Whitelaw (atypically) asked Beckett during London rehearsals for *Footfalls* in 1976 whether or not May had committed suicide, the playwright (typically) replied, "No . . . she is just not there." Ruby Cohn, *Just Play: Beckett's Theater* (Princeton: Princeton University Press, 1980), p. 200.

a stronger need to crush that will, until—as Beckett says in his staging notes for *Not I*—the main character's "vehement refusal to relinquish third person" effectively locks her into her circular story, ever returning to the narrative past for some semblance of meaning.[16]

Beckett's handling of dramatic action differs from that of Ibsen, Shepard, and Pinter. In Ibsen and Shepard the action of the play is not circular but bifurcated in various ways, in part because their narratives about the past serve as clues to the present, disclosing secrets that offer revelations. Nora in *A Doll's House* and Vince in *Buried Child,* for example, reveal through their first-person narratives information that clarifies, if complicates, their present situations. In Beckett the past is vaguer, not so much a clue as one of many retellings of the effort of the will to survive, to signify something, if only through its own destruction. In contrast, Pinter favors a filmic double exposure of his action, a dual enactment and creation of past and present—as when Kate and Anna slip into their girlhood in *Old Times* and Kate's jealous husband attempts to pull them back to his present. Pinter's plays move toward a precise if complex definition, whereas Beckett's raise more questions with each passing moment.

Beckett's spiraling structure and narrative devices touch not only the action but also the characters in *Footfalls.* The playwright uses his narration in part to remind us of the written word and therefore to suggest the primacy of the playwright. In *Footfalls* May presses "the reader" to remember Amy; in *Ohio Impromptu* the Reader actually appears onstage, eyes glued to the text; and even in *Catastrophe* the idea of a playwright is present in a note-taking Assistant. But by calling attention to narratives, and especially to the written word, onstage, Beckett does more than remind us of the playwright; he also calls attention to, and thereby empowers, the character as storyteller, thus ironically granting the actor, through the character, the presence he himself seeks to retain. He counteracts this process either by repeating the stories within the plays (as if to suggest the character's willful lack of inventiveness) or by splitting the narrator into two characters, who are, therefore, less powerful in and of themselves. Often he even forces a storyteller offstage, allowing only

16. Samuel Beckett, *Not I,* in *Collected Short Plays,* p. 215.

the voice onstage, as with the Woman's Voice in *Footfalls*. Like Zeami, he splits this storytelling voice between the *shite* and the *waki* or chorus, who have access to the *shite*'s innermost thoughts. In *What Where* the Voice of Bam is represented onstage by a megaphone; in his early play *Krapp's Last Tape* Beckett actually places the tape recorder that plays Krapp's past stories onstage, as Krapp listens to his own voice from the past. In *Not I* the Mouth and the Auditor; in *Rockaby* the (taped) Voice of the woman and the Woman; in *Ohio Impromptu* the Reader and the Listener: Beckett reworked this splitting and fusion of characters in countless ways.[17]

Beckett's scripts do not focus on character development, then, like Ibsen's; or a sudden revelation of character in the moment, as in Pinter; or even on a kaleidoscopic experience of various aspects of character, as in Shepard. Instead Beckett creates a static willfulness of character, an impasse between (1) the "immobile" part of the narrative voice, which wants to return to the past to retell the same story (a voice that is paradoxically often linked to a character's circular or repeated *movements* onstage); and (2) the part of the voice that feels the desire to move, to develop or intensify that same story (a voice frequently and ironically connected to a character's *immobilized* state onstage). In *Footfalls,* for example, May vacillates between (1) standing still as "V," the Voice, develops the story, and (2) pacing in a silencing or holding pattern within that same story. In *Not I* the Auditor's arms rise during the silences; in *Ohio Impromptu* the Listener's insistent knock occurs at breaks in the Reader's story, as physical movement seems forever to miss its connection with the specific voice that might be capable of complementing it and granting it true presence.

In production this static willfulness of character creates certain paradoxes in terms of the physical makeup of the actor as character, her movement, and her manner of speaking; these paradoxes become clearer when seen in terms of *nō* performance traditions. For example, when the male *nō* actor dons his customary mask, he is believed to be transformed into the character, as he "first denies the existence of physical facial expressions and then goes a step further to deny within his consciousness the existence of the mask."[18] Al-

17. For a discussion of the *shite* and *waki* in a number of Beckett's other plays, see Takahashi, "Qu'est-ce qui arrive?" pp. 103–6.
18. Komparu, *Noh Theater,* p. 17.

though Beckett's actors do not usually wear actual masks, Beckett frequently stipulates that his characters must resemble one another as closely as possible, as in *What Where* and *Ohio Impromptu*. And the most prominent Beckett-influenced American and British productions of his plays have repeatedly featured a select group of actors, including Billie Whitelaw and David Warrilow, who have developed an acting style that includes as one of its striking features masklike faces that are paradoxically immensely expressive.

As May in the New York production of *Footfalls*, for example, Whitelaw followed precisely the strategy of the *nō* actor described earlier, first denying the existence of mere realistic physical facial expressions by immobilizing her face, erasing the customary manifestations of realism, then denying that very immobility. (See figure 11.) Her face remained visibly "not there," until suddenly every muscle strained toward her final, hollow line "It all," which prompts her disappearance from the stage. Similarly, in *Rockaby* Whitelaw presented the Woman as a stuffed doll, masklike except for those moments when the light in her eyes seemed brighter as she called for "more" and when she slowly but surely allowed first her eyes and then the face within her "mask" to die at the close of the play. Those who saw David Warrilow perform in *Catastrophe* will recognize the same phenomenon of the mask: his Protagonist was a faceless victim until the final moment when his spirit seemed to escape his mask (indeed, his skull) to confront the audience with his transcendent accusatory stare. In promoting this *nō*-like mask work, these actors are paradoxically suggesting the Beckett character's frustrated desire for the oblivion of the "Not-I" and, at the same time, the character's terrible need and invincible will to break through the mask and mean something against all odds.

In Beckett, as in *nō*, the mask in performance is intimately connected with movement. Both Zeami and Beckett suggest the otherworldliness, the ghostlike presence of their actors by seeking to eliminate mimetic facial expression and by tightly controlling their actors' movements to an extent only hinted at in Pinter. Kunio Komparu maintains that the *nō* masks enable the actor to control the remainder of performance work more completely, thus evoking the true spirit of the character: "By covering the at best unruly facial expressions of the actor, expressions likely to waver in the concentration and excitement of performance, the mask frees him to commu-

Figure 11. Billie Whitelaw in *Footfalls* (1976), photo by Martha Swope

nicate a more accurate sense of the state of mind of the character through the movements of a highly trained body. . . . Noh masks . . . are thought of as having some spiritual, mystical significance. In this they approach the real meaning of 'mask' (which derives from the medieval Latin word for spectre): identifying the performer with the spirit of the character assumed."[19]

The mystical quality of many Beckett productions emerges from a variety of contributing factors, but certainly two of those elements are the masklike disposition of the actors' faces and their accompanying movements, which often seem as tightly choreographed and ritualized as the dances of a *nō* performer. The various torturers and tortured characters in *What Where*, going through their paces like May in *Footfalls*, for example, are enacting a dance of death that precedes them in its rules of movement, just as the *nō* characters reenact ancient dance patterns in an attempt to evoke the spirit of nature itself. The effect of these *nō*-like ritualized movements is often ghostly, to borrow the term Beckett used to describe Whitelaw's hunched shuffling in *Footfalls*, and is heavily dependent on the actor's restraint, her ability to control her body as tightly as she does her face—to internalize Beckett's surveillance.

According to Komparu the *nō* actor relies on the principle of restraint, and "the influence of Zen Buddhist thought is evident in this approach: each movement is reduced to its minimum, and therein lies the discovery of its perfection."[20] In *nō*, of course, this notion of restraint calls to mind the carefully perfected traditional dances and encoded gestures of the beautifully clad *nō* masters, and in Beckett it suggests gray-robed creatures who move little because they are simply unable to move more, and because there is nothing to be done. But Beckett actors may learn from the formalized composure of their *nō* counterparts. Zeami believed that "no matter how slight a bodily action, if the motion is more restrained than the emotion behind it, the emotion will become the substance and the movements of the body its function, thus moving the audience."[21] A standard rule of acting, this dictum is carried to its extreme in *nō*

19. Ibid., p. 224.
20. Ibid., p. 216.
21. Zeami Motokiyo, "A Mirror Held to the Flower" (*Kakyō*), in Rimer and Masakazu, *On the Art of the Nō Drama*, p. 75.

and in Beckett, until in fact "the times of action in Noh [and in Beckett] exist for the sake of the times of stillness."[22] May rarely walks and talks simultaneously, for example, and her unwilling pacing serves in large part to highlight her parallel desire to stop "revolving it all," her wish to remain still.

Acting in Beckett, like acting in *nō*, may be "a matter of doing just enough to create the *ma* that is a blank space-time where nothing is done, and that *ma* is the core of the expression, where the true interest lies."[23] After all, the presence of both May and Miyasudokoro serves to call attention to their absence from the space-time constructs that the Voice and the *waki* attempt to establish, as tenuous and shifting and dreamlike as those realities are. As a result, the Beckett actor, like the *nō* performer, is prompted to think in terms of oppositional gestures, not to create the social context or demonstrate choices as in Brecht Collective acting but rather to evoke the mystery of paradox. Under Beckett's direction in *Footfalls* Whitelaw used the same simple but oppositional gesture throughout much of her performance: she reached across her chest, clutching her hunched shoulder with one hand and grasping at her throat with the other, suggesting simultaneously a desperate attempt to comfort and sustain the child (or the voice) within her and an equally powerful effort to strangle herself, to slow herself down to a complete halt. She also contrasted her measured footfalls with the "exact sharp sound [Beckett] desired."[24] These strategies parallel Zeami's dictum supporting opposition in gesture: "When [an actor] moves himself about in a powerful way, he must stamp his foot in a gentle way. And when he stamps his feet strongly, he must hold the upper part of his body quiet."[25]

This restrained, oppositional approach to movement in performance supplements what Beckett and Zeami both identified as the key to the success of any movement onstage: novelty. Zeami associates *hana*, the flowering of an actor's artistic abilities, with fascination

22. Komparu, *Noh Theater,* p. 216.

23. Ibid., p. 73. See also p. 70: "Noh is sometimes called the art of *ma*. This word can be translated into English as space, spacing, interval, gap, blank, room, pause, rest, time, timing, or opening."

24. Cohn, *Just Play,* p. 269.

25. Zeami Motokiyo, "Teachings on Style and the Flower" (*Fūshikaden*), in Rimer and Masakazu, *On the Art of the Nō Drama,* p. 58.

and hence with the controlled novelty that he can create within each
nō gesture.[26] Beckett seeks actors who can find and then repeat a
novel gesture, perhaps to accentuate the circular quality of his narratives. He once complained that "producers don't seem to have any
sense of form in movement. The kind of form one finds in music,
for instance, where themes keep recurring. When in a text, actions
are repeated, they ought to be made unusual the first time, so that
when they happen again—in exactly the same way—an audience
will recognize them from before."[27]

Perhaps the most curious element of movement in *nō* and Beckett
performances, however, is the paradox presented by the *i-guse*, the
"non-dance."[28] At the climactic moment of the first part of *Nonomiyo*
Miyasudokoro crosses center stage to perform her *i-guse*, or seated
dance. "The beauty of this section of the play," writes Komparu, "lies
not in the grace of the dance movements but in the intense *yugen*
[grace] created by the actor as he quietly sits, concentrating with all
his heart on portraying the intricate and delicate beauty of the dance
without moving. This is an unusual form of acting based upon an
aesthetic of paradox, as the normal method of portraying the beauty
of this dance is by dancing it as in a *mai-guse* (dance *kuse*)."[29] Similarly, the immobile actor playing May can focus on her "dance" by
concentrating on the Voice's narrative about her. But whereas the *nō*
actor highlights the beauty of Miyasudokoro's *i-guse*, the Beckett
actor might be more likely to heighten the pain of May's *i-guse*.[30] In
both cases, however, mask and movement merge, and a third element, the voice, comes into play.

26. Yamazaki Masakazu, "The Aesthetics of Ambiguity: The Artistic Theories of
Zeami," in Rimer and Masakazu, *On the Art of the Nō Drama*, p. xxxiv.

27. Cohn, *Just Play*, p. 231.

28. Takahashi, "Qu'est-ce qui arrive?" pp. 104–5, mentions the *i-guse* in Beckett's
Eh Joe.

29. Komparu, *Noh Theater*, p. 314.

30. The *nō* actor, is, of course, male, and Beckett actor female, which helps explain
the probable choice of different emphases. Notice that this reading of Beckett's staging contrasts sharply with those critics who associate stillness with stasis, or who, like
Mary Doll, focus on the character's desire to leave the body to become pure soul. In
my view body and spirit are inextricable, as are motion and stillness. See Mary A. Doll,
"Walking and Rocking," in *Make Sense Who May: Essays on Samuel Beckett's Later Works*,
ed. Robin J. Davis and Lance St. J. Butler (Totowa, N.J.: Barnes and Noble, 1989), pp.
46–55.

The Beckett actor can also learn something from the *nō* performer's use of the voice, so central to the chants that characterize *nō* plays. In Beckett these *nō* chants become the slowed-down speech patterns, the repeated refrains, and the evocative sentence fragments that his characters so frequently intone: "It all" in *Footfalls* or "more" in *Rockaby*, for example. In plays by both Zeami and Beckett these chants require an atypical use of the voice. As Komparu notes, the *nō* voice "seems intense and 'swallowed' in comparison to the clear, 'projected' voice of Western singing," and the same description might fit the carefully controlled voices of many of Beckett's actors.[31] Beckett reportedly urged Rose Hill, the mother's Voice in the London and New York productions of *Footfalls*, "to speak more softly, to drain words of conventional emotion, and to time phrases like musical bars,"[32] thereby creating an analogue for the controlled, "unemotional" chant we associate with the *nō*. When he directed *Endgame* in Germany, Beckett also frequently asked his actors to eliminate vocal expression (*Ein-to-nig*) from their performances, specifying at the same time that his refrains be spoken identically: "In Beckett's *Endgame* text different characters speak the same old words, but more often they repeat their own words, and Beckett wanted such repetitions spoken identically."[33]

This does not mean that *nō* or Beckett actors are doomed to expressionless chant; rather, the emotion in the voice emerges from a nontraditional, nonrealistic framework very different from that of the Ibsen or Pinter actor. The "hollow, haunting groan" of Whitelaw's "It all" in *Footfalls* or the airy ghostliness of her "more" in *Rockaby* evoke and reveal as much emotion as a full-bodied, mimetic plea might, simply because they are as novel as the movement (or nonmovement) that accompanies them.[34]

For both the *nō* and the Beckett actor, breathing provides the technical key to this accomplishment. Zeami claimed that "to truly grasp the deep and true principles of the chant, one must first master the fundamentals of exhalation and inhalation, train the voice, learn to color the melodies, and thus arrive at immovable

31. Komparu, *Noh Theater*, p. 170.
32. Cohn, *Just Play*, p. 270.
33. Ibid., p. 242.
34. Ibid., p. 201.

heights of an art founded on a mastery of the breath."[35] While she was rehearsing for the part of the Mouth in *Not I,* Whitelaw discovered the very same centrality of the breath in acting Beckett: "In repeating the part aloud, Whitelaw conducted herself with hand, forefinger, or big toe. Until she evolved a breath rhythm, she might have a sudden dizzy spell during rehearsal: 'I would fall over at rehearsals; my jaw felt as though it had full army kit on. I know now how an athlete feels when his muscles become overtired. The jaw would not open and shut.'"[36] Although any voice coach would claim that good breath control is at the heart of every fine performance, it assumes special importance in *nō* and Beckett because of the unusual physical demands the actors commonly endure, whether in the role of the Mouth in *Not I* (shrouded in darkness, confined to absolute stillness, and strapped into a chair many feet above the ground), or the controlled dancing of Miyasudokoro.

In *nō,* of course, performance techniques such as the use of the mask, movement, and the voice are perfected by a small group of actors and musicians highly trained in the detailed, tradition-bound codes of performance. Their work demands a lifetime of dedication, and their artistic powers are perceived as intimately connected to the "interior spiritual power that lies within [them]."[37] As J. Thomas Rimer writes: "Zeami conceived of the Way of the *nō,* as he sometimes put it, in a manner similar to that of the Way of the *waka* poet or the Buddhist adept. The Way (*michi* in Japanese) suggests commitment, constant practice, and a genuine humility on the part of the one who is sincere in seeking a true path toward enlightenment or excellence."[38] This focus on inner enlightenment characterizes the actor David Warrilow's understanding of his work on Beckett, which he describes in mystical, *nō*-like terms: "There's a place in me that does Beckett, a place I go to in myself. . . . Everybody has in themselves a sanctuary that they can go to when they need deep

35. Zeami Motokiyo (notes taken down by Hata No Motoyoshi), "An Account of Zeami's Reflections on Art" (*Sarugaku dangi*), in Rimer and Masakazu, *On the Art of the Nō Drama,* p. 204.

36. Cohn, *Just Play,* p. 199.

37. Zeami Motokiyo, "Disciplines for the Joy of Art" (*Yūgaku shūdō fūken*), in Rimer and Masakazu, *On the Art of the Nō Drama,* p. 115.

38. J. Thomas Rimer, "The Background of Zeami's Treatises," in Rimer and Masakazu, *On the Art of the Nō Drama,* pp. xxi–xxii.

guidance. It's a place of natural knowing and inspiration. I have a place in me like that for this work."[39] This spiritual emphasis is coupled with a demand that the actors create for themselves a sense of ensemble, as Zeami instructed in "Learning the Way" (*Shūdōsho*): "The various skills of all the performers must be properly harmonized together."[40]

The world of Beckett production, of course, offers no centuries-old tradition dictating each element of performance, from the precise gesture to signify weeping to the moment a percussive sound should be struck. But Beckett's notation system for actors, embedded in his scripts, is as precise, and is customarily accepted to be as authoritative, as the code of *nō* performance style. There are also striking resemblances between *nō* troupes and the performance groups Beckett favored. Beckett's final scripts became more and more precise about the physical staging and movement of the characters, dictating head positions (as in *What Where*) as well as the exact sound to be produced by May's nine steps. In addition, a select group of actors tended to perform the premieres of his plays, whether in the United States, England, France, or Germany. Billie Whitelaw, David Warrilow, and Rand Mitchell acted in many Beckett productions in the United States and in England, developing a stylized acting approach that, like *nō* acting, is physically and spiritually demanding and is not based primarily on a concern with the psychological underpinnings of character. In her first Beckett role, W2 in the British premiere of *Play* in 1964, Whitelaw "never thought to ask psychological questions about her role."[41] In performing Beckett, Warrilow says, "I barely deal with psychological reality. I don't have to. I mean, I can have ideas about that but it isn't what works. What works is finding what musicians have called the 'right tone.' By 'right' I mean what works for me. I then have to trust that it'll work for somebody else—that if I get it right, if I sing it 'on key,' 'in time,' it's going to vibrate properly for someone else."[42] By discovering the rhythm, the sound of the work, both Warrilow and Whitelaw seek to

39. Quoted in Kalb, *Beckett in Performance*, pp. 221–22.
40. Rimer and Masakazu, *On the Art of the Nō Drama*, p. 163.
41. Cohn, *Just Play*, p. 198.
42. Kalb, *Beckett in Performance*, p. 224.

decode the precise signs of Beckett's ellipses and pauses, much as a *nō* performer attempts to master his encoded dances and chants: "Whitelaw now likes to recall that one of Beckett's first notes to her was that she pause for two dots rather than the three indicated in the script."[43]

As Whitelaw's disclosure reveals, Beckett clearly agreed with Zeami that "the ritual/play must be performed brilliantly, *it must be done right*, or it will not 'pacify the devils.'"[44] If the actors fulfill their roles properly, these playwrights reasoned, the audience will reach the desired relationship with them and hence with the play. Zeami calls the culmination of this phenomenon the "opening of the eyes" of the audience:

> What is called "opening the eyes" refers to the moment in a *nō* play when the deep sensations inherent in the play are suddenly experienced in one moment of profound exchange [between actor and audience]. When their "eyes are opened," the spectators receive this extraordinary impression through the aesthetic qualities related to dance movement. This moment arises from the manifestation of the artistic and spiritual power of the actor. It may seem that such a moment may bear no relation to the drama as actually composed, but in fact this visual impression of superb skill could not come about if the actual moment for its realization had not been planned for in the play itself. The one composing the text must consider with extreme care where to place the moment when the actor's visual movements can create this effect. This moment, so crucial in the play, resembles that moment when the eyes are placed in a new statue of the Buddha; thus, this moment is referred to as "opening the eyes."[45]

There is no doubt that Beckett and his directors and actors reproduced this phenomenon. Whitelaw, to cite but one example, generated a moment of union with her audience through her almost

43. Ibid.

44. Wallace Chappell, Foreword, in Rimer and Masakazu, *On the Art of the Nō Drama*, p. ix; emphasis added.

45. Zeami Motokiyo, "The Three Elements in Composing a Play" (*Sandō* or *Nōsakusho*), in Rimer and Masakazu, *On the Art of the Nō Drama*, pp. 158–59.

imperceptible movement (a veritable masked *i-guse*) at the end of her performance in *Rockaby*. The *New York Times* reviewer Frank Rich describes the moment:

> At that point, Miss Whitelaw stops rocking. The lone light that picks her face out of the blackness starts to dim, and in the longest of Beckett pauses, we watch the light within the face's hollow eyes and chalky cheeks dim too. During the long silence, the actress doesn't so much as twitch an eyelash—and yet, by the time the darkness is total, we're left with an image different from the one we'd seen a half minute earlier. Somehow Miss Whitelaw has banished life from her expression: what remains is a death mask, so devoid of blood it could be a faded, crumbling photograph. And somehow, even as the face disintegrates, we realize that it has curled into a faint baby's smile. We're left not only with the horror of death, but with the peace.[46]

The actor, through the subtlest shift from face to mask, allowed the audience to watch her disappear. In Zeami's terms, she created *ma* (the blank space-time of nothingness), despite her presence onstage, and thereby "opened the eyes" of the audience.

Beckett's own directorial work with actors tended toward the technical rather than the psychological, just as a *nō* actor's work is not primarily devoted to a probing of character psychology: "At Beckett's first meeting with the actors in a play, he never speaks about the play but plunges right into it. Work on scenes begins at once, and Beckett shakes his head at questions that stray from concrete performance. On the other hand, no practical detail is too small for his attention. . . . The spoken text must be not only letter-perfect, but punctuation perfect; he will stop an actor who elides a comma-pause."[47] In working with Whitelaw on *Footfalls*, for example, he separated May's walking from her talking and "recited the lines together [with her], each conducting as from a score." He also "demonstrated one hand at throat and the other crossed to the opposite shoulder," the dancelike paradoxical gesture that Whitelaw em-

46. Frank Rich, "Stage: A Whitelaw Beckett," *New York Times*, February 17, 1984, sec. C, p. 3.
47. Cohn, *Just Play*, p. 237.

ployed throughout her performance.[48] His "Director's Workbook" for his 1975 Berlin revival of *Waiting for Godot* also reveals the precision he expected in staging: "Beckett's many diagrams showing the movements of the characters amplify the text. This is not only traditional blocking, but concern with who faces where at every moment of time, with each actor's moment-by-moment victory over stillness, with the total stage pattern, with the counterpoint of word and gesture, with visual echoes, symmetries, and oppositions."[49] Indeed, the British director George Devine no doubt pleased the playwright by envisioning a Beckett script as "a musical score wherein the 'notes,' the sights and sounds, the pauses, have their own interrelated rhythms: and out of their composition comes the dramatic impact."[50] While applauding the success of these experienced actors and directors, may we not still probe the playwrights' insistence that the actors "do it right"? This issue, of course, necessarily involves the role of the director in Beckett productions, a role complicated by the fact of Beckett's death.

In the *nō* theatre, a director is unnecessary largely because of the precise training actors and musicians receive in decoding the various signs of the *nō* script and in performing the chants, dances, and songs of this traditional form. As Komparu remarks, "Noh is ultimately directed and conducted by the group of performers on stage, and there is no one corresponding to a director, producer, or conductor."[51] Beckett's plays do, of course, require a director, but the major productions have been staged by an astonishingly small number of directors, who often encouraged Beckett to interpret his scripts for them. As Alan Schneider writes: "[The playwright] has, after all, taken an active role in most of his French productions; and he has even managed to cross the Channel in order to be of assistance to [British] directors George Devine and Donald McWhinie. And he has regularly journeyed to Berlin himself to direct new

48. Ibid., p. 201.
49. Ibid., p. 258.
50. George Devine, quoted in *Samuel Beckett: The Art of Rhetoric*, ed. Edouard Morot-Sir, Howard Harper, and Dougald McMillan III (Chapel Hill: University of North Carolina Press, 1976), p. 294.
51. Komparu, *Noh Theater*, p. 194.

productions of his plays at the Schiller Theater."[52] Although Beckett attended Schneider's rehearsals only once (for *Film*), Schneider always traveled to Paris to seek the playwright's advice on performance issues before beginning rehearsals for his U.S. productions. Indeed, as Schneider himself notes, many directors who have repeatedly produced Beckett's plays went out of their way to seek his instructions: "In the theater . . . we most of the time seem to be trying to keep the author out but with Beckett we feel just the other way round: we want him in. To hold our hands through the darkness. To illuminate the dots, interpret the ellipses, and explain the unexplainable. . . . All of his texts—and that word included both dialogue and stage directions—have always been 'Sam's' to me, a marriage in absentia, in which I have loved, honored, and obeyed as though he were always with me."[53] Schneider's desire for explication, for guidance, and the intimate reverence of the old-fashioned "wifely" marriage metaphor strongly suggest the secondary position he assumed as Beckett's director. Furthermore, as the playwright's scripts became more and more specific and pared down, there was less for a director to do. As Ruby Cohn wrote in 1980, "Publicly [the French director Roger] Blin has always expressed admiration for Beckett, but it is rumored that he has not directed the recent plays because Beckett's scenic directions leave no creative scope for the director."[54]

Certainly Beckett felt that there should be strict limitations on the legal as well as the aesthetic freedoms allowed any director of his scripts, even his early ones.[55] His censorial response to JoAnne Akalaitis's 1984 American Repertory Theatre (ART) staging of *Endgame* received more press coverage than most such incidents, but it was by no means an isolated event. While other playwrights might deplore and even denounce a director's production of one of their works, Beckett often acted legally to halt, disclaim, or demand revisions of stagings he felt to be violations of his scripts. Jonathan Kalb describes the Beckett director's situation: "Even more than with other authors, the subject of directing Beckett is inextricably bound up

52. Alan Schneider, "Working with Beckett," in Morot-Sir et al., *Samuel Beckett*, p. 272.

53. Ibid., p. 273.

54. Cohn, *Just Play*, p. 190.

55. See, for example, Kalb, *Beckett in Performance*, pp. 71–94.

with questions of faithfulness to text, mostly because this ordinarily reticent author has been extraordinarily vocal in his objections to faithlessness. Not entirely by accident, he had the good fortune of seeing many of his premieres staged by two paradigms of loyalty— Roger Blin and Alan Schneider—who not only adhered to the very specific instructions in his scripts but also made frequent public comments about the propriety of that strictness."[56] Like many Beckett scholars, Kalb strongly prefers this faithful tradition of Beckett directing and, despite his attempts at objectivity, condescends toward "underground" directors who "express their love of and respect for Beckett's work by overlaying their ingenious illustrative ideas on it."[57] Directorial interpretation, it is often argued, answers questions that Beckett wanted unanswered: if the setting becomes more specific in terms of time or place in production, or if, for example, as in Akalaitis's *Endgame,* an African-American actor is cast in a role originally played by a Caucasian, the script is violated. Many thorny issues emerge if we accept the idea that playwrights have the legal right to prevent individualized or deconstructive stagings of their scripts, and racial equality in casting is surely one of the most serious.

Without validating Beckett's supposed legal rights as an author, one may perhaps best understand him as the authorizing agent in the production of his scripts. He served in that capacity precisely because the director's and actors' position with regard to him as playwright is at the heart of every Beckett play. Their proposed powerlessness in the face of his performance conventions and yet their power in the face of his total dependence on them for a stage life; their inability to act and yet the necessity of their acting: these constitute Beckett's metaphor for life. And if the absent author of the life of these characters is "not there" in some sense, or if there seem to be two authors (a director as well as a playwright), the production may indeed be shorn of certain vital resonances. But this issue is, or should be, an artistic matter, not a legal one.

To cite just one example of what I regard as a successful directorial approach to Beckett that differs from Beckett's own, let me

56. Ibid., p. 71.
57. Ibid., p. 77.

mention Peter Sellars's 1986 Kennedy Center production of *Two Figures in Dense Violet Light*. The final event of the American National Theatre Season at the Center's Free Theatre in the Theatre Lab, this production featured three texts: Beckett's *Ohio Impromptu,* Ezra Pound's translation of Zeami's phantasmal *nō* play *Tsunemasa,* and Wallace Stevens's poem "Angel Surrounded by Paysans." Although these texts feature male characters, Sellars's directorial approach may be appropriated by directors working with female characters and actors in Beckett. Sellars cast David Warrilow as the Reader and Richard Thomas as the Listener in *Ohio Impromptu,* which they performed twice. The first staging took place in total darkness, with the Reader's voice emerging from behind the audience, so that the audience initially performed the role of listener to Warrilow's Reader, envisioning its own production. As this radio-play version of the play proceeded, the Reader's voice eventually seemed to come from the audience itself: I experienced the curious sensation, in the darkened theatre, that the Reader's voice was coming from within me. The audience was then ushered, in slow-moving columns in a darkness and silence that made us resemble the characters in *What Where,* to an adjacent space to witness another performance of *Ohio Impromptu,* now lit by the violet rays of dusk, reaching the stage through floor-to-ceiling windows behind the audience. Warrilow and Thomas could be discerned in faded saffron gowns, Roman togas with a vaguely Buddhist glow, futuristic feel, and holy aura. Warrilow as the Reader and Thomas as the Listener were seated next to each other at a plain table, their unadorned heads bowed, their left arms resting on the table top. They evoked, simultaneously, echoes of the roots of Western and Eastern civilization, the tenuous world of reality and the spirit. The audience's eyes fought to adjust to the light; momentarily we could not be sure of their reality. The voice this time clearly came from the Reader, at once a holy man and a scholar. The Listener was separate and yet a shadow of the Reader. The scene was, in the words of the *Washington Post* critic David Richards, "a Robert Wilson tableau."[58] Nothing of Beckett's mystery or paradox was lost, and something was gained: by matching Beckett's vision with an

58. David Richards, "Leaving Them Wondering: Sellars' Ambitious, Ambiguous 'Two Figures,'" *Washington Post,* August 12, 1986, sec. C, p. 2. Materials pertaining to this production may be found at the Kennedy Center Performing Arts Library. I am grateful to Walter Zvonchenko and to Vicki Risner-Wolff for their assistance.

equally resonant one of his own, Sellars had expanded the scope of the two characters' exploration and asked the audience to rethink the source of the voices.

In the third curtained space to which the audience moved, the stage was lit only by a shaft of light from a partially open (or partially closed) door. The effect echoed the lighting of *Footfalls*. Warrilow, the Priest of the *nō* play, was seated at the table. Echoing the Readers in the two earlier performances, he invoked a Spirit, this time Zeami's Tsunemasa and, at the same time, Stevens's angel of reality. Ever so gradually Thomas was revealed in the doorway, in a motionless gesture that "extend[ed] a promise of redemption," to quote Richards, but in a voice that warned of the tenuousness of that possibility: "Am I not, / Myself, only half of a figure of a sort, / A figure half seen, or seen for a moment, a man / Of the mind, an apparition apparelled in / Apparels of such lightest look that a turn / Of my shoulder and quickly, too quickly, I am gone?"[59] Tsunemasa himself, like the Priest who has summoned him and like Stevens's angel, is uncertain about his reality. Thomas explored the liminal zone between appearance and reality, being there and not there, East and West.

When I attended this production, I had already written most of this chapter, and was intrigued by Sellars's independent but similar line of thinking about Beckett's work. The audience filed out of the theatre into the night, onto the outdoor terrace of the Kennedy Center, where we could see our reflections in the window. Through those reflections we could still see the motionless actors, in their evocative gowns. Only then were we given programs, the customary guides to the viewing of any production. And only then could we decode fully the tickets we had carried with us through the production: in hieroglyphics suggesting ancient Egyptian times, the three separate boxes on the ticket showed the sign first for an ear, then an eye, then a kneeling figure that signified, I later discovered, a holy man or a dead man. The audience's movements echoed the characters' own movements as we circled back to the site where we had begun the evening.

In the power vacuum created by Alan Schneider's untimely death,

59. Wallace Stevens, "Angel Surrounded by Paysans," in *Poems by Wallace Stevens*, intro. Samuel French Morse (New York: Vintage Books, 1959), p. 153.

Beckett strove to prevent many interpretations of his scripts, to maintain control in the United States over what he saw as a performance situation requiring actors and directors trained in following his particular tradition of approaching the script. Robert Scanlan articulated this point of view at the December 1989 meeting of the Beckett Society, held soon after the playwright's death. Scanlan perceived the integral relationship between the structure of Beckett's dramatic action, its meaning, and the performance style it encodes. His explanation is worth quoting at some length because it articulates many of the issues raised and critiqued in this chapter:

> Recognition of formal accomplishments, and respect for them as values in their own right, are defining acts of a culture. . . . Is the willful marring of forms—through the addition of visual material or bold new concepts of performance—not a disregard for the *meaning* of these plays? We in the critical profession seem to be increasingly intimidated by current trends of post-modernism and a few ill-digested caveats derived from "deconstructive" artistic procedures, and equally timid about a mission as teachers: that there are criteria of excellence to be learned from the example of masters, to be practiced, and to be eventually mastered, if that is within our power.[60]

Because Beckett's scripts attempt to locate the origin of the voice, Scanlan contends, they require special handling. Unlike Shakespeare's scripts, which can survive and even flourish in postmodern stagings, Beckett's scripts must be staged "right." The 1988 Mike Nichols *Waiting for Godot* violated Beckett's performance code, according to Scanlan, because, like Akalaitis's *Endgame,* it substituted "American equivalencies . . . for every aspect of the original," and thereby diminished Beckett's work.[61] (Unlike Akalaitis and the ART, Nichols reportedly sought Beckett's approval prior to his production and thereby quelled any potential objections.) To illustrate further the effects of directorial license on Beckett's scripts, Scanlan reports on the Comédie Française's 1988 production of *Fin de partie.* Beckett

60. Robert Scanlan, "Performing Voices: Recent Stagings of Beckett's Work," paper delivered at the Modern Language Association meeting, December 28, 1989, Washington, D.C., p. 3.
61. Ibid., p. 4.

learned of the Parisian director's concept just before the production opened and demanded that the production be modified to satisfy his criticisms, but traces of the director's concept remained and "spoiled" the production.

All of these illustrations strengthen the sense that Beckett viewed himself, and is perceived by many if not most Beckett scholars, as the supreme playwright as author: he devised a structural method and system of stage directions that prompted a certain carefully circumscribed performance style from directors and actors involved in the premieres of his works. Partly because of his stature, he was able to circumvent the ascending power of directors who later tried to authorize new performance styles for his plays. It mattered very much to Beckett "who is speaking," and it still matters to the community of Beckett scholars, who can be expected to protect his authorship even more fiercely in his absence. As Jonathan Kalb claims, Beckett is "the last best hope of the Author in the theatre."[62]

The University of Maryland Visual Press's videotaped productions of Beckett's scripts, "Beckett Directs Beckett," signal the playwright's acquiescence in the marketing of Beckett as supreme author. The fact that Beckett allowed this academically affiliated television production company to use his name as director as well as playwright reveals his eagerness to retain control of his legacy in the face of unruly directors. According to Mitchell Lifton, co-producer of the series with John Fuegi, "Beckett has said, and I think I am quoting him quite exactly, 'This is my last word on the subject of these three plays,'" *Waiting for Godot, Krapp's Last Tape,* and *Endgame.* Fuegi calls these productions, which incorporate Beckett's last textual revisions, the *"ausgabe letzter hand . . .* the edition last touched by the hand of the artist. . . . The *televised* version of *Waiting for Godot* will stand as the true Beckett, [Fuegi] says, replacing the printed text published in 1954 by the Grove Press. Because the actors are following Mr. Beckett's every direction, the televised text 'is better than the Grove Press edition.'"[63] Donald Gibson, the director of general programs for the National Endowment for the Humanities, which, along with the University of Maryland, provided the seed money for

62. Kalb, *Beckett in Performance,* p. 162.

63. Quoted in Patricia Meisol, "Talking Books: UM's Alternative Press Is Putting Texts on TV," *Baltimore Sun Magazine,* November 13, 1988, pp. 17, 16.

"Beckett Directs Beckett," acknowledges that this project raises a major question about the idea of text, the question "whether television can be used instead of or in addition to books to transmit complex ideas."[64] But of course the question concerning text is much more complicated, even if we set aside for a moment the issue of a mass television audience as opposed to a circumscribed theatre audience. For example, in what sense can there even be future productions of these three scripts if we are to understand "script" to mean the videotaped text? And which taped version does the press wish to validate, since there are, in fact, two versions of each production, one in French and one in English? Indeed, the project raises several questions, not only about the idea of text but also about the concept of the author in the theatre. If, as Fuegi and Lifton hope, the revised videotaped versions come to be accepted as more authoritative than the original printed scripts, what role is left for the director or actor to play in Beckett's "theatre"? Any staging or taping from now on must be viewed as "unauthorized."

As a matter of fact, Beckett was not present on the set during the Paris taping for this series but rather called in daily from his apartment, leaving the actual work to his colleague, the German director Walter Asmus, who was demoted to the title of "'realizateur'—the man who calls the technical shots."[65] This new world of televised text, as promoted by the Visual Press, thus retitles the director, elevating the absent playwright, by virtue of his detailed stage directions and verbal guidance, to that title, and to the position of sole authorizing agent of the work. This exemplifies one logical extension of the tradition of the playwright's influence over the performance text not only through unique structural and performance conventions but also through precise stage directions: Beckett's *spoken* guidelines also serve as directives protecting his presence in the text. Beckett thereby problematized the position of the director as well as the actor in his theatre.

A further difficulty resides in the curious nature of the resulting artwork, a televised play. Because Beckett's scripts rely on the paradox of the actor/character's simultaneous presence and absence in

64. Ibid., p. 16.
65. Ibid., p. 17.

the theatre, they evoke a more complicated performance situation when they are staged rather than videotaped. Ironically, this effort to capture the author function forever may subvert the very thing that gives life to Beckett's scripts: the live actor. The Beckett series is of special note because it is an international project headed by well-respected, well-established scholars, and as such is being monitored by other groups, both private and governmental, that want to take advantage of the financial as well as the pedagogical opportunities of this type of experiment. It is a virtual litmus test of who controls the authorial function in the theatre, the playwright or the director. The scholarly and public reaction to it should be very revealing.[66]

The critical examination of the position of the female actor in the Beckett theatre also promises to reveal contradictory problems as well as opportunities. Currently, however, the emphasis seems to be on the opportunities, as feminists herald Beckett's genius at investigating the complexities of womanhood. Linda Ben-Zvi, for example, cites Beckett's adamant stance against cross-gender casting not as his refusal of a common theatrical means to critique gender codes but rather as an indication of "his keen awareness of, and commitment to revealing, those elements that fix his people in place and tie them to stultifying gender roles."[67] For instance, Winnie in *Happy Days* is "thus not only a woman; she is the physical embodiment of the *condition* of being a woman in her society. Not a stereotype, she is the

---

66. "The Visual Press is being launched at a time when European companies are storing up a cache of quality international television programming in an attempt to dominate the new market they expect will develop with the 1992 integration of the European Economic Community. On both sides of the Atlantic, producers are finding that cultural programs are cheaper to make, and easier to finance and market, if they are international in scope; governments want to be listed in the screen credits" (ibid., p. 16). The U.S. Librarian of Congress, James Billington, for example, was deeply committed to moving the Library into the realm of producing cable television shows, as was evident in his announcement of the Global Library Project to be aired, eventually daily, on the "Mind Extension University channel." Although the initial programming may be devoted to informative shows about the Library itself, Elizabeth Kastor reports that Billington "went on to say that producers contracted by the library could take advantage of lectures, performances, and seminars held at the library." Elizabeth Kastor, "Library to Produce Cable Series," *Washington Post*, October 11, 1989, sec. B, p. 4. These developments signal just some of the elements that may soon force us to rethink our understanding of the author's function in the theatre.

67. Linda Ben-Zvi, ed., *Women in Beckett: Performance and Critical Perspectives* (Urbana: University of Illinois Press, 1990), p. x.

result of stereotypic views of women." Beckett's gender critique, which reflects an understanding of real women's lives as well as the social construct of woman, becomes especially apparent in the late plays, according to Ben-Zvi.[68] Unfortunately, Ben-Zvi's argument ignores the fact that Beckett's presentation of the social construct of woman ties those *conditions*—those elements that fix women—to mystical, ever-returning *universal forces.* There is no way out for any of these representations of woman, nor for the men who court, ignore, jilt, or threaten them. Never has the representation of womanhood strayed further from the historically tied and therefore alterable social interactions of the Brecht Collective characters. Nor is there an escape for Beckett's female actors, unalterably subject to the playwright's *nō*-like performance style.

Elin Diamond, however, asserts that "the hysteric and the presymbolic (or 'semiotic') maternal" appear in Beckett's late plays, as in French feminism, as sites of resistance to the patriarchal symbolic. The Mouth in *Not I* refuses "*the fiction* of ego-agency" that would cure her disruptive and therefore subversive hysteria; in declining the use of first-person discourse, she illuminates her awareness of a symbolic order that denies her agency.[69] Diamond posits the Listener—at first possibly, and then certainly—as male: "The (male?) figure in the priestly djellaba, face averted, listens as though to an analysand, with sympathy, with '*helpless compassion*,' silently urging Mouth to staunch her verbal flow with an object-representation—an 'I'—however fictional and provisional. The djellaba figure acts the role of mental healer, who cannot modify the culture that makes his patient sick (he is '*helpless*'), but attempts to, as Kristeva puts it, 'prevent [her] *jouissance,* [her] truth, and replace it with the plausibility of reasonable discourse'" (p. 211). This figure's censoring potential gains ground through another, internalized censor within Mouth, which Diamond identifies as "the Other—the Law, the Symbolic Order, or (in Beckett, always), God" (p. 211).

As Diamond herself recognizes, however, the struggle of Mouth, as the figuration of the hysteric, against these censors is doomed to failure because (as Catherine Clement has demonstrated) viewers of

68. Ibid., p. xiii.
69. Elin Diamond, "Speaking Parisian: Beckett and French Feminism," in Ben-Zvi, *Women in Beckett*, p. 211. All subsequent references are cited by page in the text.

the hysteric's symptomatic outbursts become inured to her, and she ends up enclosed within the family circle, ignored by them. The second reason the hysteric's struggle is not heroic, according to Diamond, is that "there is no narrative at all, nor are there discrete discourses"; because Mouth's eruptions "are not small victories so much as evidence of the conundrum of enunciation: the I of discourse *in* discourse; it is *not I,* it seems, who speaks" (p. 212). What does this conclusion, this reading, mean for real women onstage and in the audience? Is it even possible to read *Not I* this way in the theatre itself?

The very physicality of the actor and spectator complicate Beckett's script, strengthening both its feminist critique and its power to harm actual women. When the audience members see a particular mouth enacting Mouth, they may very well distance themselves from her disjointed, hysterical spurts of language; they may even perceive the way in which the language is disembodied, in which the discourse seems to speak itself. But they are nonetheless simultaneously aware that there is a real, individual female actor onstage—up *there* onstage there is an I as well as a Not I, and both the real and the scripted I are at once the collective I of the audience (that is, of the posited "universal" female experience) and the Not I, signaling the uniqueness of each particular female's negotiation of competing if not discrete discourses. And what if the Listener is understood to be a female, engaging in a sympathetic response to the Mouth, trying to help her survive? That rather changes the nature of spectatorship.

If female actors and spectators simply adopt the role of the hysteric, they will be forever relegated to silence as anything other than pathetic figures critiquing the patriarchy. What of the possibility of creating new conditions that might promote agency for real women? Women may very well need to assume ego agency, even though it is a fiction, for to do otherwise is to remain a hysteric, bound in the symbolic darkness, visible only as a gaping wound. According to Teresa de Lauretis, there are competing discourses, not just one univocal order, and in the negotiation there is hope for real women to gain a voice.

Diamond's second example of female resistance within Beckett resides in the fact that, in *Footfalls* and *Rockabye,* he "stages a crisis posed by feminist theories of the maternal: how [to] celebrate and separate from the mother's body?" (p. 213). This reading, too, presents some difficulties, largely those implicit in the theories that give it shape: Julia Kristeva's theory of the maternal "semiotic," Hélène Cixous's theory of *l'écriture féminine*, and Jane Gallop's competing concept of the phallic mother. Kristeva and Cixous collapse the nurturing function with the universalized biological female, and Gallop identifies the resultant power of the maternal as male, or "phallic." The first two theorists mystify the image of the mother, locking real women into an impossible role, and the third erases real women from the all-encompassing power that is supposedly tied to that role. Diamond's explication of the way in which these theorists illuminate Beckett's scripts enables us to perceive not just sites of resistance but also the shortcomings of Beckett's theatre for female actors and spectators.

The "slippage" in Diamond's own summary of Kristeva's "semiotic" reveals the essentialism lurking in this theory. "The mother, or more accurately the maternal function, because of her 'pre-Oedipal' or pre-cultural role in nurturing, gendering, and socializing the infant, has become a metaphoric lever for dislodging patriarchal structures. . . . Kristeva locates the semiotic in the pre-verbal moment of mother-child bonding, when the child is most dependent on the maternal body" (p. 212). Starting out with "the mother," a female, Diamond pries that role from biological females with the qualification "or more accurately the maternal function," only to return to the female pronoun "her," which reinscribes the essentialism inherent in linking the female, and only the female, to the process of nurturing the infant. Furthermore, parent-child bonding, mystified in Kristeva as a "*pre*-cultural" absolute for women, may very well be for real women an active effort, an accomplishment rather than the dramatic "given" of having given birth. Actual women frequently feel subjected to impossible standards through this cultural norm of the mystical universal bonding between mother and child. Feminists have the responsibility to keep the "maternal function" separate from as well as connected to the female body. To the extent, then, that Beckett colludes with Kristeva in representing the mother as the "alliteration, repetition, melody, harmony" that subvert the symbolic narrative, he may be said to reinscribe a myth that disables as well as enables. As an accomplishment, parent-child bonding can be applauded in the theatre, but as a mystical, preverbal moment—especially as Cixous's woman-"song before the law"—perhaps it should not be. In Kristeva, furthermore, the patriarchy suddenly becomes *necessary* to break this mystical mother-child bond, this Lacanian Imaginary. Beckett's "W," the woman in the rocker in *Rockabye,* may certainly be viewed as "Beckett's radical contribution to [the] feminist discussion of the phallic mother—she who, as mother and primary nurturer, seems omnipotently in control of life (she is the rocker) but who, as a female subject, cannot emerge from her internal monologue to change or control her representation (she is rocked)" (p. 215). But that image onstage effectively masks any potential agency that might be exercised by real females—actors or spectators.

In Beckett's last plays the daughters, bereft of the mother's nurture, jilted by potential suitors (whether divine or romantic), enact a curious double life: they are at once erased and exalted. When Ben-Zvi asked Billie Whitelaw how she would summarize the qualities of Beckett's women, she replied that she and the playwright had a private joke about "May, or is it Amy, [who] suddenly says she is dreadfully un . . . and she can't finish the word—dot dot dot. . . . I will tell him, 'I'm dreadfully un . . . this morning, dreadfully un . . .' Maybe you could say all Beckett's women are dreadfully un."[70] Dreadfully un, then, Beckett's characters, especially in *Footfalls,* nonetheless stand as saintly symbols of a kind of forgiveness.[71] Irena Jun, a Polish actor, contends that in Beckett "certain aspects of womanhood have been raised as problems applying to all human beings. . . . In many cases Beckett has chosen Woman as his medium to express the essence of Human Being. . . . One can imagine . . . a man walking up and down a room and improvising a story in [the] form of a dialogue. It is all possible. But those situations would strike you as false. What follow is that some aspects of [the] human condition can only be expressed by the image (medium) of a female fig-

70. Interview with Ben-Zvi, in Ben-Zvi, *Women in Beckett,* p. 10.

71. Ruby Cohn writes: "Beckett was brought up a Christian; he could not sustain his faith, but he nevertheless dramatizes an 'Amen' to a 'loving God and the fellowship of the Holy Ghost.' And he does this by exalting woman." Cohn, "The Femme Fatale on Beckett's Stage," in Ben-Zvi, *Women in Beckett,* p. 162.

ure."[72] Productions and readings that keep separate this awareness of the individual and the universal, rather than collapsing them, seem most profitable for feminists.

Beckett's female actors face the possibility of a very real liberation and a seriously injurious attack. Released from the strictures of being attractive, they can be virtuosos instead, achieving pleasure in that disciplined mastery. When Whitelaw worried about sounding uninteresting in *Not I,* Beckett counseled, "Let it be boring."[73] Although she could fake her way through other roles, she could not do so with Beckett, Whitelaw admits, clearly celebrating that fact, just as the early Ibsen actors enjoyed the challenge of creating the style suggested by Ibsen's scripts. Jun voices her satisfaction in being able to transform her body into a "perfect instrument."[74] As for Brenda Bynum in *Come and Go,* there was room to "be herself in the text," to quote interviewer Lois Overbeck, if she submitted to the required discipline: "If you accept those restrictions, it is like a world in a grain of sand; you get inside those parameters and you find so much, a new universe."[75] For Bynum, that discovery constitutes the "life-affirming" quality of Beckett's scripts.

But there is a rather dark underside to the story of the relationship between Beckett and female actors: not only do these actors suffer unusual physical pain in staging the playwright's vision of woman, but also by following the prescribed Beckett style of performing, they participate in the process of disembodying themselves. The Beckett veteran Whitelaw admits, "Every damn play of Beckett's that I do involves some sort of physically or mentally excruciating experience."[76] A paralyzed jaw in *Not I,* a spine injury in *Footfalls*—there is a price to pay. And all the while Beckett remains the supreme "*nō* master," saying a line in rehearsal, then asking the actor to repeat it precisely.[77]

Ironically, of course, Beckett's real desire was to rid himself of the actor, female or male, entirely. "Not for me these Grotowskis and

72. Interview with Antoni Libera, in Ben-Zvi, *Women in Beckett,* p. 50.

73. Interview with Ben-Zvi, in Ben-Zvi, *Women in Beckett,* p. 5.

74. Interview with Libera, in Ben-Zvi, *Women in Beckett,* p. 48.

75. Interview with Lois Overbeck, in Ben-Zvi, *Women in Beckett,* p. 52.

76. Interview with Ben-Zvi, in Ben-Zvi, *Women in Beckett,* p. 5.

77. The actor Shivaun O'Casey, among many others, refers to this process in her interview with Rosette Lamont, in Ben-Zvi, *Women In Beckett,* p. 31.

Methods," Beckett is quoted as saying: "The best possible play is one in which there are no actors, only the text. I'm trying to find a way to write one."[78] The *nō*-like training demanded by Beckett's preferred performance style comes as close as possible to accomplishing this feat. As Ed Menta notes, "The Beckettian self-annihilation of the actor with reference to the text can be compared to the rigorous Zen training of the Noh actor, with its inherent eradication of ego and enhancing of humility."[79] Beckett sees the "text" as mind, the actor as body, and he wants to purge the theatre of bodies, leaving live, skinned minds to enact their (sometimes humorous) torture. This desire for "only the words" (or perhaps for the collapse of the body into the words) seizes from the hands of female actors and audiences a very useful tool: the tension between the iconicity of the actor/character and the physical presence of the actor as a wedge disrupting that iconicity. In the theatre we are always, to a greater or lesser extent, aware that we are *in* the theatre, that real actors enact a fiction. If our awareness of the real actor is diminished, our ability to see the act as a fiction may also be diminished. Despite the surface similarity of Beckett's theatre to certain of the "denaturing" effects of Brecht, in Beckett we are about as far from the Brecht Collective theatre as possible. And if we watch female actors evacuate their bodies in front of our very eyes, if we as spectators are asked to celebrate their virtuosity in accomplishing that feat, where does that leave us in terms of creating a sense of agency for women?

Beckett is dealing with a metaphysical world, one might object, not (or at least not just) a material one. Granted. But the metaphysical world is fashioned to reflect the "universal" within real women's lives, and therein lies the danger for Beckett's female actors and audiences.

Increasingly in the last years of his life Beckett tried, however unknowingly, to encourage a performance style like that of the *nō* theatre through every means at his command: through his spiraling structures, his novelistic narrative devices, his production notes, and his careful endorsement of certain actors and directors. And yet he did not have the venerable tradition of the *nō* to sustain his demands.

78. Deirdre Bair, *Samuel Beckett: A Biography* (New York: Harcourt, Brace, Jovanovich, 1978), p. 527.
79. Menta, "Samuel Beckett in a Noh Light," p. 58.

To ensure that his work remains vital, his followers may eventually have to relinquish their now tenuous hold (in his behalf) on the authorial function, to allow directors to take up the admittedly difficult challenge of collaborating with Beckett, perhaps by exploring even further his *nō* connections, as Peter Sellars did, or by discovering values in the scripts that lead to other, quite different performance styles. These performance texts, in turn, may well complicate the current theorizing about Beckett's women. But even Samuel Beckett cannot accomplish Zeami's feat of making the director (or the actor) disappear.

Afterword

Any useful idea of the theatre, particularly one serviceable to feminists eager for social change, has to demonstrate its flexibility and efficacy in response to specific performance situations. The approach adopted in the present study attempts to address that demand. The theatre is a site of struggle where meaning is created through the intricate interactions of various factors: the structure and representational system of the script and the critical assessment of its authority; the actor's—particularly the female actor's—invention of an acting style that initiates a specific relationship between the actor, the character, and the audience; the director's mediation between the provinces of playwright, actor, and audience; the audience's active and potentially resistant rendering of the performance text; and the critics' establishment of a lens through which the work may be viewed; not to mention the designers, architects, city planners, and publicists whose work also merits investigation. This approach enables us to retrieve the accomplishments of female actors of the past century, who—even in producing scripts by male playwrights—have managed to originate acting styles that make visible and critique the performative nature of the idea of woman.

Any acting style that enables female actors and spectators to become conscious of performance, of the existence and nature of codes of behavior engendered by a patriarchal cultural system and the presence of alternative, competing codes, may be potentially illuminating for women, whether that style is Brechtian, naturalistic, a combination of the two, or any other available or yet-to-be discovered style. By focusing on acting styles and by analyzing actors' work within actual performance situations, this book documents that female actors and spectators may gain power even in circumstances heretofore regarded as impossible, and, conversely, that circumstances previously regarded as fairly auspicious need not necessarily lead to feminist subversion. This fact encourages female actors, onstage and off, to act with originality and with a keen awareness of all the shifting, contradictory, and unpredictable factors in any performance situation.

At a time when the entire feminist project is under siege in the wider community, it is pragmatic to acknowledge, generate, and imagine as many subversive positions as possible. One need not posit an ideal position for female actors or spectators, since different situations of necessity require different approaches. And though it is imperative both to foster and to critique the work of female actors in plays by women, it is equally worthwhile to investigate the work of female actors in plays by men. Such an investigation prompts women of all backgrounds, in the theatre and in the cultural scene at large, to create their own individual styles of performance, their own ways of intervening in scenarios sketched by absent male playwrights—nudging or provoking audiences to rewrite as the case may merit. As Judith Butler notes, each of us manifests a unique style: "one does one's body, and indeed, one does one's body differently from one's contemporaries and from one's embodied predecessors and successors as well," though this process of embodying possibilities "is never fully self-styled, for living styles have a history, and that history conditions and limits possibilities."[1] Contemporary women may live in an already scripted space, but the history of

1. Judith Butler, "Performative Acts and Gender Constitution: An Essay in Phenomenology and Feminist Theory," in *Performing Feminisms: Feminist Critical Theory and Theatre,* ed. Sue-Ellen Case (Baltimore: Johns Hopkins University Press, 1990), p. 272. Butler's concern is to prevent the reification of "an implicitly heterosexual framework for the description of gender, gender identity, and sexuality" (p. 281), and I support her effort. I also think that her call "to expand the cultural field bodily through subversive performances of various kinds" (p. 282) invites all women to push at the boundaries of their bodies, making their "audiences" conscious of and resistant to the performative nature of gender.

shifting acting styles proves that they can invent, even in unlikely places, new ways of performing themselves and of transforming their fellow players.

This shifting—and variously occupied—figure of the female actor, creating ever new styles of performance, making visible her position with a given culture, creating and changing her own subjectivity, merits recognition as a valuable fiction as well as a historical reality.

Index